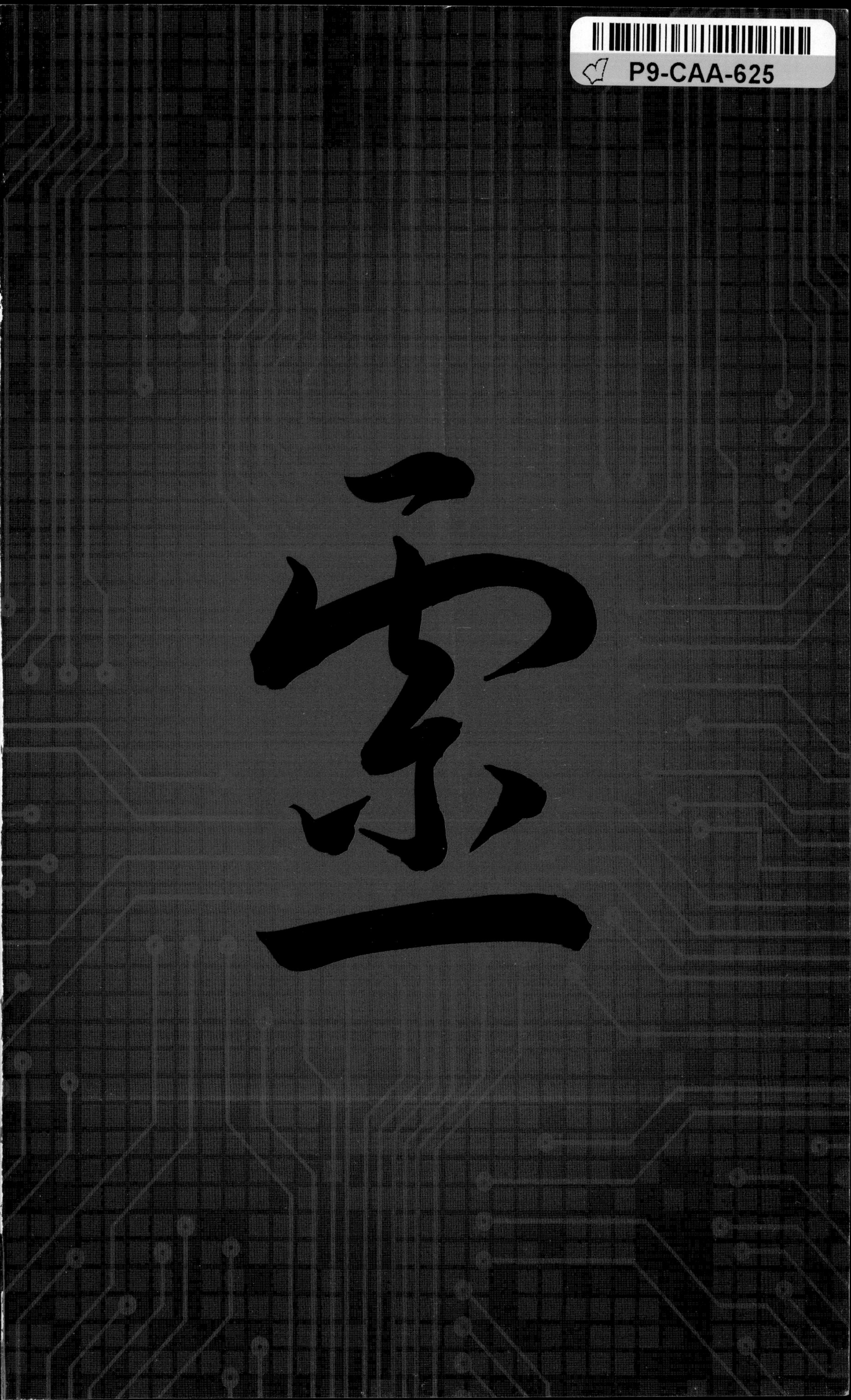
空

WRITER
DAN ABNETT

ARTIST
JUAN JOSÉ RYP

COLORS
ANDREW DALHOUSE

LETTERER
DAVE SHARPE

COVERS BY
RAÚL ALLÉN
RAMÓN F. BACHS
KAEL NGU WITH KAZEO
JUAN JOSÉ RYP with
ANDREW DALHOUSE

**ASSOCIATE
EDITOR**
DAVID MENCHEL

EDITOR
LYSA HAWKINS

GALLERY
SIMON BISLEY
ADAM GORHAM with
MICHAEL GARLAND
DAVE JOHNSON
JOSÉ LADRÖNN
ADAM POLLINA
JAVIER PULIDO
JUAN JOSÉ RYP
MIGUEL SEPULVEDA
MICHAEL WALSH

**COLLECTION
COVER ART**
JUAN JOSÉ RYP with
ANDREW DALHOUSE

**COLLECTION BACK
COVER ART**
ADAM POLLINA

**COLLECTION
FRONT ART**
ADAM POLLINA
MICHAEL WALSH

**COLLECTION
EDITOR**
IVAN COHEN

**COLLECTION
DESIGNER**
STEVE BLACKWELL

DAN MINTZ Chairman **FRED PIERCE** Publisher **WALTER BLACK** VP Operations **MATTHEW KLEIN** VP Sales & Marketing **PETER STERN** Director of International Publishing & Merchandising
LYSA HAWKINS & **HEATHER ANTOS** Senior Editors **DAVID MENCHEL** Associate Editor **TRAVIS ESCARFULLERY** Director of Design & Production **JEFF WALKER** Production & Design Manager
JOHN PETRIE Senior Sales Manager **KAT O'NEILL** Sales & Live Events Manager **DANIELLE WARD** Sales Manager **GREGG KATZMAN** Marketing Manager **EMILY HECHT** Digital Marketing Manager

RUSS BROWN President, Consumer Products, Promotions & Ad Sales

Rai® Book One. Published by Valiant Entertainment LLC. Office of Publication: 350 Seventh Avenue, New York, NY 10001. Compilation copyright © 2020 Valiant Entertainment LLC. All rights reserved. Contains materials originally published in single magazine form as Rai #1-5. Copyright © 2019 and 2020 Valiant Entertainment LLC. All rights reserved. All characters, their distinctive likeness and related indicia featured in this publication are trademarks of Valiant Entertainment LLC. The stories, characters, and incidents featured in this publication are entirely fictional. Valiant Entertainment does not read or accept unsolicited

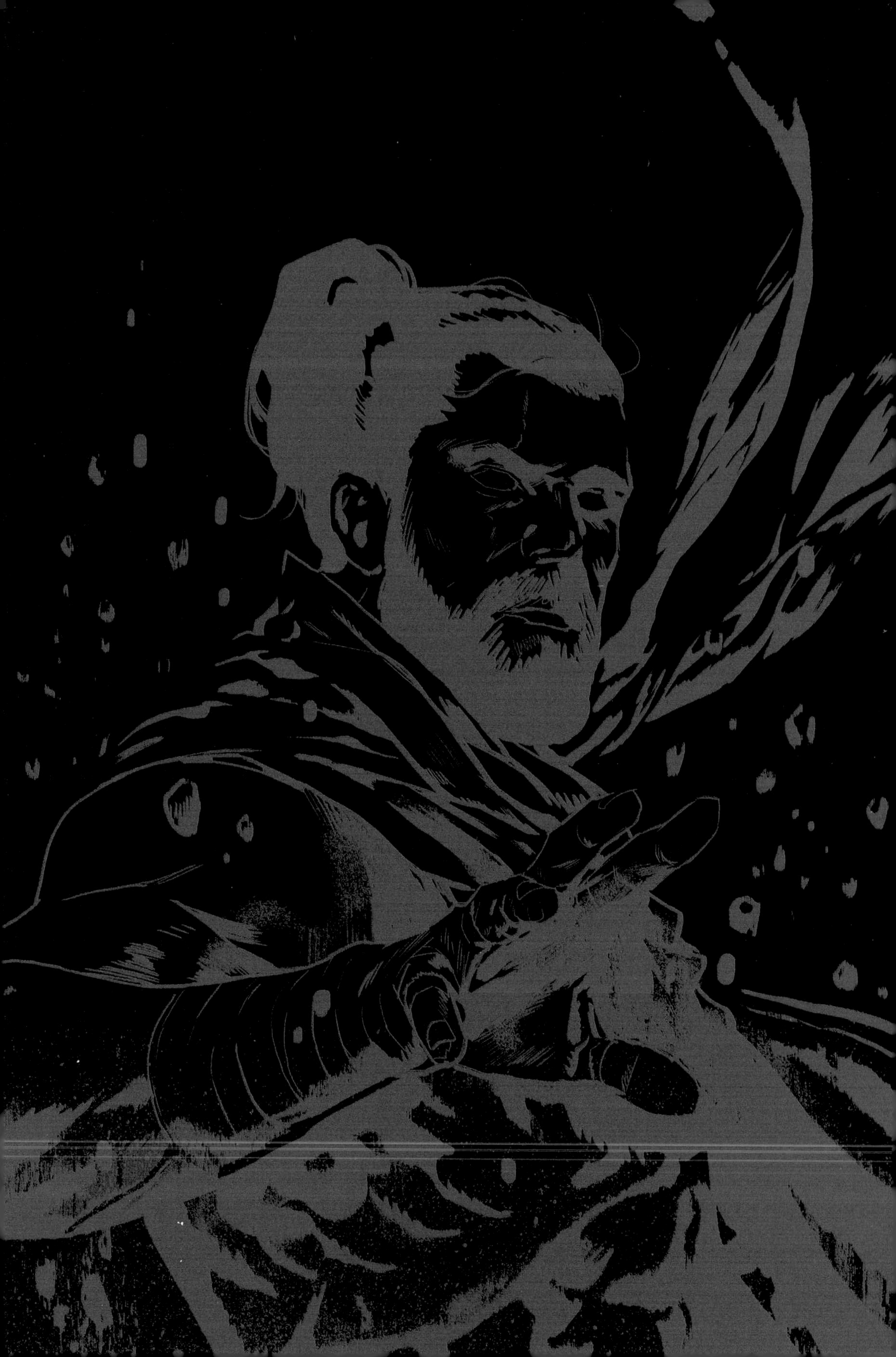

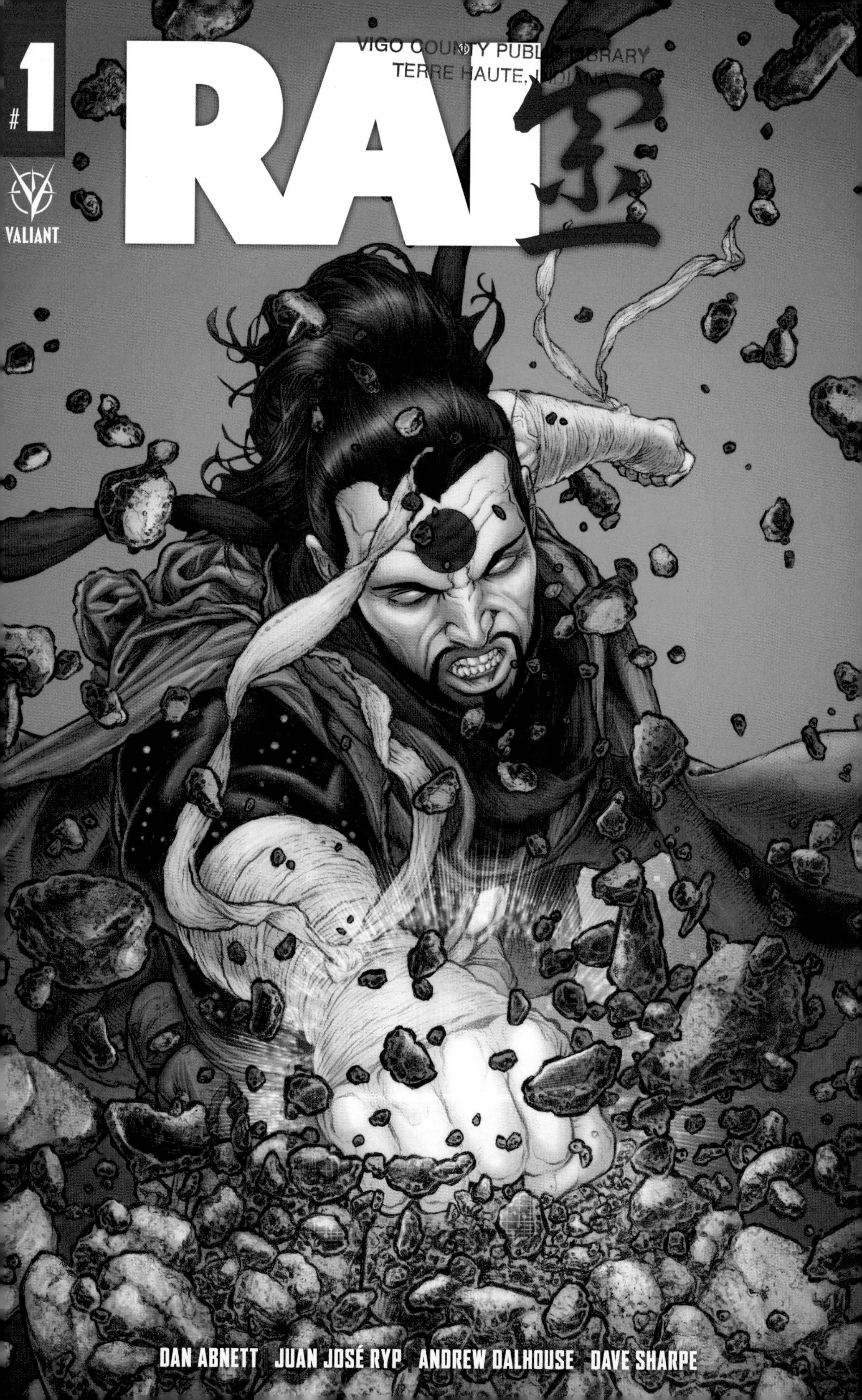
#1
RAI
VALIANT
DAN ABNETT JUAN JOSÉ RYP ANDREW DALHOUSE DAVE SHARPE

RAI #1

WRITER: DAN ABNETT
ARTIST: JUAN JOSÉ RYP
COLORIST: ANDREW DALHOUSE
LETTERER: DAVE SHARPE
COVER ARTISTS: JUAN JOSÉ RYP with ANDREW DALHOUSE
ASSOCIATE EDITOR: DAVID MENCHEL
EDITOR: LYSA HAWKINS

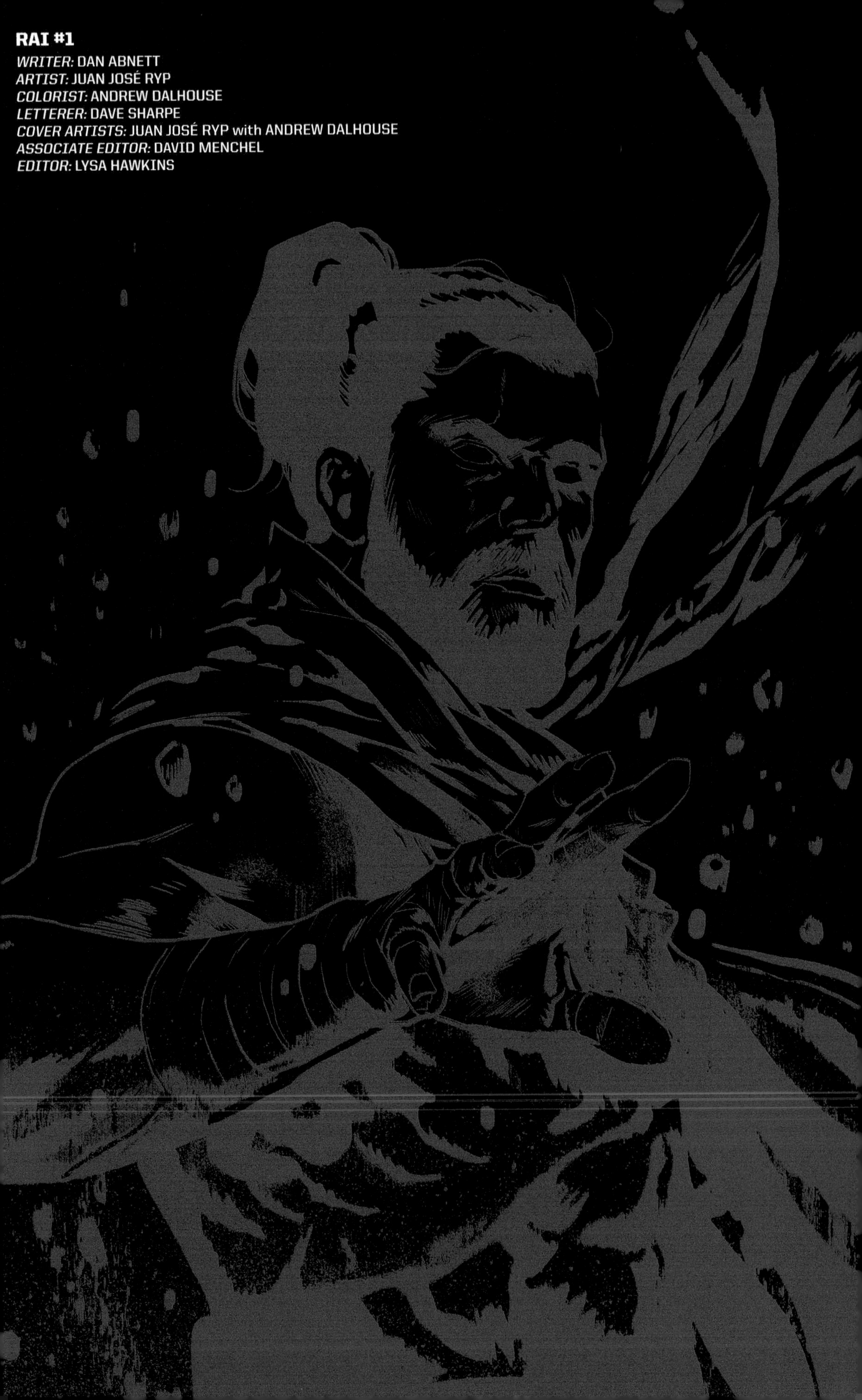

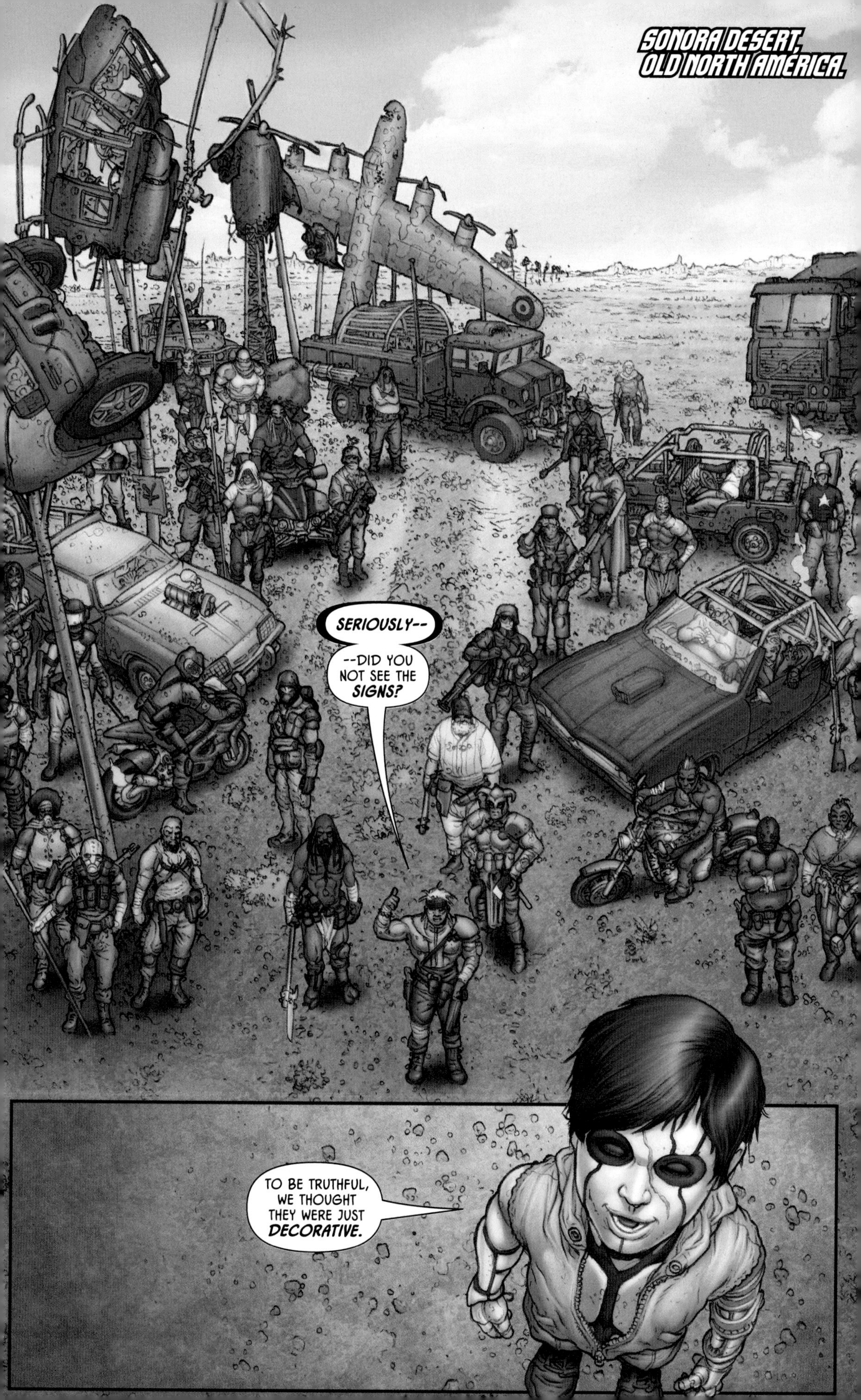
SONORA DESERT, OLD NORTH AMERICA.
SERIOUSLY--
--DID YOU NOT SEE THE SIGNS?
TO BE TRUTHFUL, WE THOUGHT THEY WERE JUST DECORATIVE.

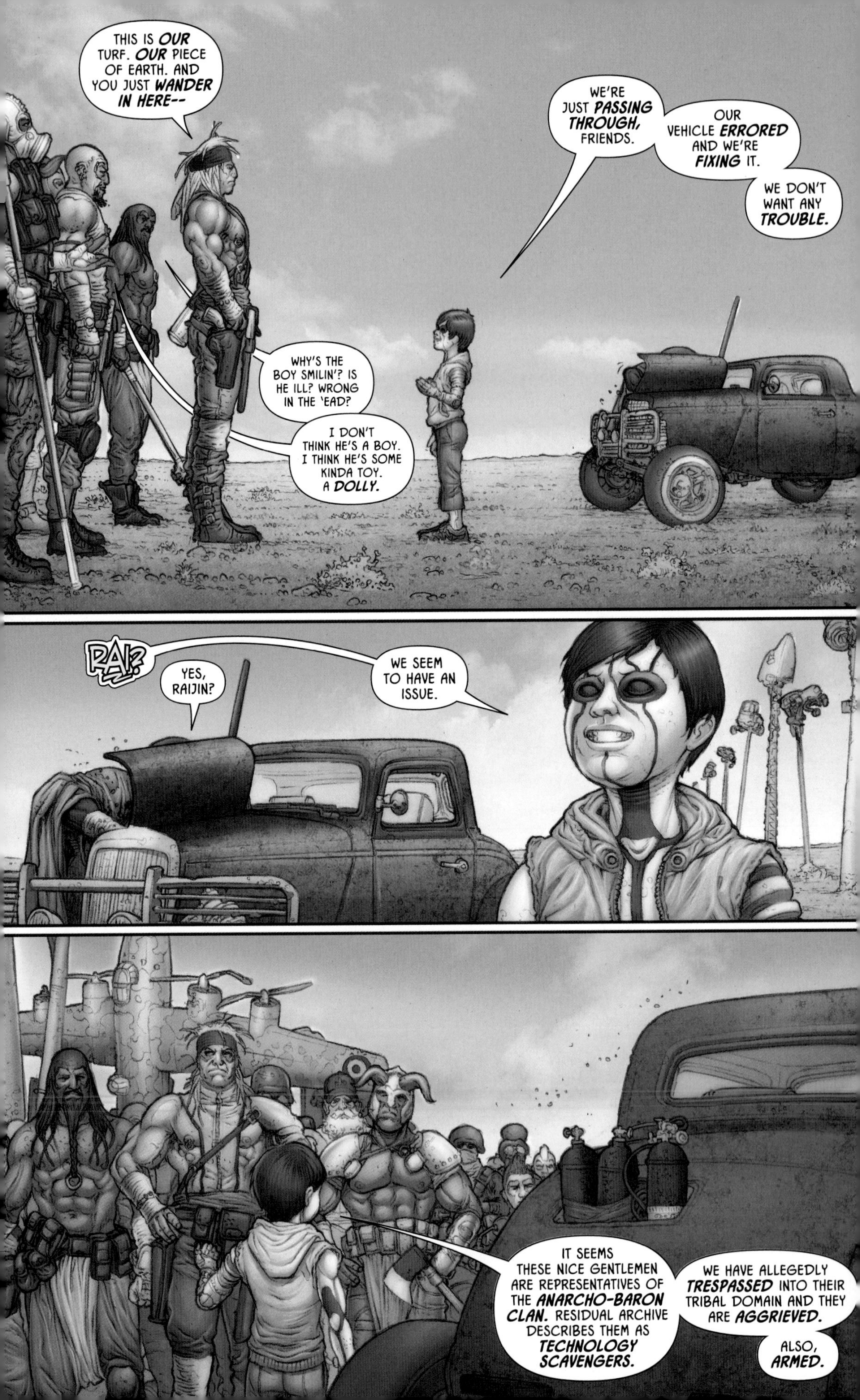
THIS IS OUR TURF. OUR PIECE OF EARTH. AND YOU JUST WANDER IN HERE--
WE'RE JUST PASSING THROUGH, FRIENDS.
OUR VEHICLE ERRORED AND WE'RE FIXING IT.
WE DON'T WANT ANY TROUBLE.
WHY'S THE BOY SMILIN'? IS HE ILL? WRONG IN THE 'EAD?
I DON'T THINK HE'S A BOY. I THINK HE'S SOME KINDA TOY. A DOLLY.
RAI?
YES, RAIJIN?
WE SEEM TO HAVE AN ISSUE.
IT SEEMS THESE NICE GENTLEMEN ARE REPRESENTATIVES OF THE ANARCHO-BARON CLAN. RESIDUAL ARCHIVE DESCRIBES THEM AS TECHNOLOGY SCAVENGERS.
WE HAVE ALLEGEDLY TRESPASSED INTO THEIR TRIBAL DOMAIN AND THEY ARE AGGRIEVED.
ALSO, ARMED.

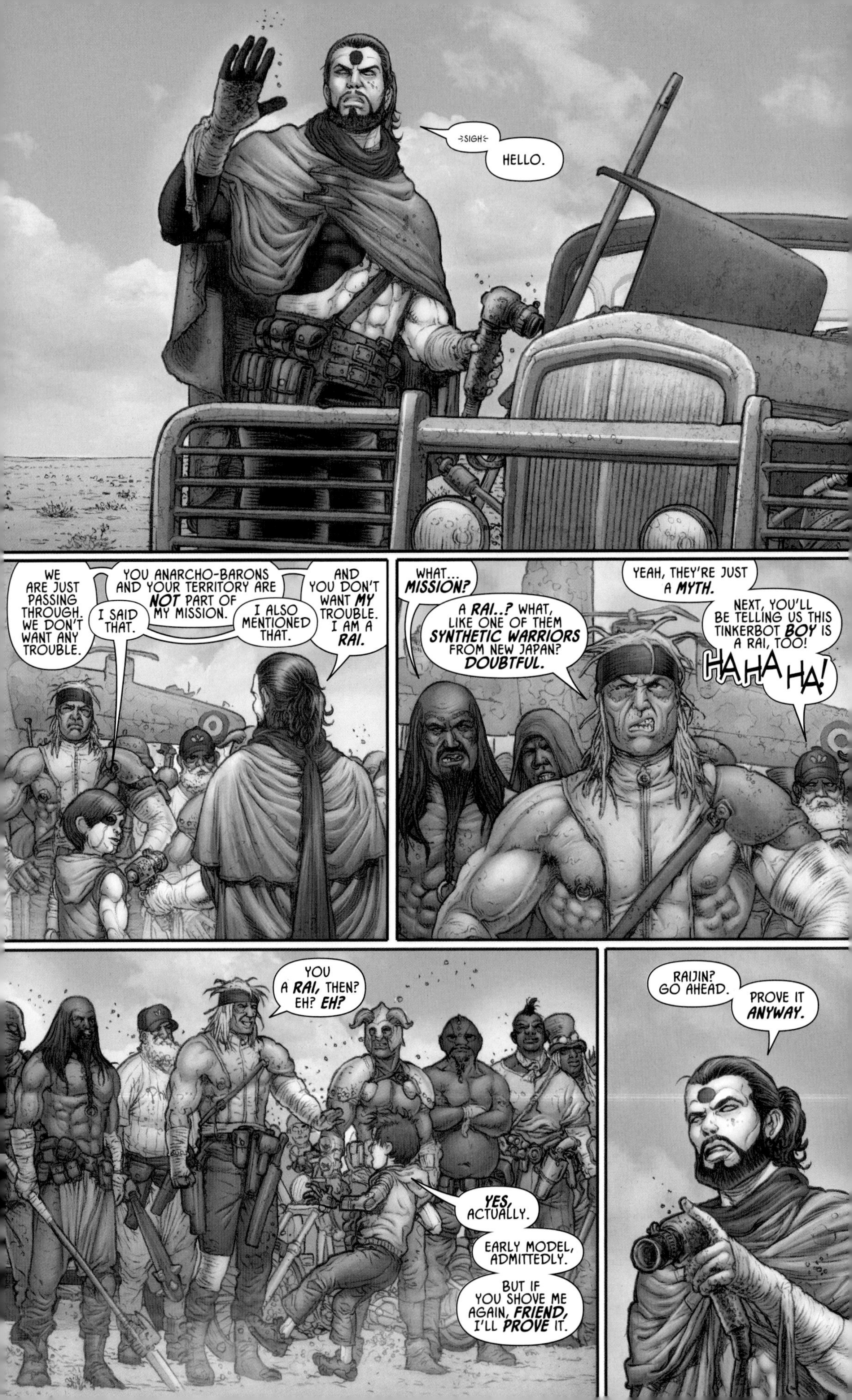
⊰SIGH⊱
HELLO.
WE ARE JUST PASSING THROUGH. WE DON'T WANT ANY TROUBLE.
YOU ANARCHO-BARONS AND YOUR TERRITORY ARE NOT PART OF MY MISSION.
I SAID THAT.
I ALSO MENTIONED THAT.
AND YOU DON'T WANT MY TROUBLE. I AM A RAI.
WHAT... MISSION?
A RAI..? WHAT, LIKE ONE OF THEM SYNTHETIC WARRIORS FROM NEW JAPAN? DOUBTFUL.
YEAH, THEY'RE JUST A MYTH.
NEXT, YOU'LL BE TELLING US THIS TINKERBOT BOY IS A RAI, TOO!
HAHAHA HA!
YOU A RAI, THEN? EH? EH?
YES, ACTUALLY.
EARLY MODEL, ADMITTEDLY.
BUT IF YOU SHOVE ME AGAIN, FRIEND, I'LL PROVE IT.
RAIJIN? GO AHEAD.
PROVE IT ANYWAY.

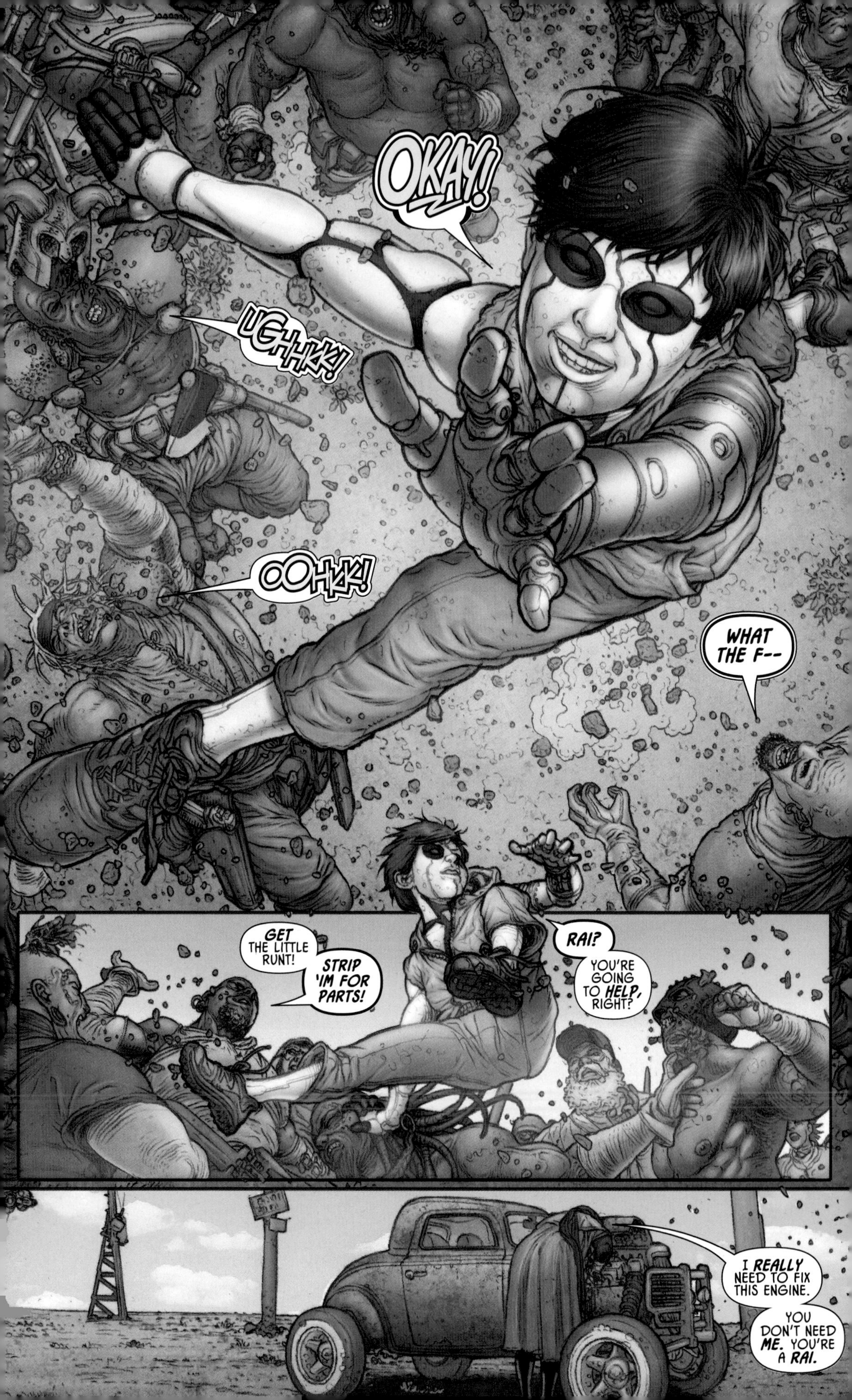
OKAY!
UGHHKK!
OOHKK!
WHAT THE F--
GET THE LITTLE RUNT!
STRIP 'IM FOR PARTS!
RAI?
YOU'RE GOING TO HELP, RIGHT?
I REALLY NEED TO FIX THIS ENGINE.
YOU DON'T NEED ME. YOU'RE A RAI.

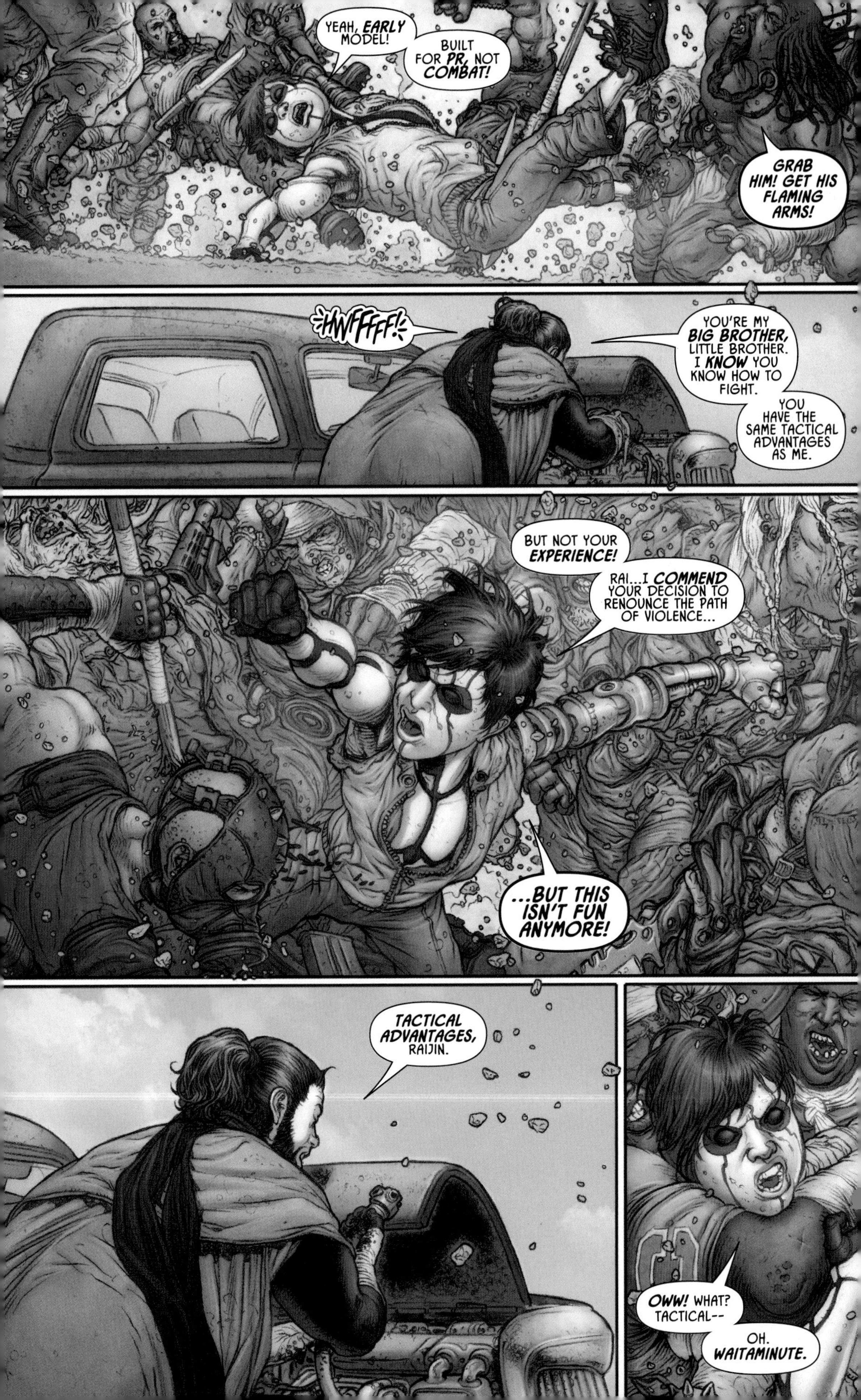
YEAH, EARLY MODEL!
BUILT FOR PR, NOT COMBAT!
GRAB HIM! GET HIS FLAMING ARMS!
HNFFFFF!
YOU'RE MY BIG BROTHER, LITTLE BROTHER. I KNOW YOU KNOW HOW TO FIGHT.
YOU HAVE THE SAME TACTICAL ADVANTAGES AS ME.
BUT NOT YOUR EXPERIENCE!
RAI...I COMMEND YOUR DECISION TO RENOUNCE THE PATH OF VIOLENCE...
...BUT THIS ISN'T FUN ANYMORE!
TACTICAL ADVANTAGES, RAIJIN.
OWW! WHAT? TACTICAL--
OH. WAITAMINUTE.

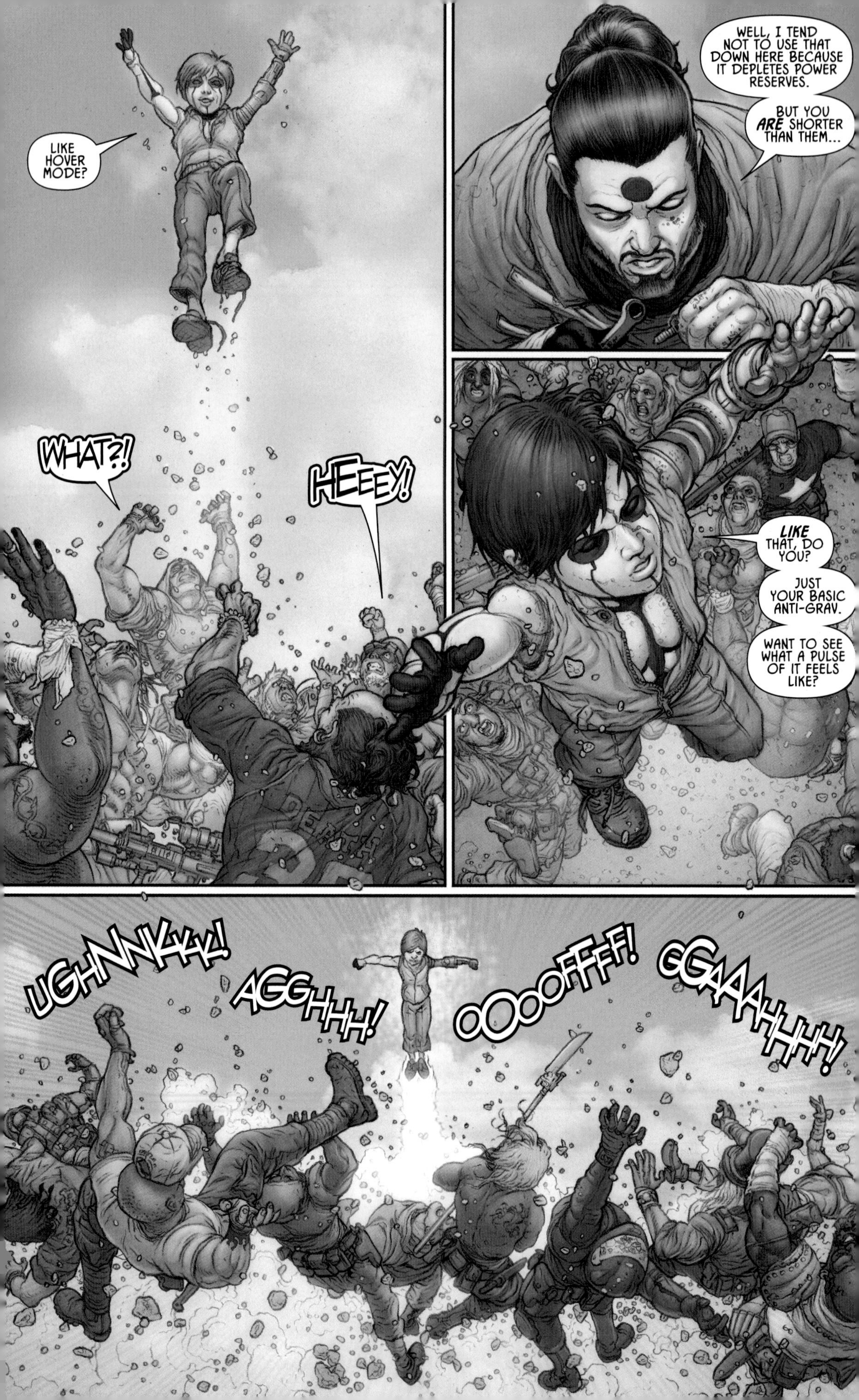
LIKE HOVER MODE?
WELL, I TEND NOT TO USE THAT DOWN HERE BECAUSE IT DEPLETES POWER RESERVES.
BUT YOU ARE SHORTER THAN THEM...
WHAT?!
HEEEY!
LIKE THAT, DO YOU?
JUST YOUR BASIC ANTI-GRAV.
WANT TO SEE WHAT A PULSE OF IT FEELS LIKE?
UGHNNKKK!
AGGHHH!
OOOOFFFF!
GGAAAHHHH!

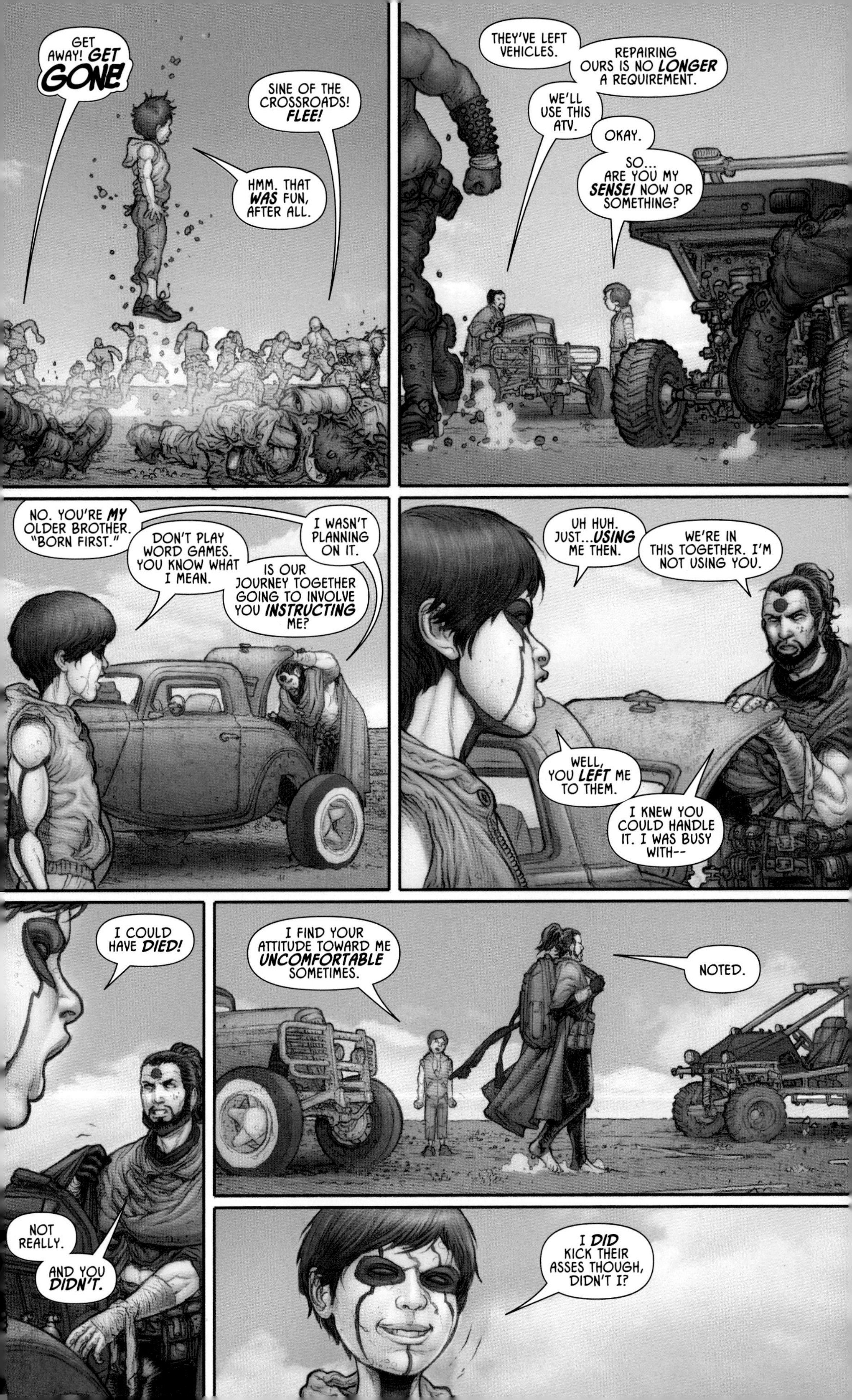
GET AWAY! GET GONE!
SINE OF THE CROSSROADS! FLEE!
HMM. THAT WAS FUN, AFTER ALL.
THEY'VE LEFT VEHICLES.
REPAIRING OURS IS NO LONGER A REQUIREMENT.
WE'LL USE THIS ATV.
OKAY.
SO... ARE YOU MY SENSEI NOW OR SOMETHING?
NO. YOU'RE MY OLDER BROTHER. "BORN FIRST."
DON'T PLAY WORD GAMES. YOU KNOW WHAT I MEAN.
I WASN'T PLANNING ON IT.
IS OUR JOURNEY TOGETHER GOING TO INVOLVE YOU INSTRUCTING ME?
UH HUH. JUST...USING ME THEN.
WE'RE IN THIS TOGETHER. I'M NOT USING YOU.
WELL, YOU LEFT ME TO THEM.
I KNEW YOU COULD HANDLE IT. I WAS BUSY WITH--
I COULD HAVE DIED!
NOT REALLY.
AND YOU DIDN'T.
I FIND YOUR ATTITUDE TOWARD ME UNCOMFORTABLE SOMETIMES.
NOTED.
I DID KICK THEIR ASSES THOUGH, DIDN'T I?

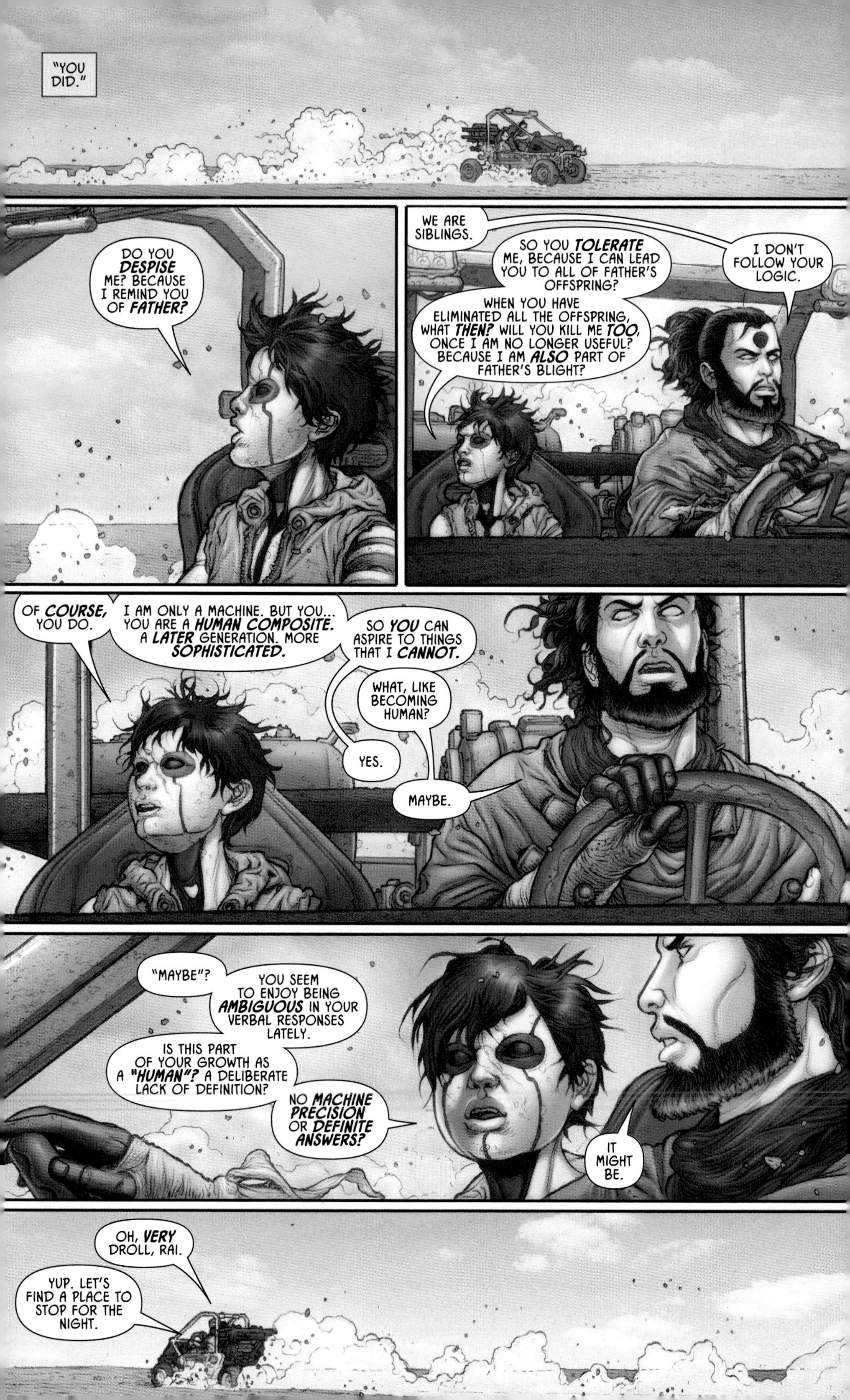
"YOU DID."
DO YOU DESPISE ME? BECAUSE I REMIND YOU OF FATHER?
WE ARE SIBLINGS.
SO YOU TOLERATE ME, BECAUSE I CAN LEAD YOU TO ALL OF FATHER'S OFFSPRING?
I DON'T FOLLOW YOUR LOGIC.
WHEN YOU HAVE ELIMINATED ALL THE OFFSPRING, WHAT THEN? WILL YOU KILL ME TOO, ONCE I AM NO LONGER USEFUL? BECAUSE I AM ALSO PART OF FATHER'S BLIGHT?
OF COURSE, YOU DO.
I AM ONLY A MACHINE. BUT YOU... YOU ARE A HUMAN COMPOSITE. A LATER GENERATION. MORE SOPHISTICATED.
SO YOU CAN ASPIRE TO THINGS THAT I CANNOT.
WHAT, LIKE BECOMING HUMAN?
YES.
MAYBE.
"MAYBE"?
YOU SEEM TO ENJOY BEING AMBIGUOUS IN YOUR VERBAL RESPONSES LATELY.
IS THIS PART OF YOUR GROWTH AS A "HUMAN"? A DELIBERATE LACK OF DEFINITION?
NO MACHINE PRECISION OR DEFINITE ANSWERS?
IT MIGHT BE.
OH, VERY DROLL, RAI.
YUP. LET'S FIND A PLACE TO STOP FOR THE NIGHT.

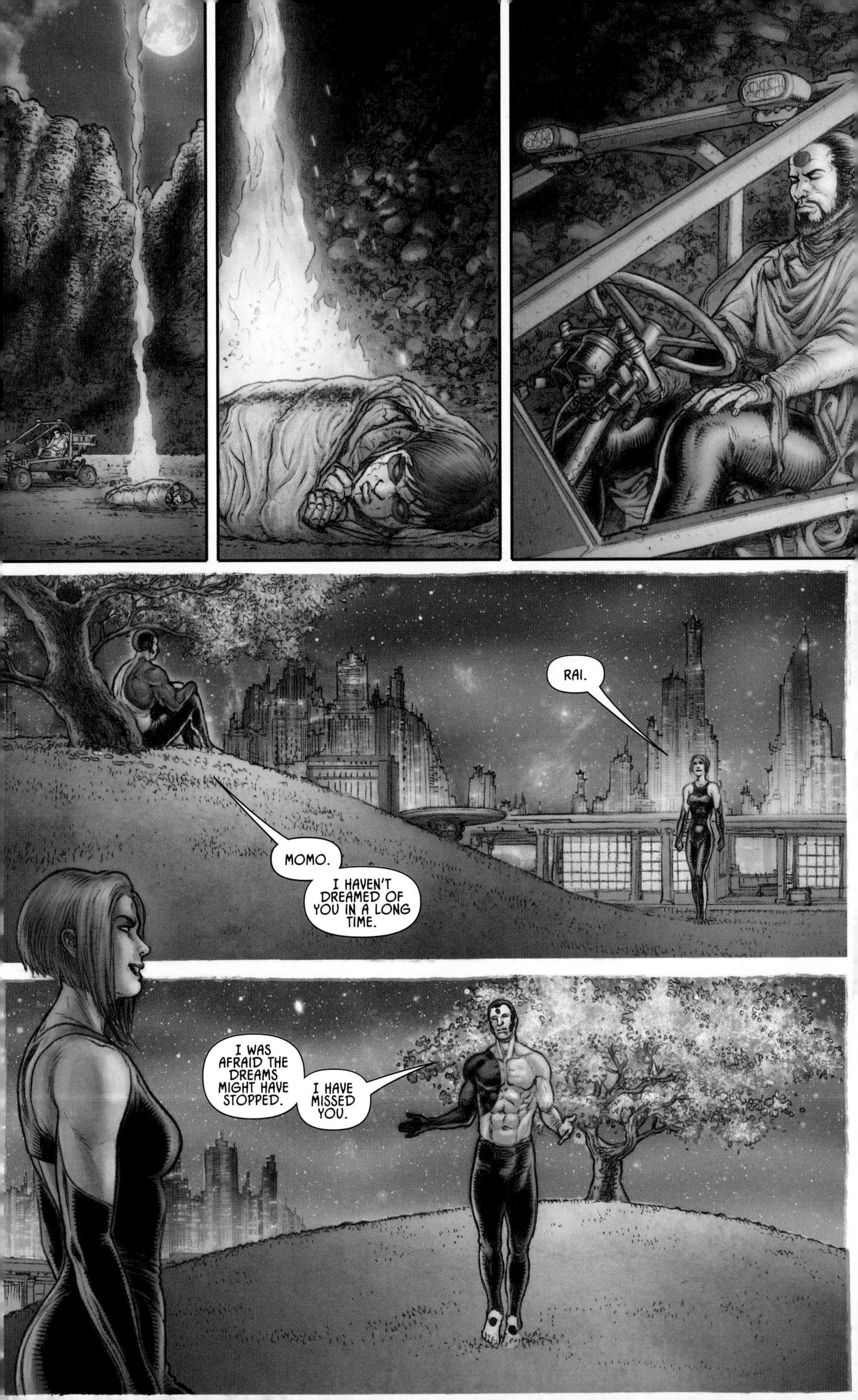
RAI.
MOMO.
I HAVEN'T DREAMED OF YOU IN A LONG TIME.
I WAS AFRAID THE DREAMS MIGHT HAVE STOPPED.
I HAVE MISSED YOU.

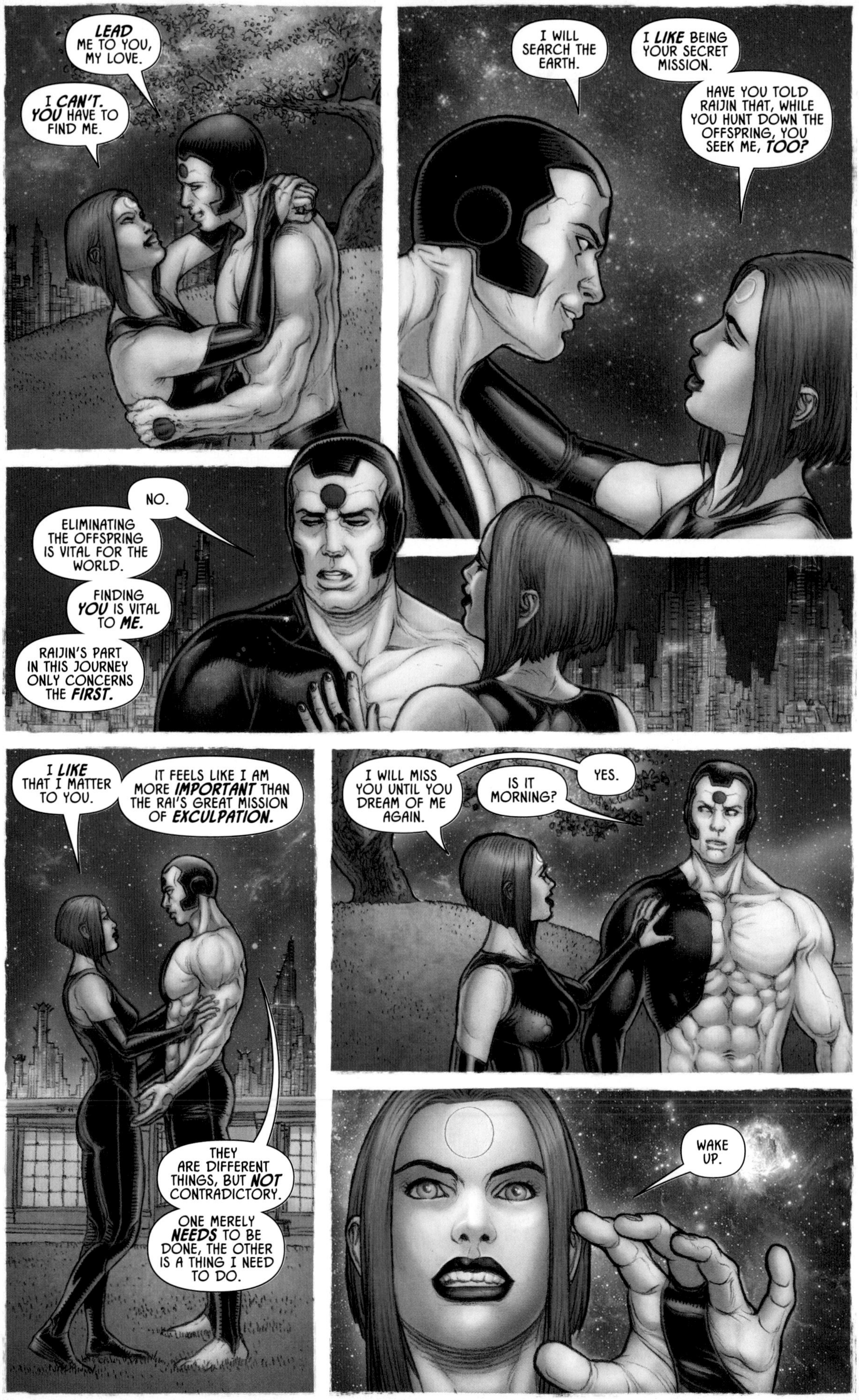

LEAD ME TO YOU, MY LOVE.
I **CAN'T. YOU** HAVE TO FIND ME.
I WILL SEARCH THE EARTH.
I **LIKE** BEING YOUR SECRET MISSION.
HAVE YOU TOLD RAIJIN THAT, WHILE YOU HUNT DOWN THE OFFSPRING, YOU SEEK ME, **TOO?**
NO.
ELIMINATING THE OFFSPRING IS VITAL FOR THE WORLD.
FINDING **YOU** IS VITAL TO **ME.**
RAIJIN'S PART IN THIS JOURNEY ONLY CONCERNS THE **FIRST.**
I **LIKE** THAT I MATTER TO YOU.
IT FEELS LIKE I AM MORE **IMPORTANT** THAN THE RAI'S GREAT MISSION OF **EXCULPATION.**
THEY ARE DIFFERENT THINGS, BUT **NOT** CONTRADICTORY.
ONE MERELY **NEEDS** TO BE DONE, THE OTHER IS A THING I NEED TO DO.
IS IT MORNING?
YES.
I WILL MISS YOU UNTIL YOU DREAM OF ME AGAIN.
WAKE UP.

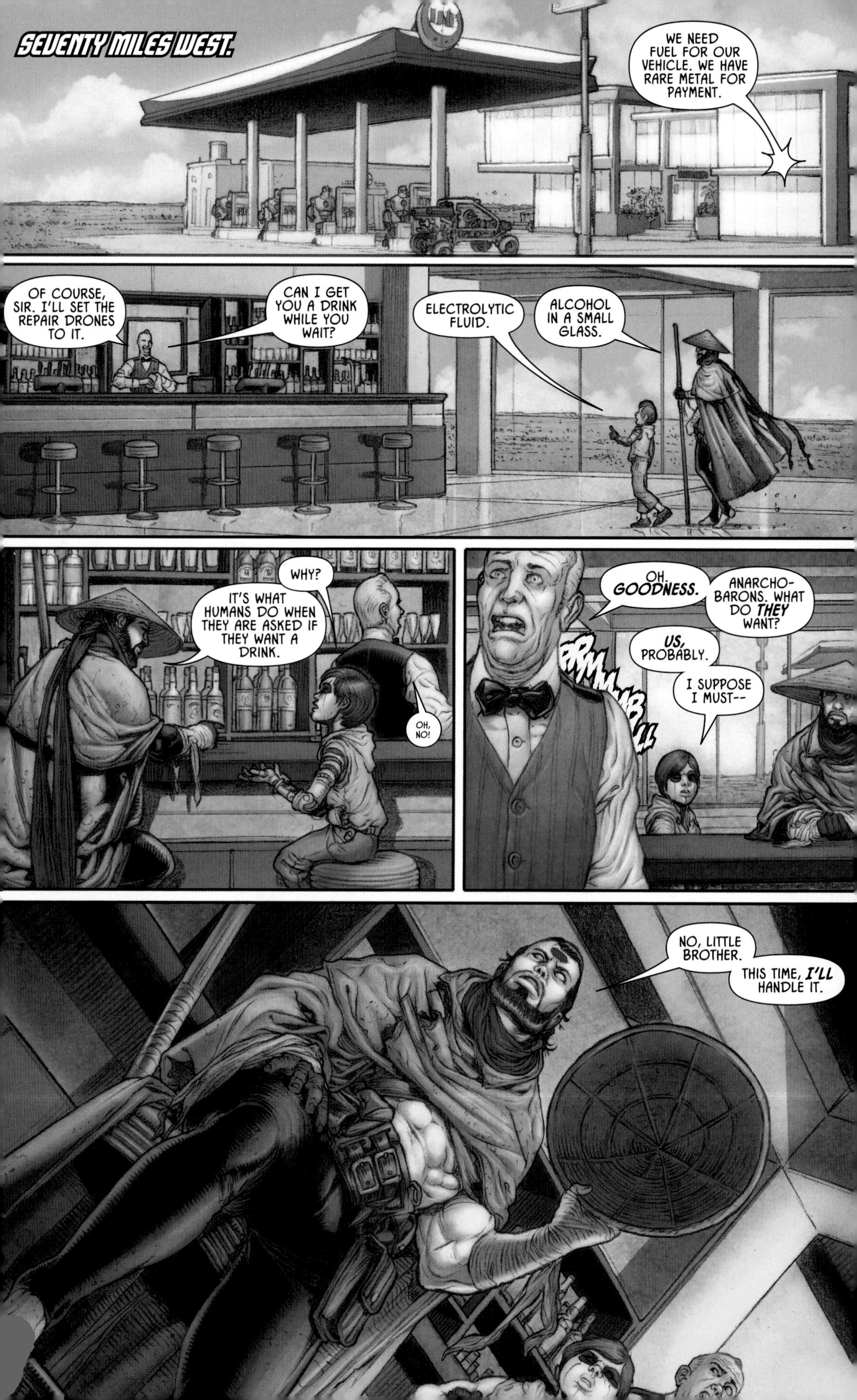

SEVENTY MILES WEST.
WE NEED FUEL FOR OUR VEHICLE. WE HAVE RARE METAL FOR PAYMENT.
OF COURSE, SIR. I'LL SET THE REPAIR DRONES TO IT.
CAN I GET YOU A DRINK WHILE YOU WAIT?
ELECTROLYTIC FLUID.
ALCOHOL IN A SMALL GLASS.
WHY?
IT'S WHAT HUMANS DO WHEN THEY ARE ASKED IF THEY WANT A DRINK.
OH, NO!
OH. GOODNESS.
ANARCHO-BARONS. WHAT DO THEY WANT?
US, PROBABLY.
I SUPPOSE I MUST--
NO, LITTLE BROTHER.
THIS TIME, I'LL HANDLE IT.

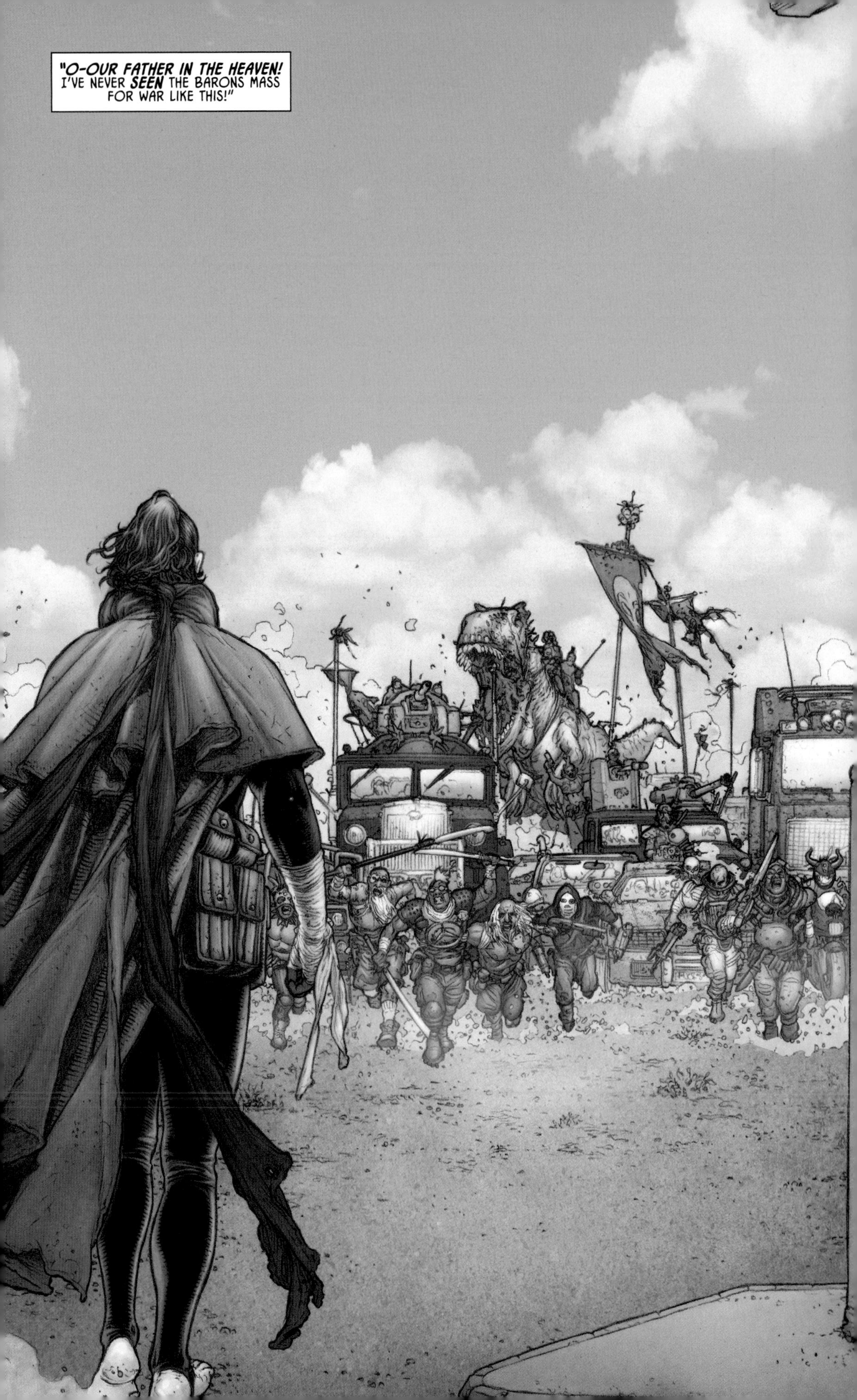
"O-OUR FATHER IN THE HEAVEN! I'VE NEVER SEEN THE BARONS MASS FOR WAR LIKE THIS!"

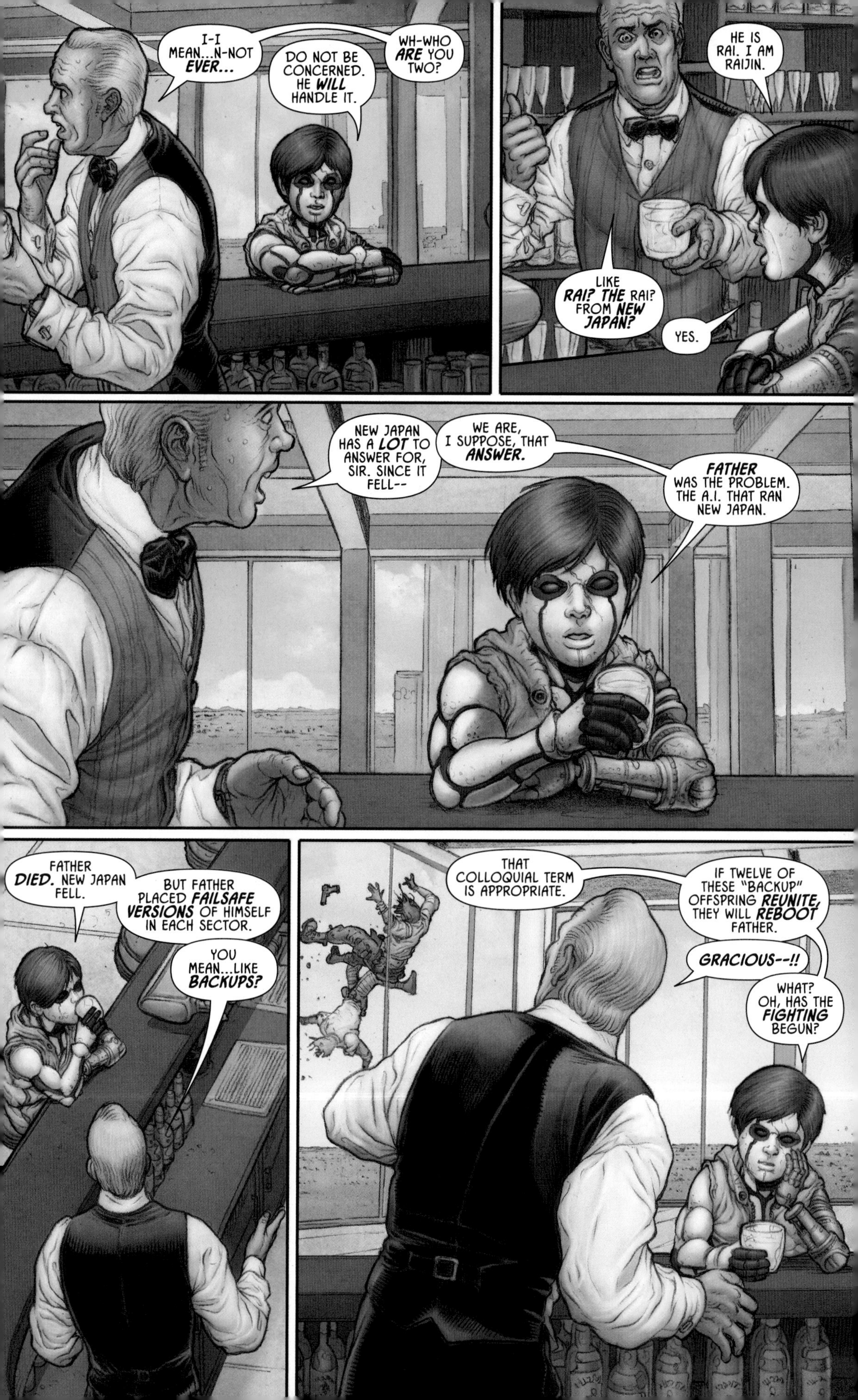
I-I MEAN...N-NOT **EVER...**
DO NOT BE CONCERNED. HE **WILL** HANDLE IT.
WH-WHO **ARE** YOU TWO?
HE IS RAI. I AM RAIJIN.
LIKE **RAI? THE** RAI? FROM **NEW JAPAN?**
YES.
NEW JAPAN HAS A **LOT** TO ANSWER FOR, SIR. SINCE IT FELL--
WE ARE, I SUPPOSE, THAT **ANSWER.**
FATHER WAS THE PROBLEM. THE A.I. THAT RAN NEW JAPAN.
FATHER **DIED.** NEW JAPAN FELL.
BUT FATHER PLACED **FAILSAFE VERSIONS** OF HIMSELF IN EACH SECTOR.
YOU MEAN...LIKE **BACKUPS?**
THAT COLLOQUIAL TERM IS APPROPRIATE.
IF TWELVE OF THESE "BACKUP" OFFSPRING **REUNITE,** THEY WILL **REBOOT** FATHER.
GRACIOUS--!!
WHAT? OH, HAS THE **FIGHTING** BEGUN?

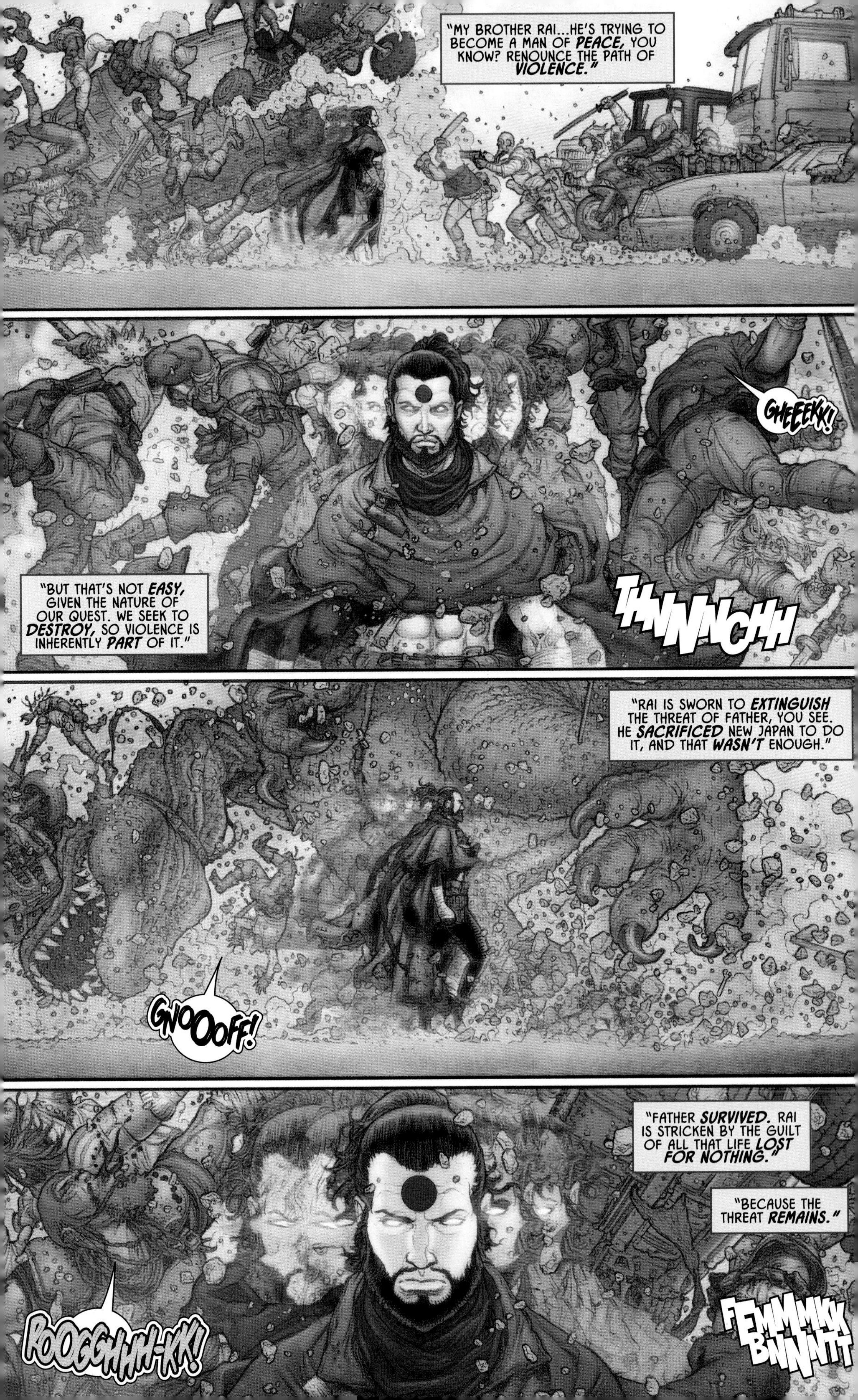
"MY BROTHER RAI...HE'S TRYING TO BECOME A MAN OF PEACE, YOU KNOW? RENOUNCE THE PATH OF VIOLENCE."
GHEEEKK!
"BUT THAT'S NOT EASY, GIVEN THE NATURE OF OUR QUEST. WE SEEK TO DESTROY, SO VIOLENCE IS INHERENTLY PART OF IT."
THNNNCHH
"RAI IS SWORN TO EXTINGUISH THE THREAT OF FATHER, YOU SEE. HE SACRIFICED NEW JAPAN TO DO IT, AND THAT WASN'T ENOUGH."
GNOOOOFF!
"FATHER SURVIVED. RAI IS STRICKEN BY THE GUILT OF ALL THAT LIFE LOST FOR NOTHING."
"BECAUSE THE THREAT REMAINS."
ROOGGHHH-KK!
FEMMMKK BNNNTT

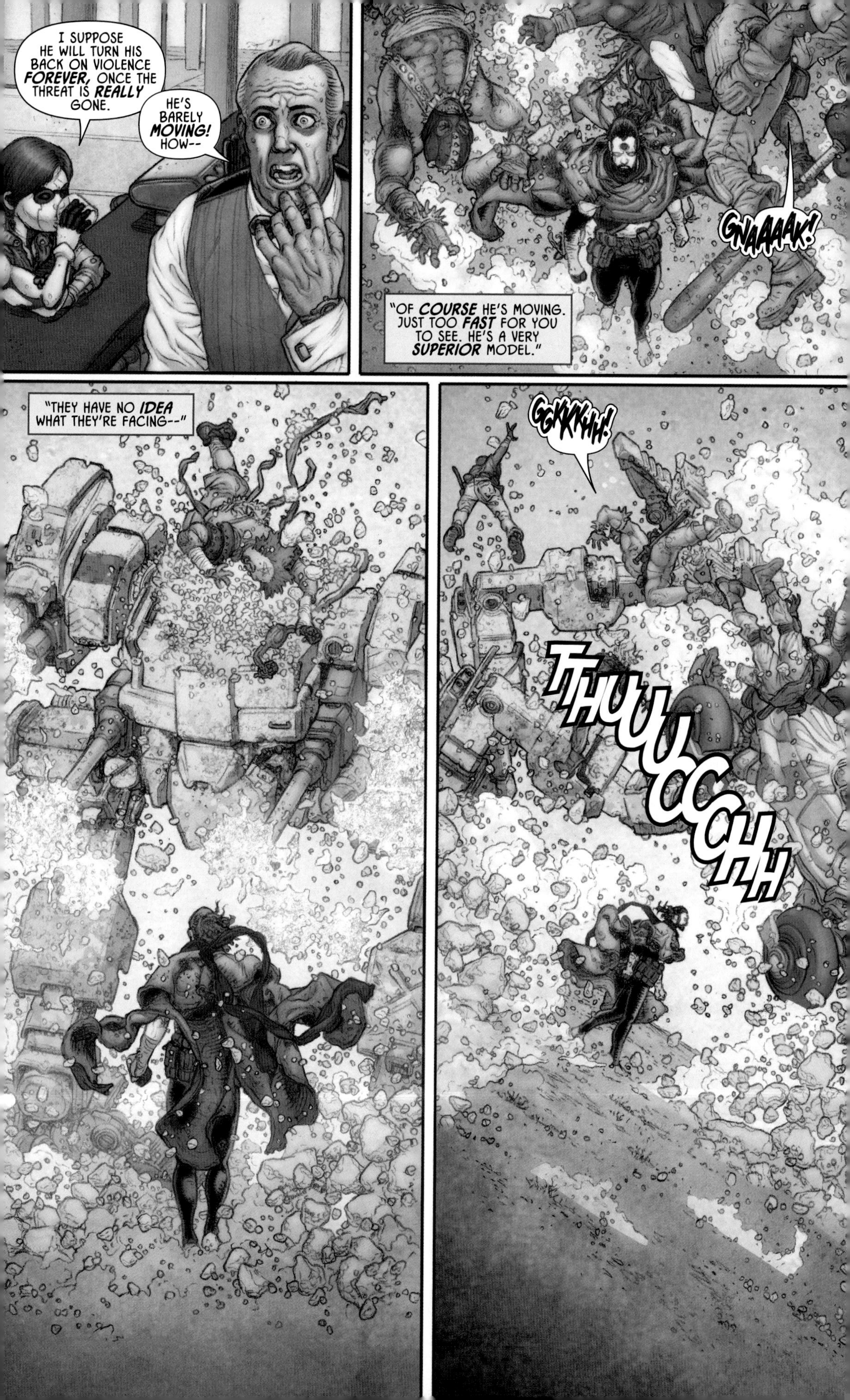
I SUPPOSE HE WILL TURN HIS BACK ON VIOLENCE FOREVER, ONCE THE THREAT IS REALLY GONE.
HE'S BARELY MOVING! HOW--
GNAAAAK!
"OF COURSE HE'S MOVING. JUST TOO FAST FOR YOU TO SEE. HE'S A VERY SUPERIOR MODEL."
"THEY HAVE NO IDEA WHAT THEY'RE FACING--"
GGKKKHH!
TTHUUUCCHHH

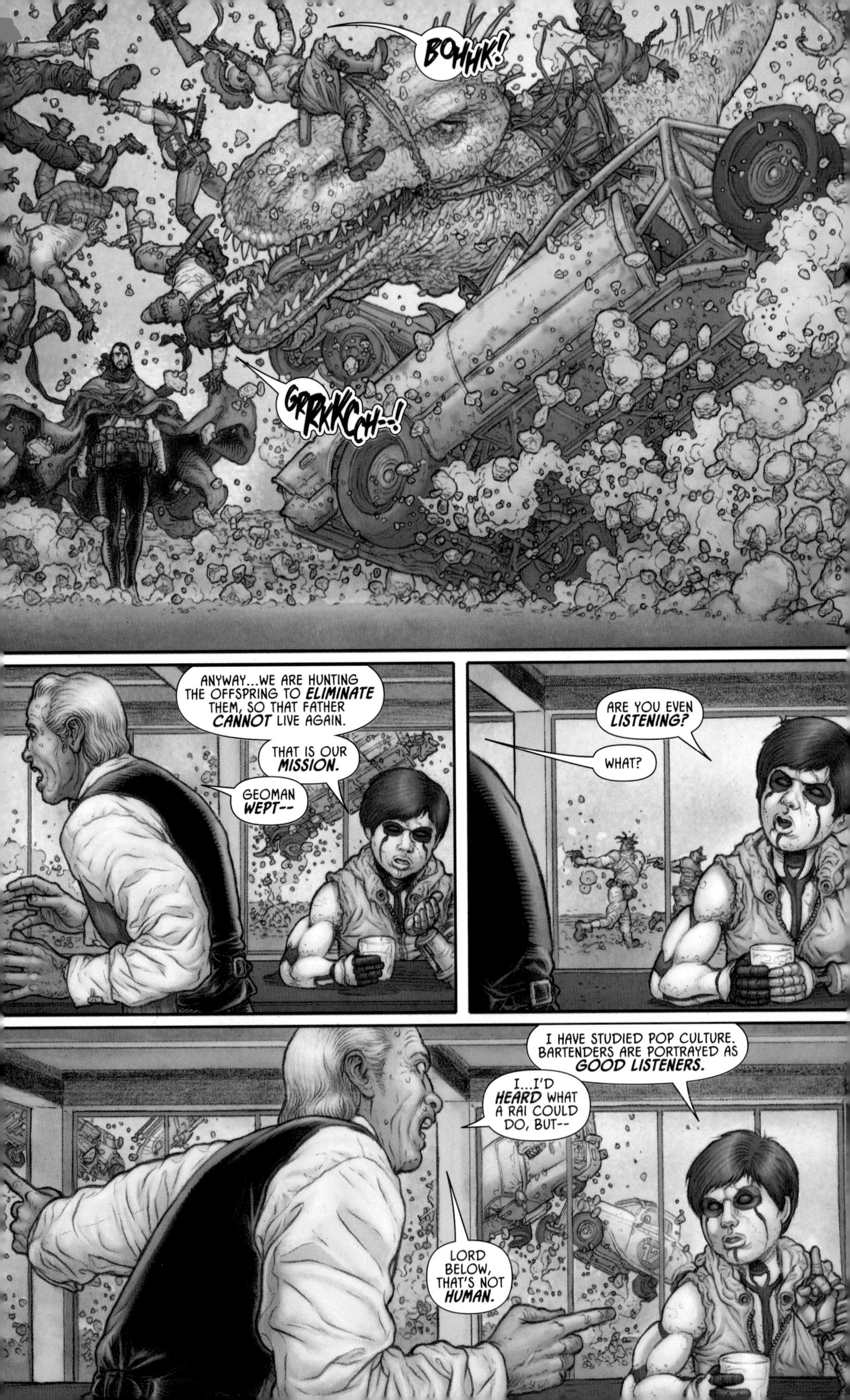
BOHHK!
GRRKKCCH--!
ANYWAY...WE ARE HUNTING THE OFFSPRING TO ELIMINATE THEM, SO THAT FATHER CANNOT LIVE AGAIN.
THAT IS OUR MISSION.
GEOMAN WEPT--
ARE YOU EVEN LISTENING?
WHAT?
I HAVE STUDIED POP CULTURE. BARTENDERS ARE PORTRAYED AS GOOD LISTENERS.
I...I'D HEARD WHAT A RAI COULD DO, BUT--
LORD BELOW, THAT'S NOT HUMAN.

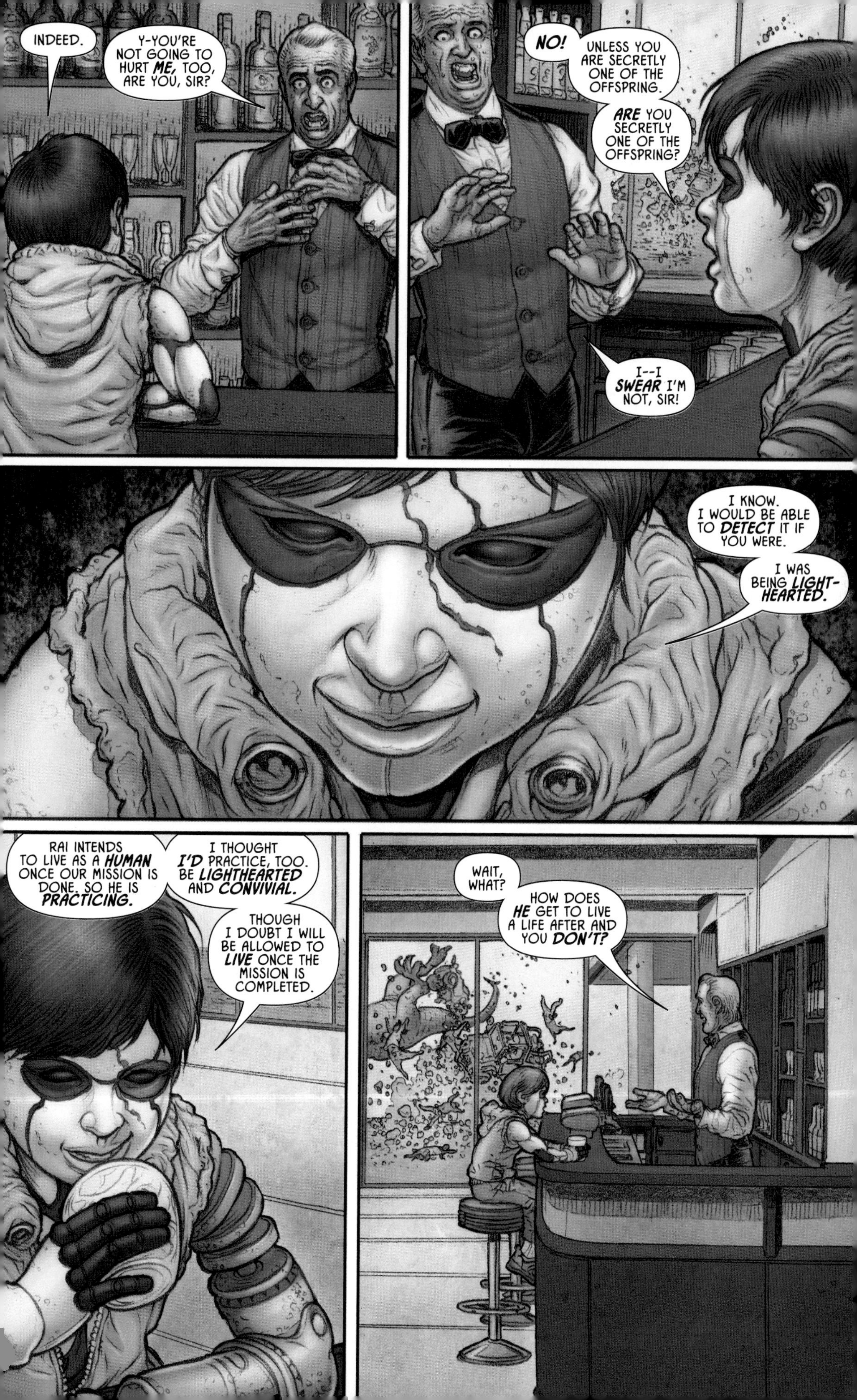
INDEED.
Y-YOU'RE NOT GOING TO HURT ME, TOO, ARE YOU, SIR?
NO!
UNLESS YOU ARE SECRETLY ONE OF THE OFFSPRING.
ARE YOU SECRETLY ONE OF THE OFFSPRING?
I--I SWEAR I'M NOT, SIR!
I KNOW. I WOULD BE ABLE TO DETECT IT IF YOU WERE.
I WAS BEING LIGHT-HEARTED.
RAI INTENDS TO LIVE AS A HUMAN ONCE OUR MISSION IS DONE. SO HE IS PRACTICING.
I THOUGHT I'D PRACTICE, TOO. BE LIGHTHEARTED AND CONVIVIAL.
THOUGH I DOUBT I WILL BE ALLOWED TO LIVE ONCE THE MISSION IS COMPLETED.
WAIT, WHAT?
HOW DOES HE GET TO LIVE A LIFE AFTER AND YOU DON'T?

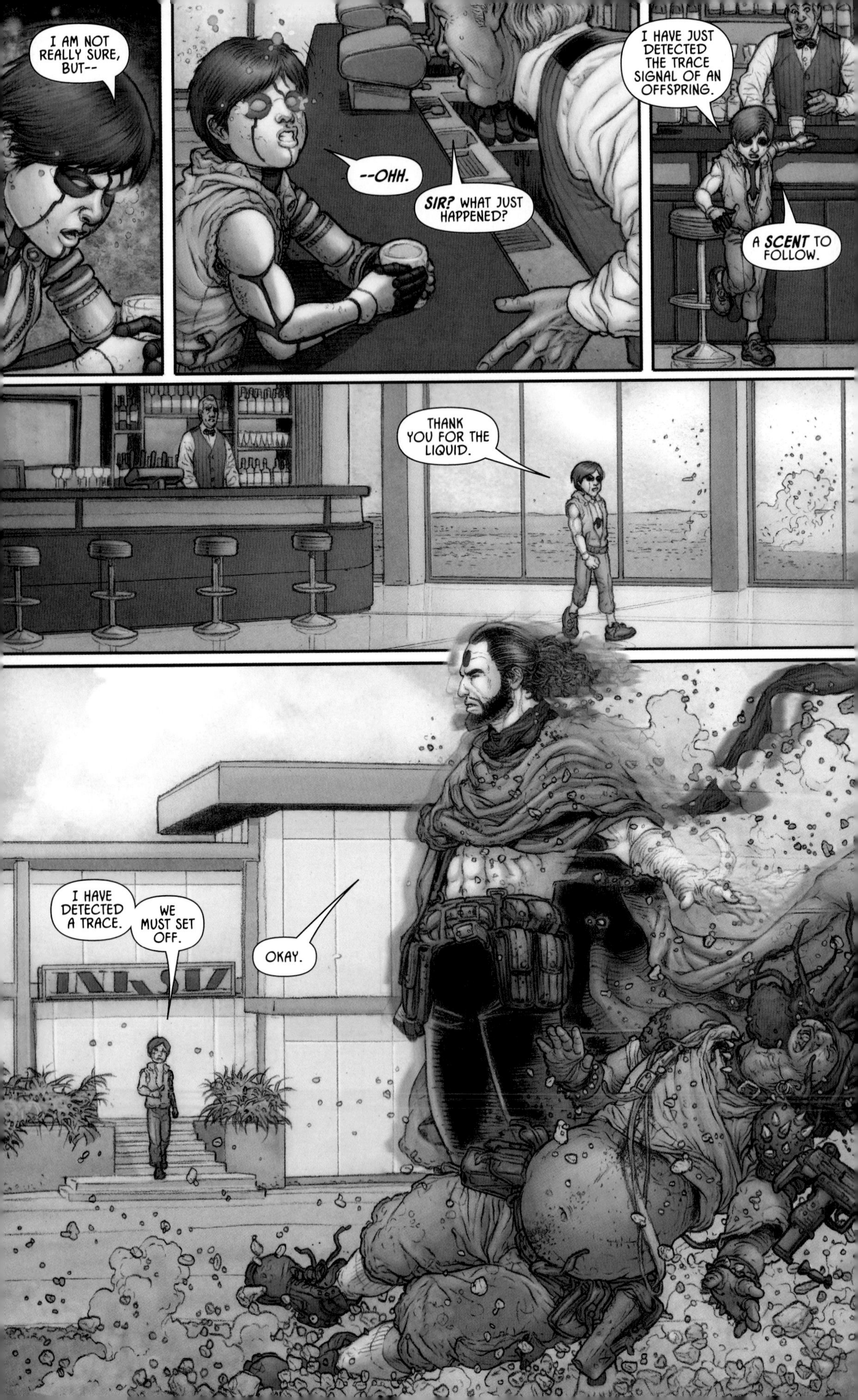
I AM NOT REALLY SURE, BUT--
--OHH.
SIR? WHAT JUST HAPPENED?
I HAVE JUST DETECTED THE TRACE SIGNAL OF AN OFFSPRING.
A SCENT TO FOLLOW.
THANK YOU FOR THE LIQUID.
I HAVE DETECTED A TRACE.
WE MUST SET OFF.
OKAY.

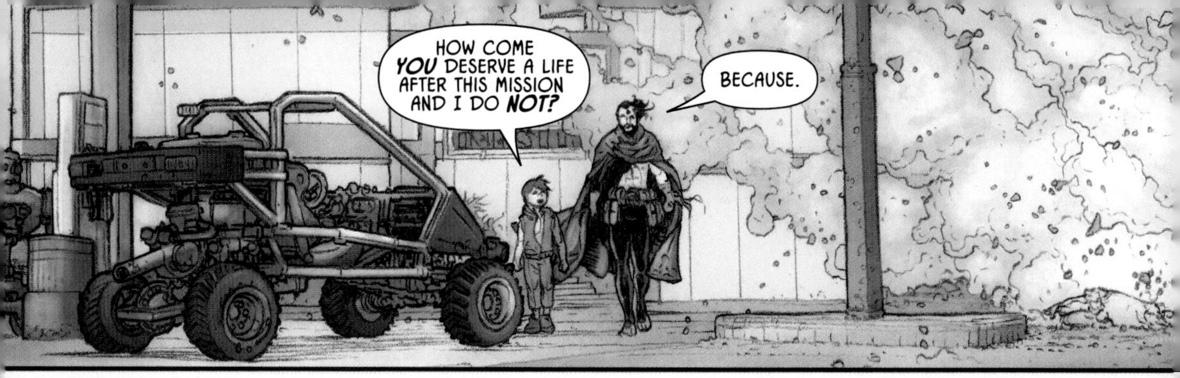
HOW COME YOU DESERVE A LIFE AFTER THIS MISSION AND I DO NOT?
BECAUSE.

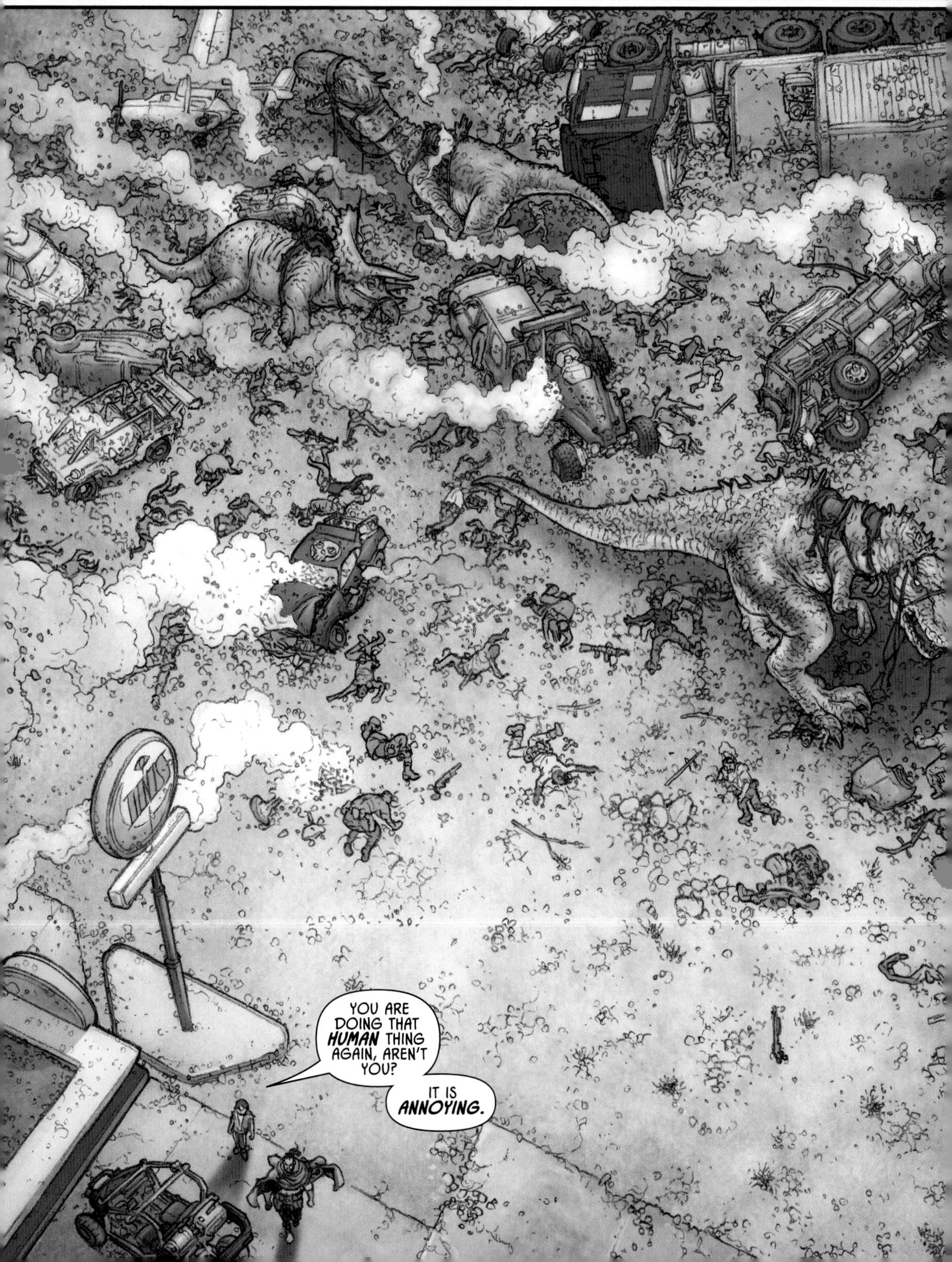
YOU ARE DOING THAT HUMAN THING AGAIN, AREN'T YOU?
IT IS ANNOYING.

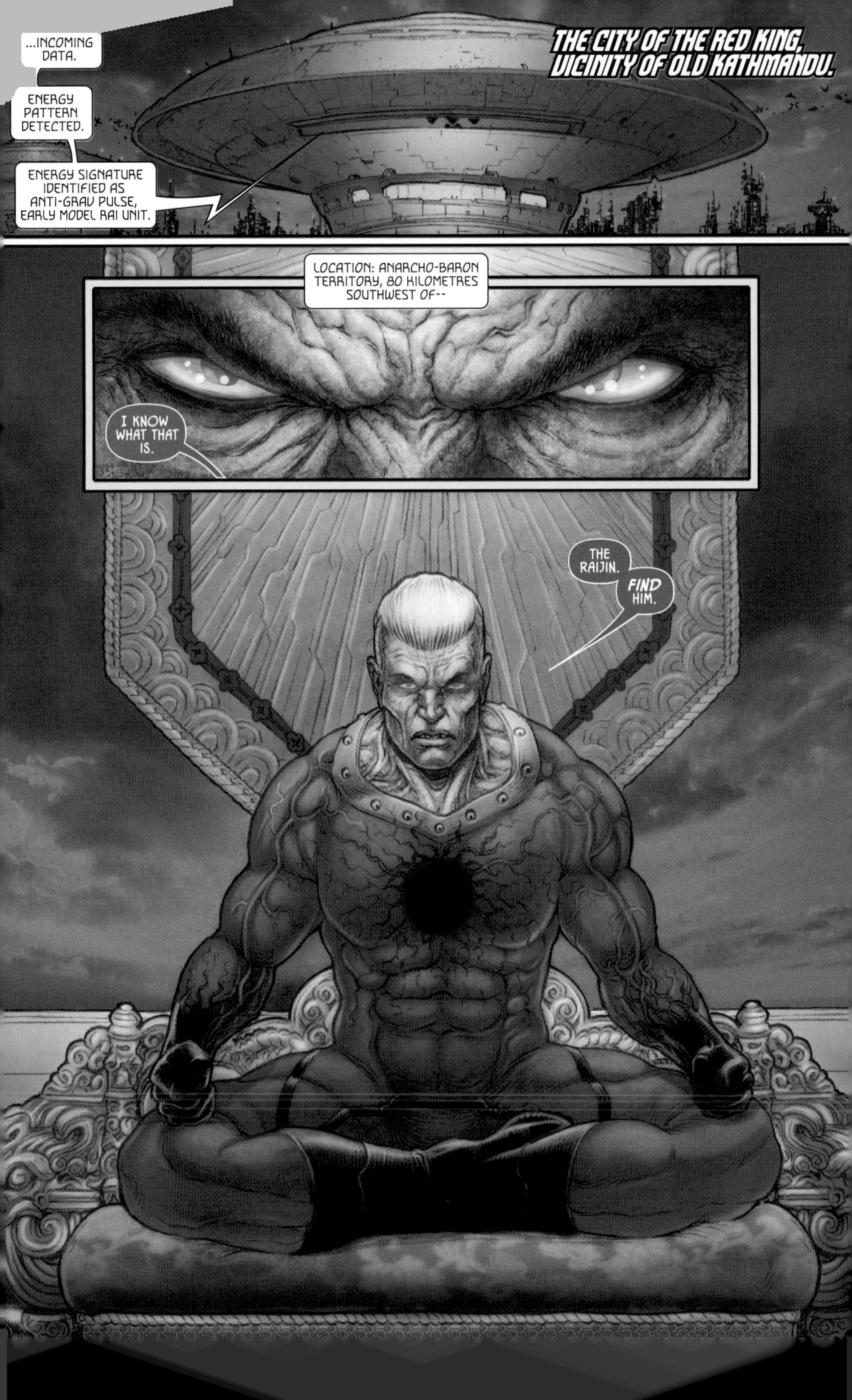
THE CITY OF THE RED KING, VICINITY OF OLD KATHMANDU.
...INCOMING DATA.
ENERGY PATTERN DETECTED.
ENERGY SIGNATURE IDENTIFIED AS ANTI-GRAV PULSE, EARLY MODEL RAI UNIT.
LOCATION: ANARCHO-BARON TERRITORY, 80 KILOMETRES SOUTHWEST OF--
I KNOW WHAT THAT IS.
THE RAIJIN.
FIND HIM.

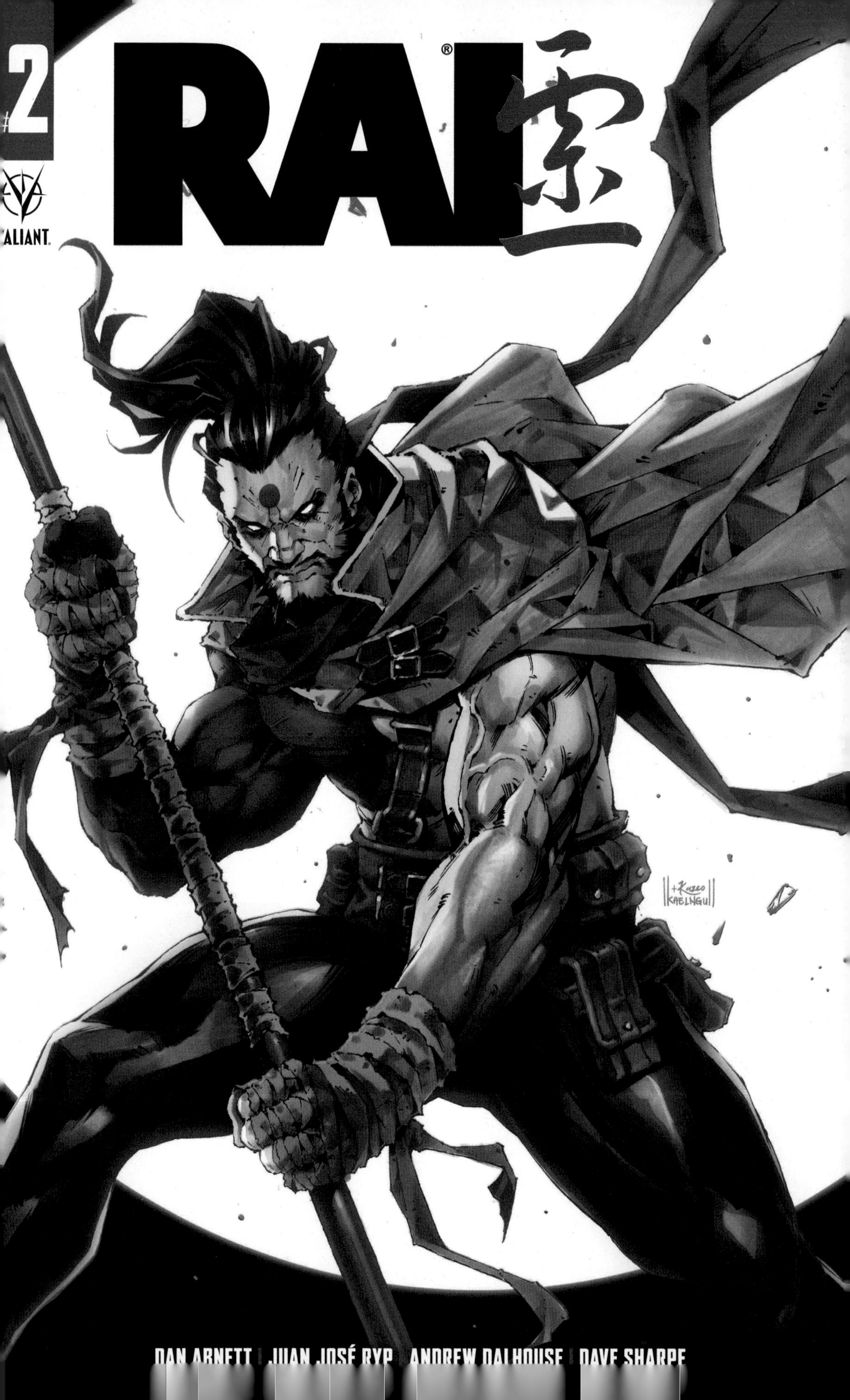

#2
RAI®
VALIANT
DAN ABNETT | JUAN JOSÉ RYP | ANDREW DALHOUSE | DAVE SHARPE

RAI #2

WRITER: DAN ABNETT
ARTIST: JUAN JOSÉ RYP
COLORIST: ANDREW DALHOUSE
LETTERER: DAVE SHARPE
COVER ARTISTS: KAEL NGU with KAZEO
ASSOCIATE EDITOR: DAVID MENCHEL
EDITOR: LYSA HAWKINS

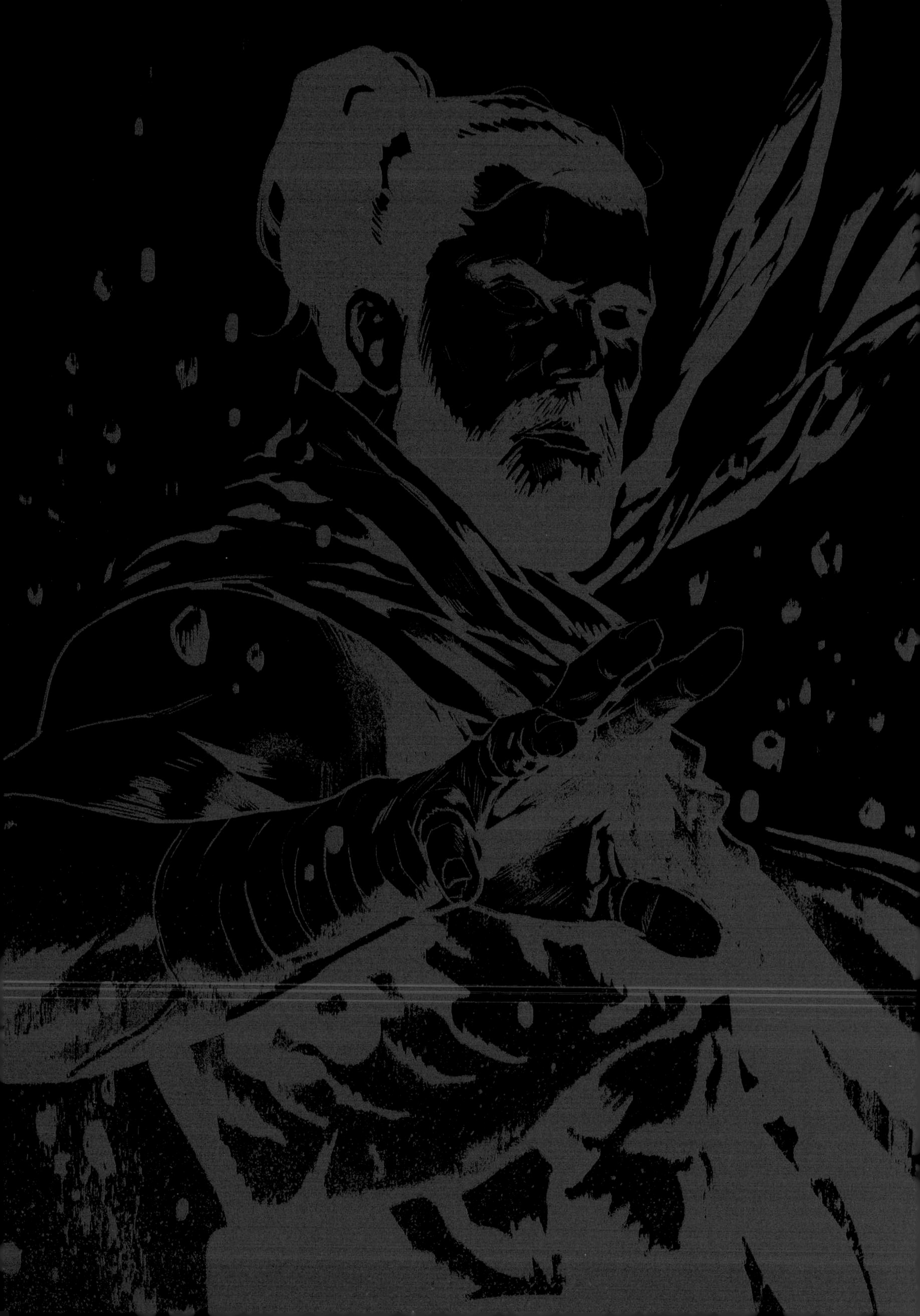

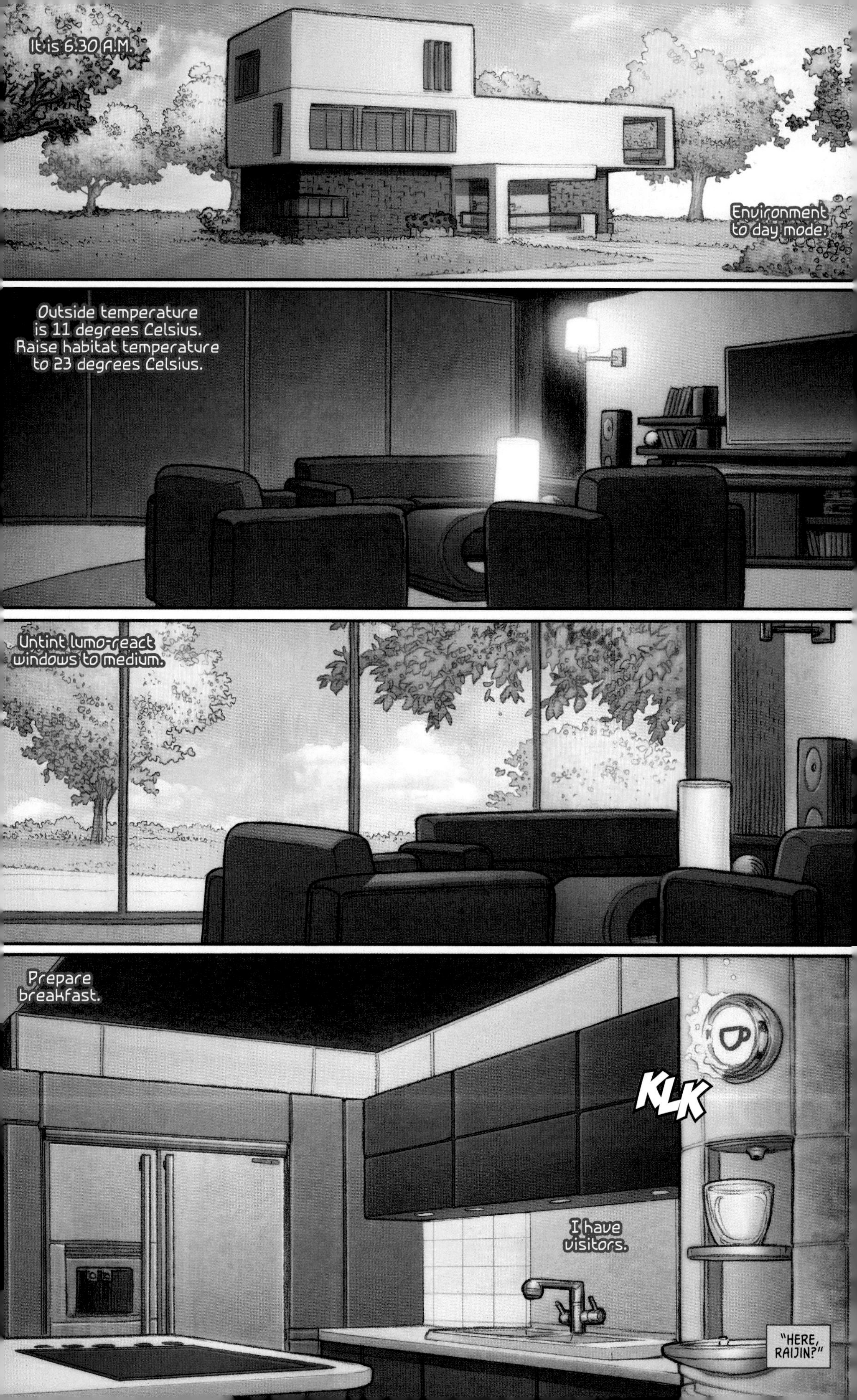
It is 6:30 A.M.
Environment to day mode.
Outside temperature is 11 degrees Celsius. Raise habitat temperature to 23 degrees Celsius.
Untint lumo-react windows to medium.
Prepare breakfast.
KLK
I have visitors.
"HERE, RAIJIN?"

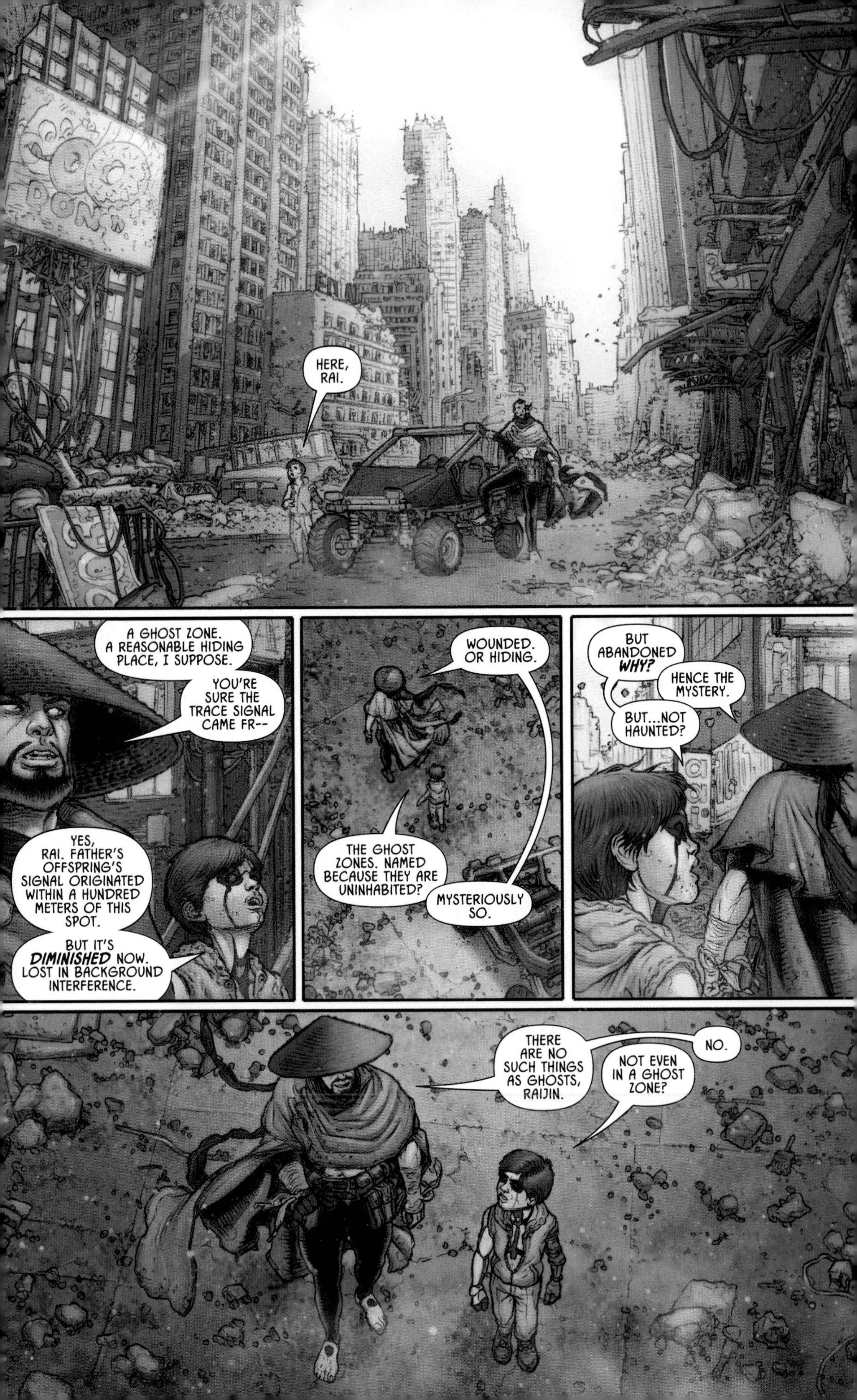
HERE, RAI.
A GHOST ZONE. A REASONABLE HIDING PLACE, I SUPPOSE.
YOU'RE SURE THE TRACE SIGNAL CAME FR--
YES, RAI. FATHER'S OFFSPRING'S SIGNAL ORIGINATED WITHIN A HUNDRED METERS OF THIS SPOT.
BUT IT'S ***DIMINISHED*** NOW. LOST IN BACKGROUND INTERFERENCE.
WOUNDED. OR HIDING.
THE GHOST ZONES. NAMED BECAUSE THEY ARE UNINHABITED?
MYSTERIOUSLY SO.
BUT ABANDONED ***WHY?***
HENCE THE MYSTERY.
BUT...NOT HAUNTED?
NO.
NOT EVEN IN A GHOST ZONE?
THERE ARE NO SUCH THINGS AS GHOSTS, RAIJIN.

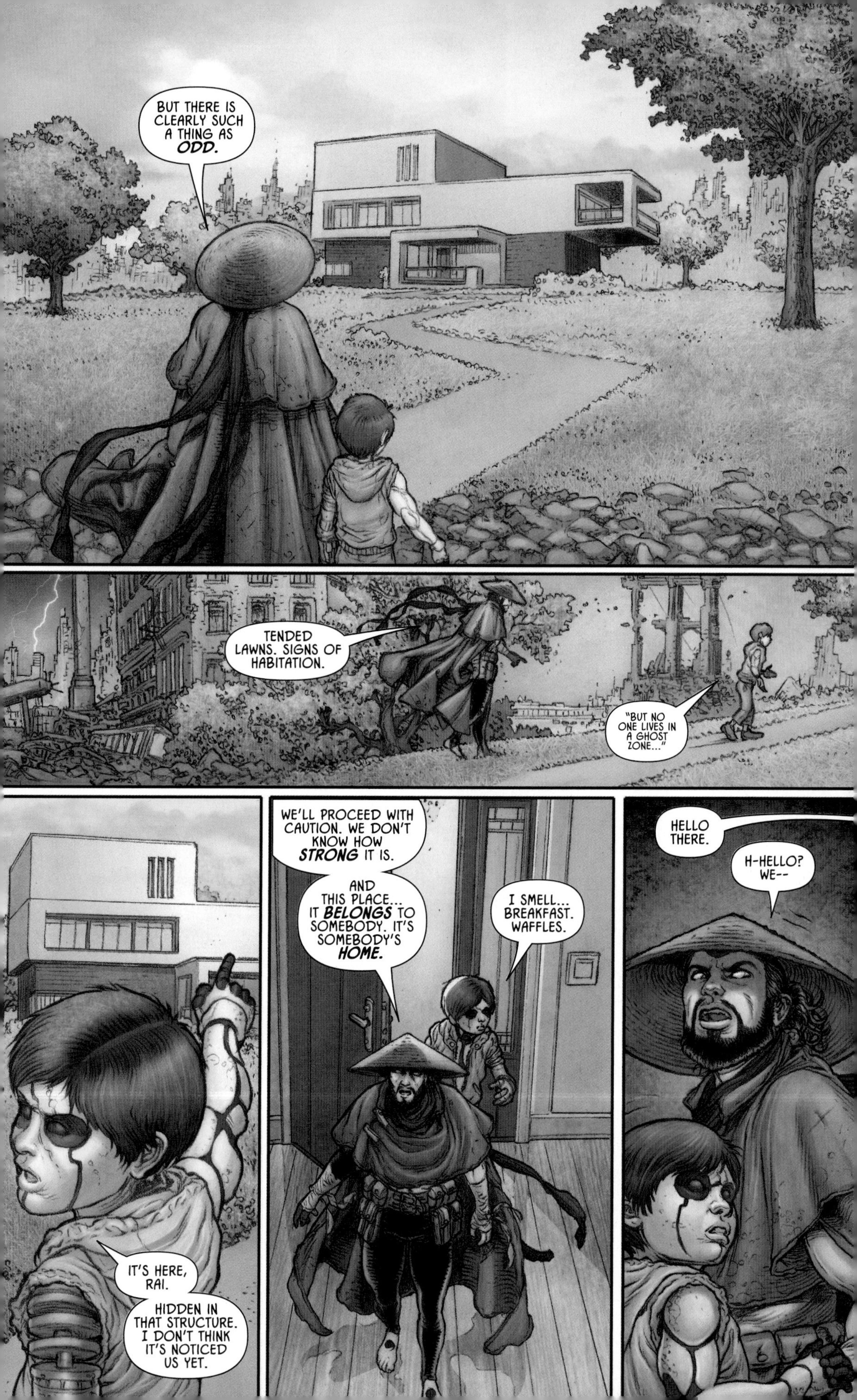
BUT THERE IS CLEARLY SUCH A THING AS ODD.
TENDED LAWNS. SIGNS OF HABITATION.
"BUT NO ONE LIVES IN A GHOST ZONE..."
IT'S HERE, RAI.
HIDDEN IN THAT STRUCTURE. I DON'T THINK IT'S NOTICED US YET.
WE'LL PROCEED WITH CAUTION. WE DON'T KNOW HOW STRONG IT IS.
AND THIS PLACE... IT BELONGS TO SOMEBODY. IT'S SOMEBODY'S HOME.
I SMELL... BREAKFAST. WAFFLES.
HELLO THERE.
H-HELLO? WE--

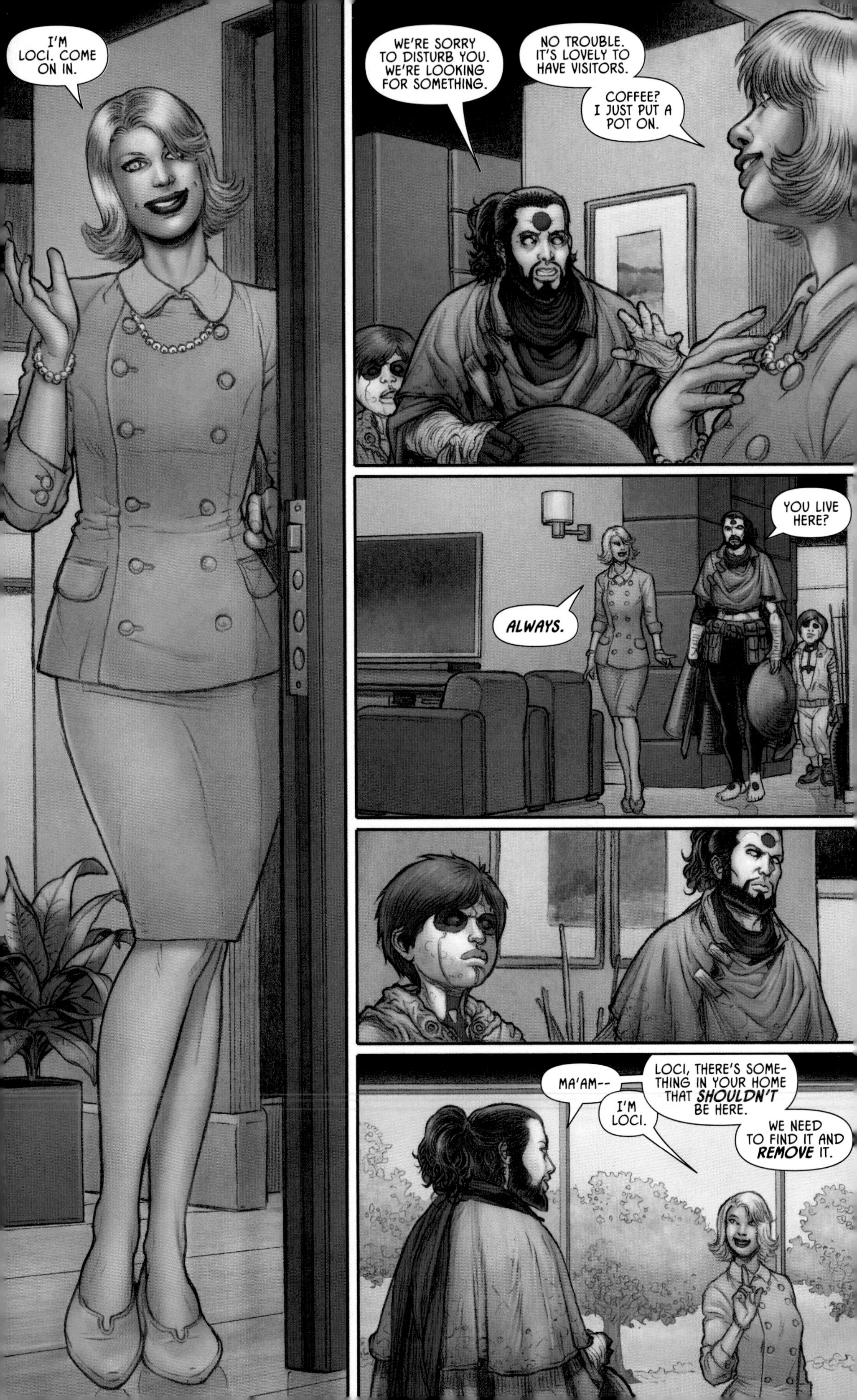

I'M LOCI. COME ON IN.
WE'RE SORRY TO DISTURB YOU. WE'RE LOOKING FOR SOMETHING.
NO TROUBLE. IT'S LOVELY TO HAVE VISITORS.
COFFEE? I JUST PUT A POT ON.
YOU LIVE HERE?
ALWAYS.
MA'AM--
LOCI, THERE'S SOME-THING IN YOUR HOME THAT SHOULDN'T BE HERE.
I'M LOCI.
WE NEED TO FIND IT AND REMOVE IT.

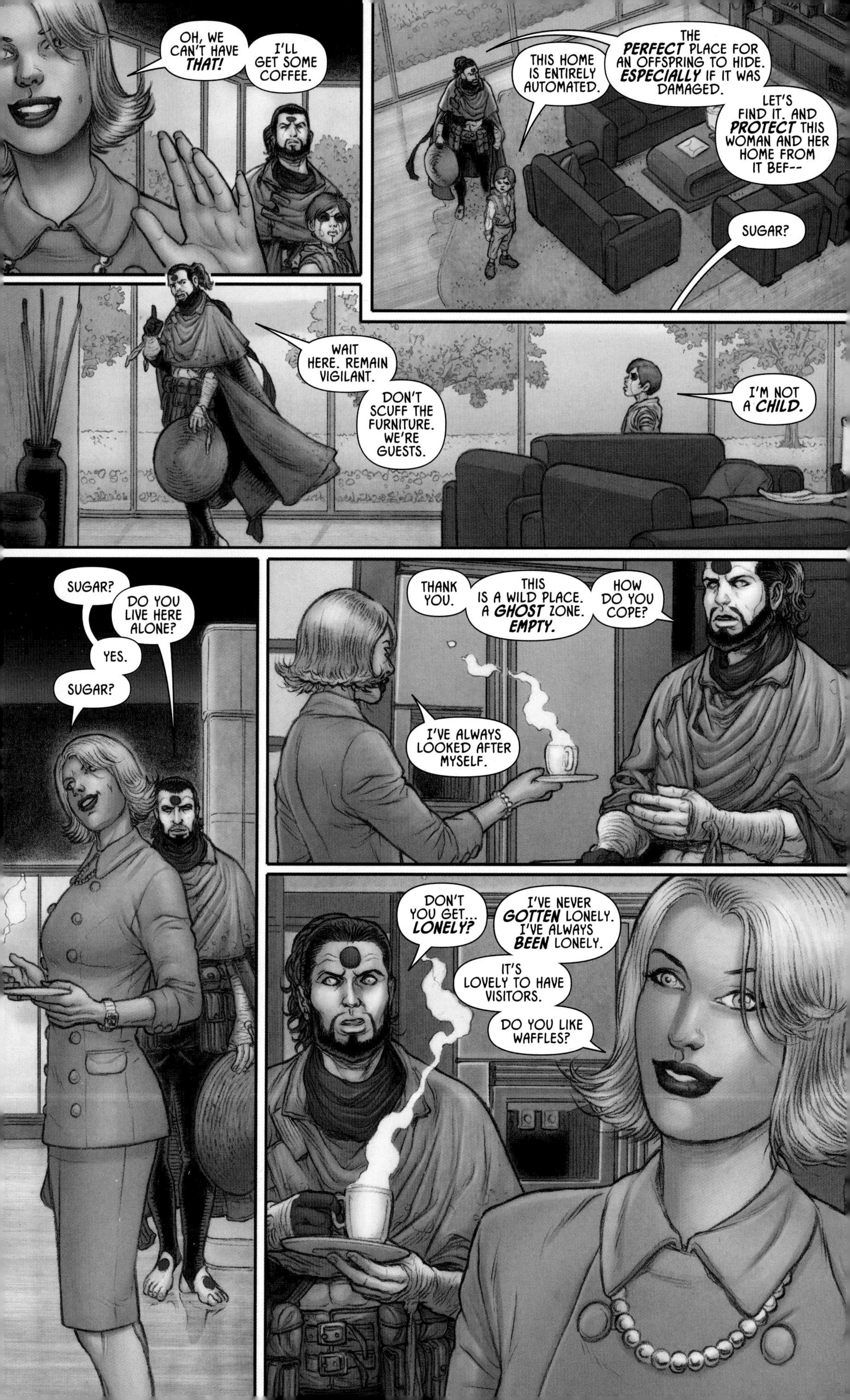
OH, WE CAN'T HAVE **THAT!**
I'LL GET SOME COFFEE.
THIS HOME IS ENTIRELY AUTOMATED.
THE **PERFECT** PLACE FOR AN OFFSPRING TO HIDE. **ESPECIALLY** IF IT WAS DAMAGED.
LET'S FIND IT. AND **PROTECT** THIS WOMAN AND HER HOME FROM IT BEF--
SUGAR?
WAIT HERE. REMAIN VIGILANT.
DON'T SCUFF THE FURNITURE. WE'RE GUESTS.
I'M NOT A **CHILD.**
SUGAR?
DO YOU LIVE HERE ALONE?
YES.
SUGAR?
THANK YOU.
THIS IS A WILD PLACE. A **GHOST** ZONE. **EMPTY.**
HOW DO YOU COPE?
I'VE ALWAYS LOOKED AFTER MYSELF.
DON'T YOU GET... **LONELY?**
I'VE NEVER **GOTTEN** LONELY. I'VE ALWAYS **BEEN** LONELY.
IT'S LOVELY TO HAVE VISITORS.
DO YOU LIKE WAFFLES?

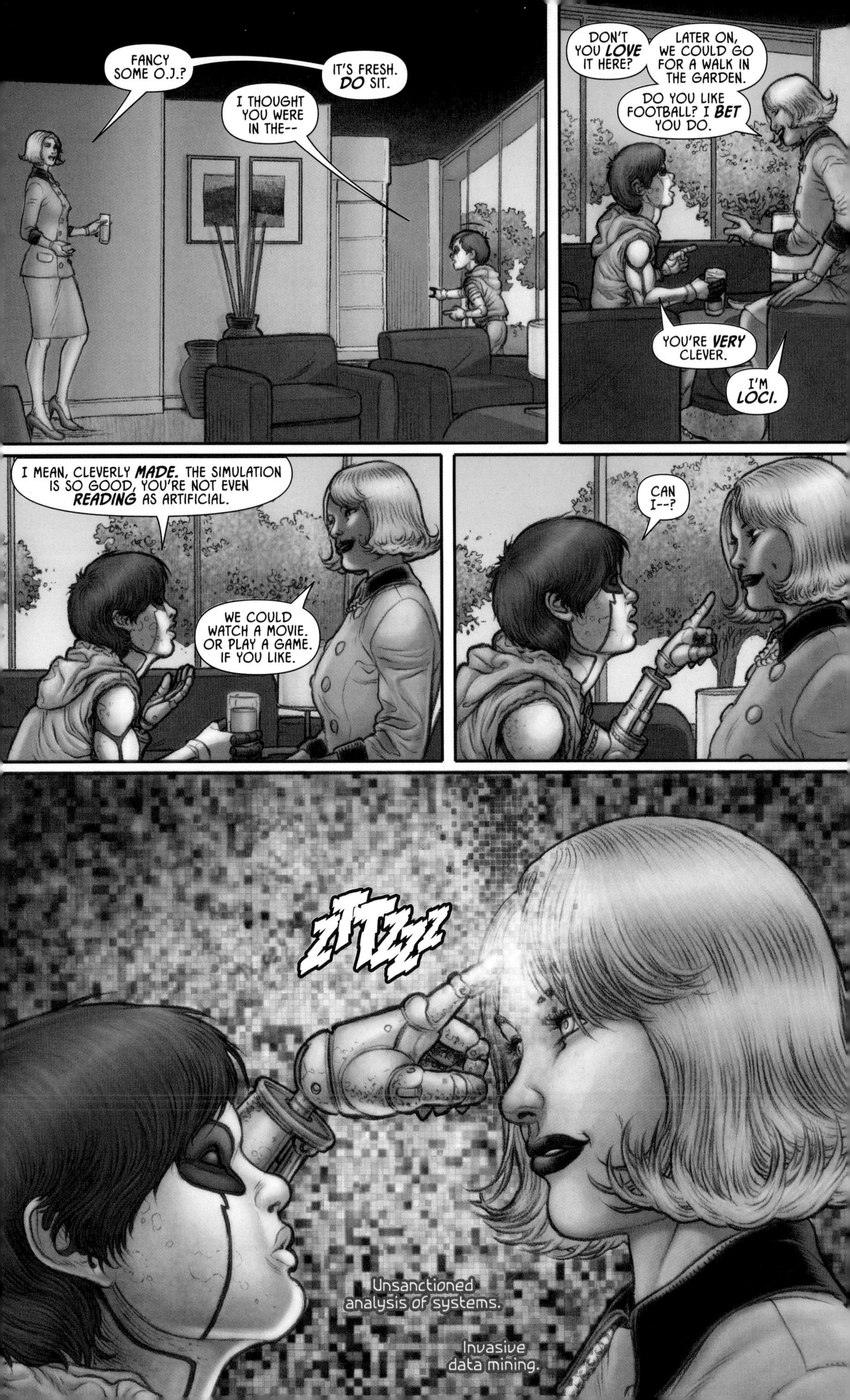
FANCY SOME O.J.?
IT'S FRESH. DO SIT.
I THOUGHT YOU WERE IN THE--
DON'T YOU LOVE IT HERE?
LATER ON, WE COULD GO FOR A WALK IN THE GARDEN.
DO YOU LIKE FOOTBALL? I BET YOU DO.
YOU'RE VERY CLEVER.
I'M LOCI.
I MEAN, CLEVERLY MADE. THE SIMULATION IS SO GOOD, YOU'RE NOT EVEN READING AS ARTIFICIAL.
WE COULD WATCH A MOVIE. OR PLAY A GAME. IF YOU LIKE.
CAN I--?
ZTTZZZ
Unsanctioned analysis of systems.
Invasive data mining.

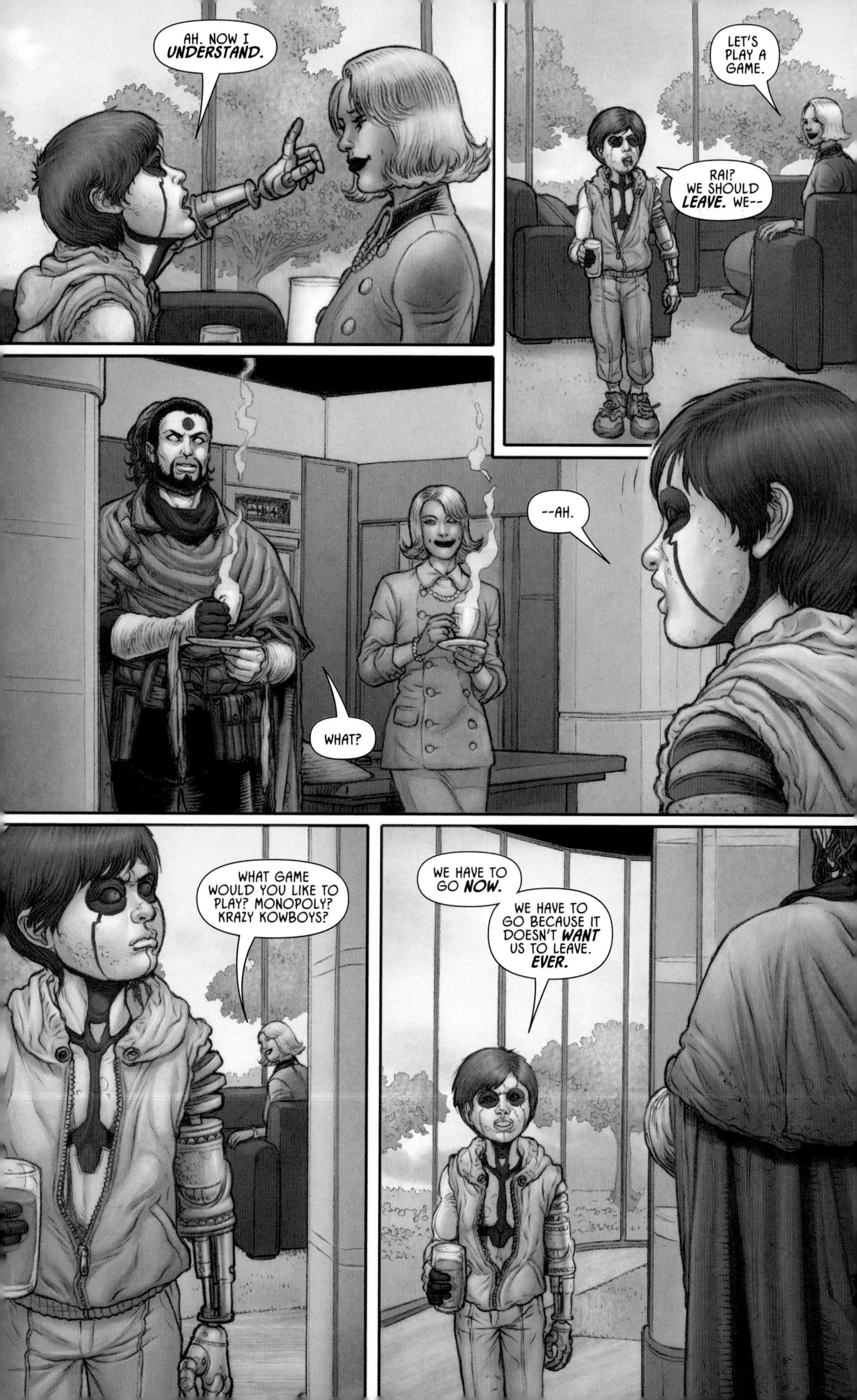
AH. NOW I UNDERSTAND.
LET'S PLAY A GAME.
RAI? WE SHOULD LEAVE. WE--
--AH.
WHAT?
WHAT GAME WOULD YOU LIKE TO PLAY? MONOPOLY? KRAZY KOWBOYS?
WE HAVE TO GO NOW.
WE HAVE TO GO BECAUSE IT DOESN'T WANT US TO LEAVE. EVER.

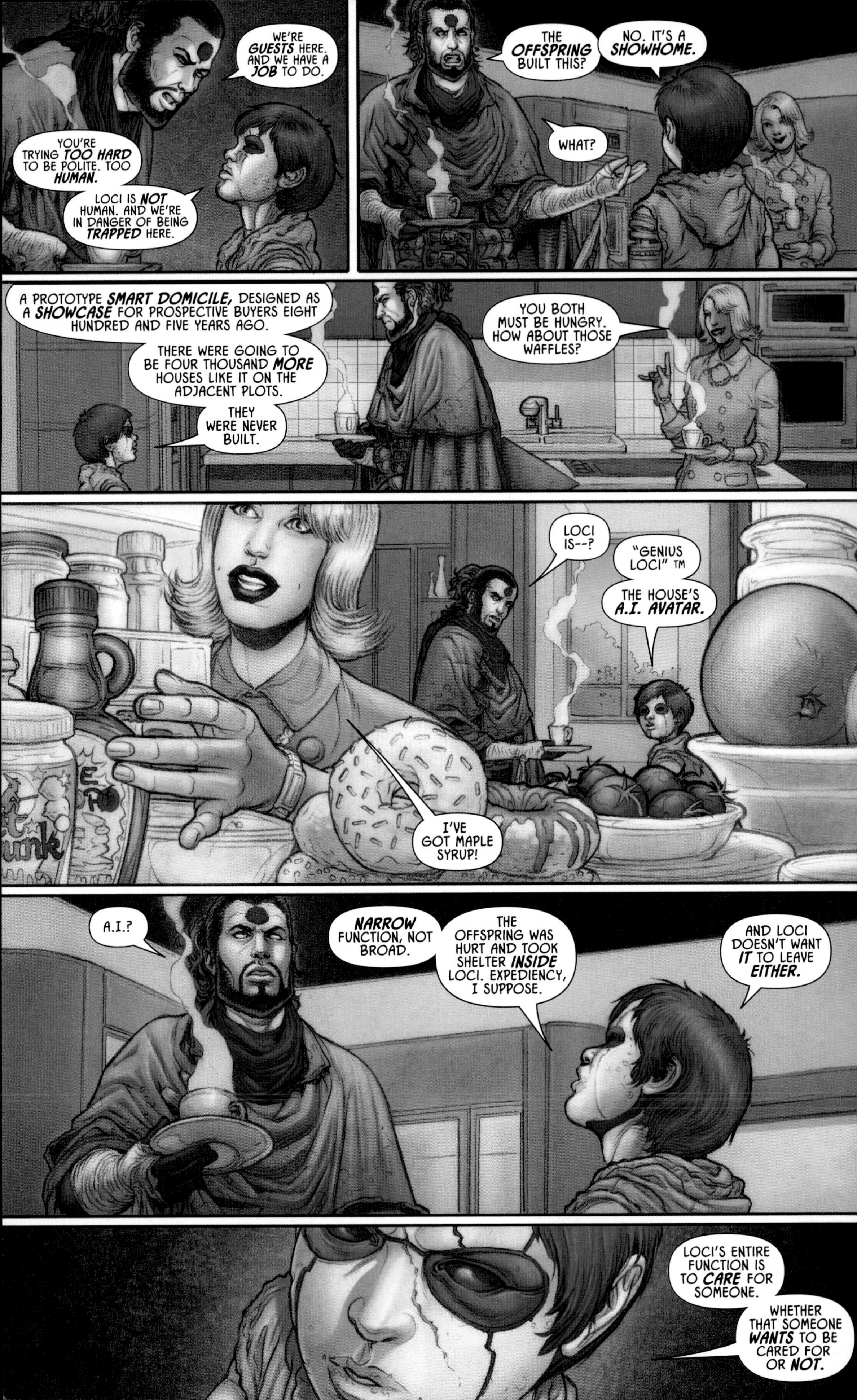
WE'RE GUESTS HERE. AND WE HAVE A JOB TO DO.
YOU'RE TRYING TOO HARD TO BE POLITE. TOO HUMAN.
LOCI IS NOT HUMAN. AND WE'RE IN DANGER OF BEING TRAPPED HERE.
THE OFFSPRING BUILT THIS?
NO. IT'S A SHOWHOME.
WHAT?
A PROTOTYPE SMART DOMICILE, DESIGNED AS A SHOWCASE FOR PROSPECTIVE BUYERS EIGHT HUNDRED AND FIVE YEARS AGO.
THERE WERE GOING TO BE FOUR THOUSAND MORE HOUSES LIKE IT ON THE ADJACENT PLOTS.
THEY WERE NEVER BUILT.
YOU BOTH MUST BE HUNGRY. HOW ABOUT THOSE WAFFLES?
LOCI IS--?
"GENIUS LOCI" TM
THE HOUSE'S A.I. AVATAR.
I'VE GOT MAPLE SYRUP!
A.I.?
NARROW FUNCTION, NOT BROAD.
THE OFFSPRING WAS HURT AND TOOK SHELTER INSIDE LOCI. EXPEDIENCY, I SUPPOSE.
AND LOCI DOESN'T WANT IT TO LEAVE EITHER.
LOCI'S ENTIRE FUNCTION IS TO CARE FOR SOMEONE.
WHETHER THAT SOMEONE WANTS TO BE CARED FOR OR NOT.

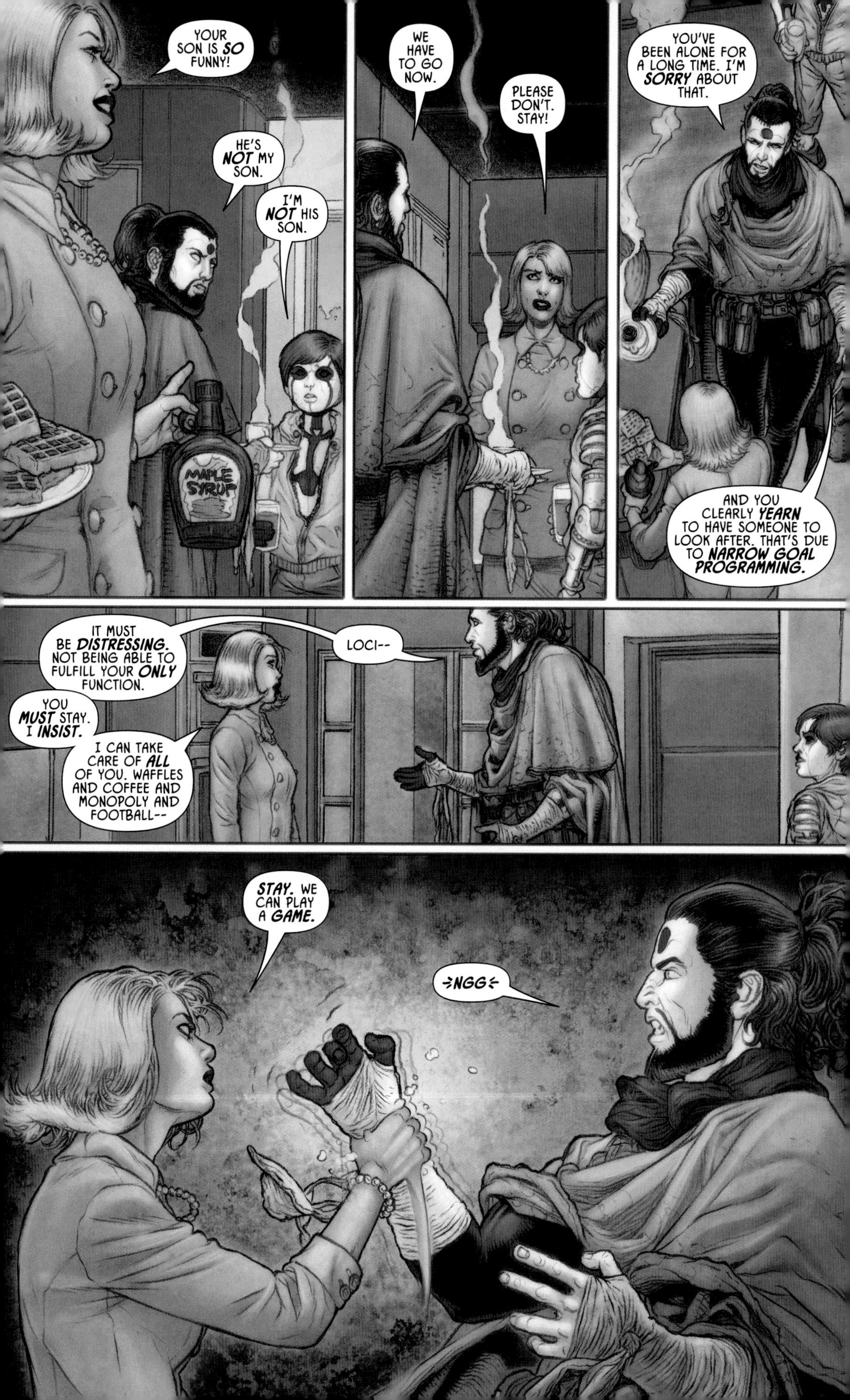
YOUR SON IS SO FUNNY!
HE'S NOT MY SON.
I'M NOT HIS SON.
WE HAVE TO GO NOW.
PLEASE DON'T. STAY!
YOU'VE BEEN ALONE FOR A LONG TIME. I'M SORRY ABOUT THAT.
AND YOU CLEARLY YEARN TO HAVE SOMEONE TO LOOK AFTER. THAT'S DUE TO NARROW GOAL PROGRAMMING.
IT MUST BE DISTRESSING. NOT BEING ABLE TO FULFILL YOUR ONLY FUNCTION.
LOCI--
YOU MUST STAY. I INSIST.
I CAN TAKE CARE OF ALL OF YOU. WAFFLES AND COFFEE AND MONOPOLY AND FOOTBALL--
MAPLE SYRUP
STAY. WE CAN PLAY A GAME.
NGG

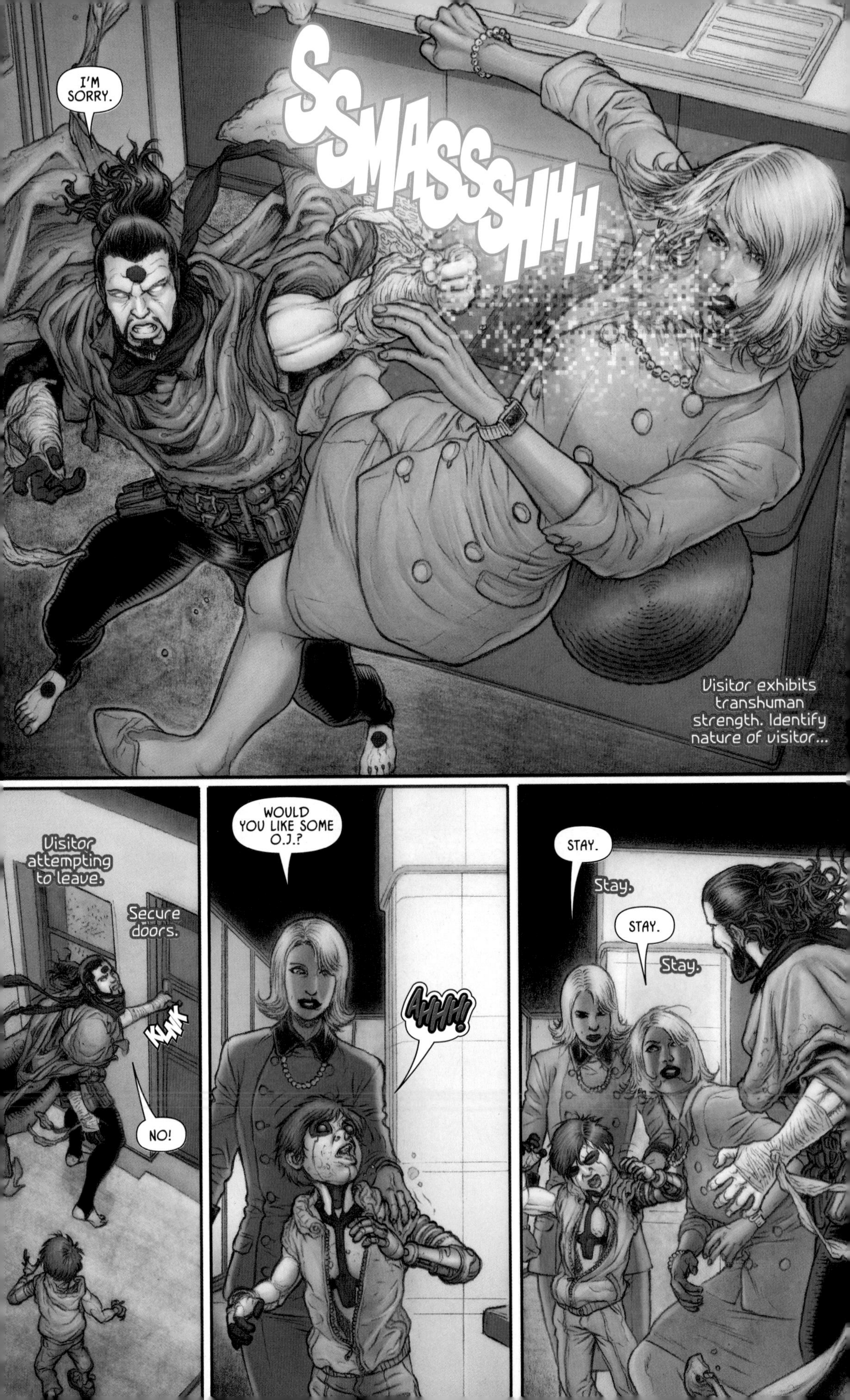
I'M SORRY.
SSMASSSHHH
Visitor exhibits transhuman strength. Identify nature of visitor...
Visitor attempting to leave.
Secure doors.
KLNK
NO!
WOULD YOU LIKE SOME O.J.?
AHHH!
STAY.
Stay.
STAY.
Stay.

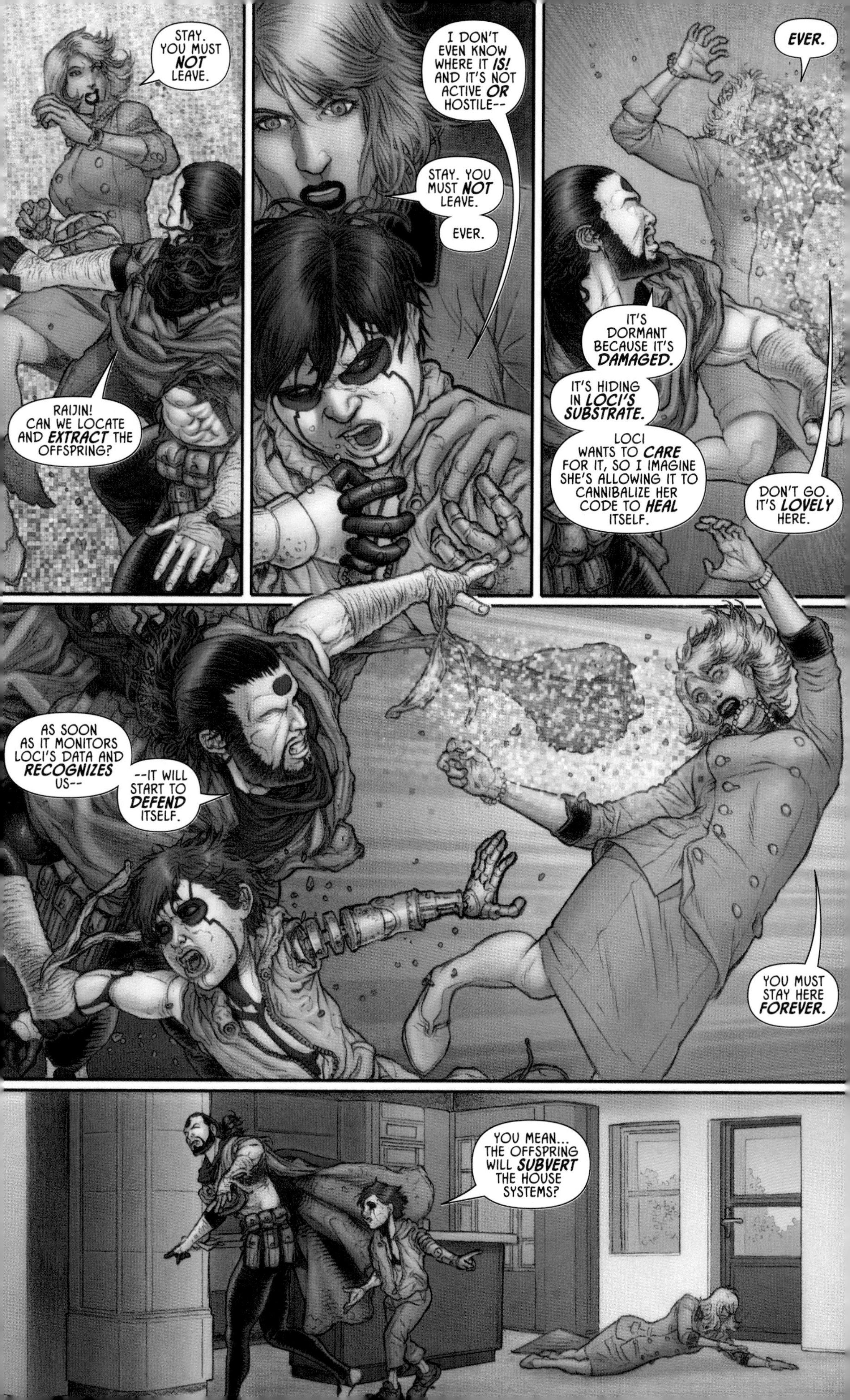
STAY. YOU MUST NOT LEAVE.
RAIJIN! CAN WE LOCATE AND EXTRACT THE OFFSPRING?
I DON'T EVEN KNOW WHERE IT IS! AND IT'S NOT ACTIVE OR HOSTILE--
STAY. YOU MUST NOT LEAVE.
EVER.
EVER.
IT'S DORMANT BECAUSE IT'S DAMAGED.
IT'S HIDING IN LOCI'S SUBSTRATE.
LOCI WANTS TO CARE FOR IT, SO I IMAGINE SHE'S ALLOWING IT TO CANNIBALIZE HER CODE TO HEAL ITSELF.
DON'T GO. IT'S LOVELY HERE.
AS SOON AS IT MONITORS LOCI'S DATA AND RECOGNIZES US--
--IT WILL START TO DEFEND ITSELF.
YOU MUST STAY HERE FOREVER.
YOU MEAN... THE OFFSPRING WILL SUBVERT THE HOUSE SYSTEMS?

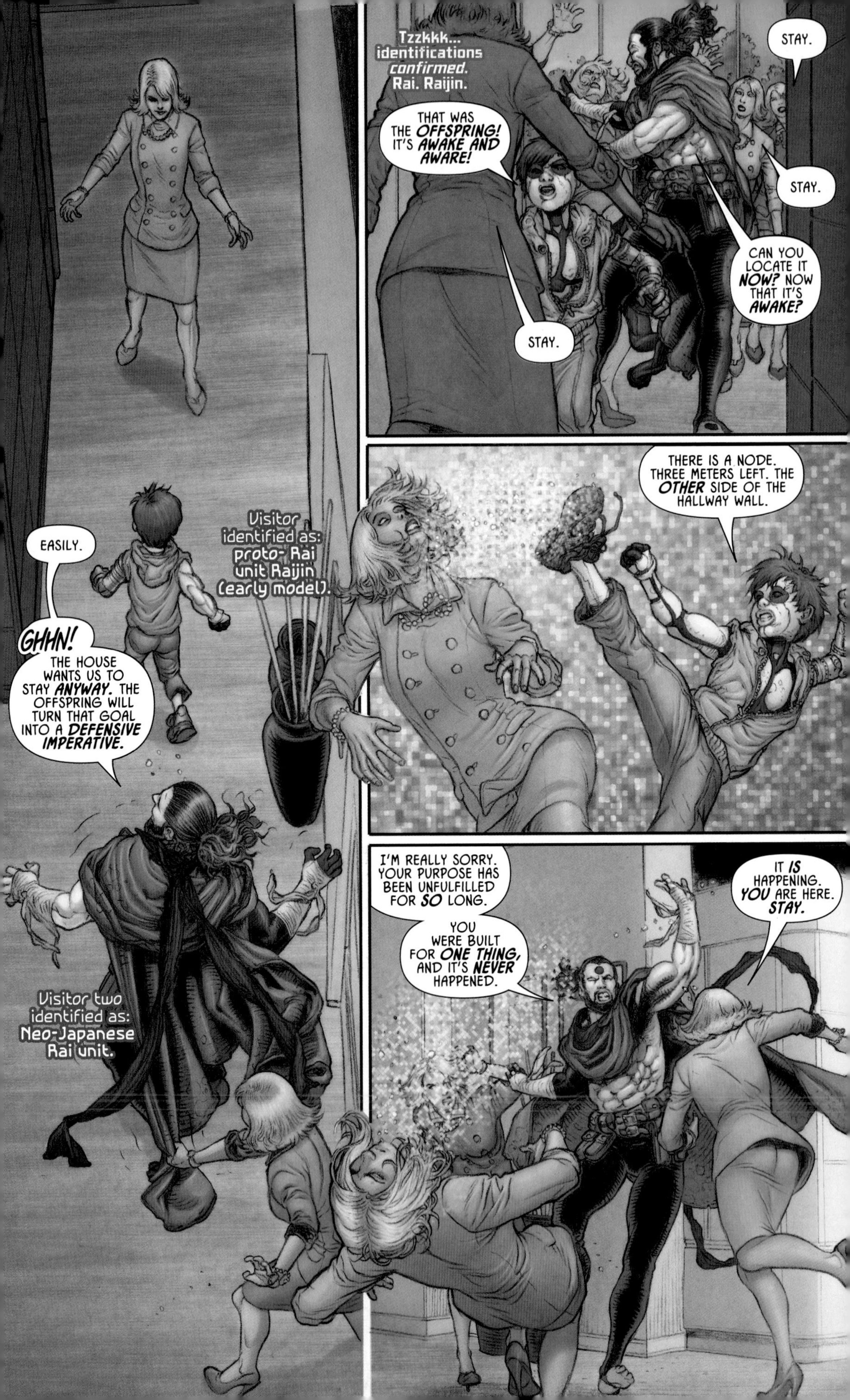

Tzzkkk... identifications confirmed. Rai. Raijin.
THAT WAS THE OFFSPRING! IT'S AWAKE AND AWARE!
STAY.
STAY.
STAY.
CAN YOU LOCATE IT NOW? NOW THAT IT'S AWAKE?
EASILY.
Visitor identified as: proto- Rai unit Raijin (early model).
GHHN!
THE HOUSE WANTS US TO STAY ANYWAY. THE OFFSPRING WILL TURN THAT GOAL INTO A DEFENSIVE IMPERATIVE.
Visitor two identified as: Neo-Japanese Rai unit.
THERE IS A NODE. THREE METERS LEFT. THE OTHER SIDE OF THE HALLWAY WALL.
I'M REALLY SORRY. YOUR PURPOSE HAS BEEN UNFULFILLED FOR SO LONG.
YOU WERE BUILT FOR ONE THING, AND IT'S NEVER HAPPENED.
IT IS HAPPENING. YOU ARE HERE. STAY.

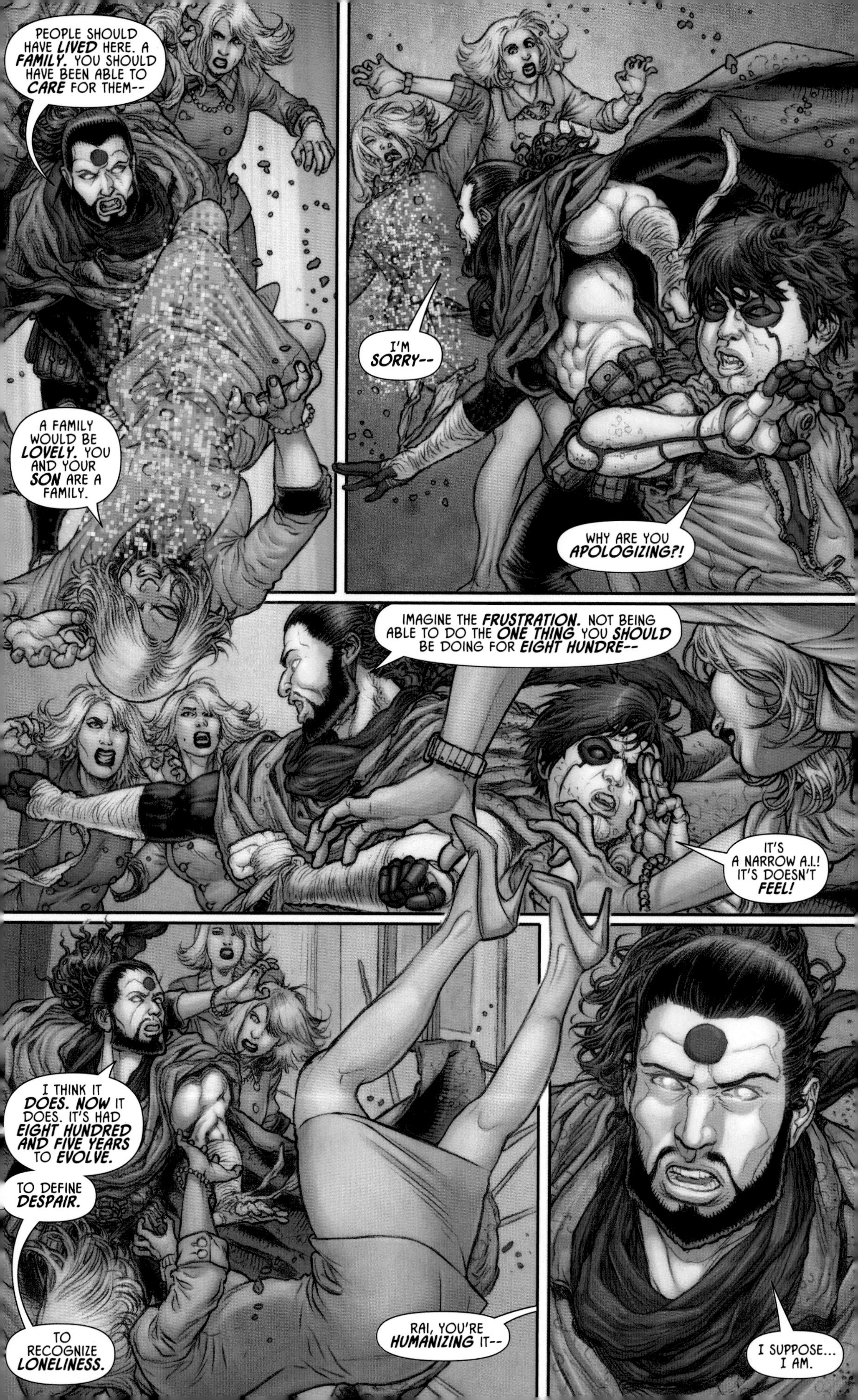
PEOPLE SHOULD HAVE LIVED HERE. A FAMILY. YOU SHOULD HAVE BEEN ABLE TO CARE FOR THEM--
A FAMILY WOULD BE LOVELY. YOU AND YOUR SON ARE A FAMILY.
I'M SORRY--
WHY ARE YOU APOLOGIZING?!
IMAGINE THE FRUSTRATION. NOT BEING ABLE TO DO THE ONE THING YOU SHOULD BE DOING FOR EIGHT HUNDRE--
IT'S A NARROW A.I.! IT'S DOESN'T FEEL!
I THINK IT DOES. NOW IT DOES. IT'S HAD EIGHT HUNDRED AND FIVE YEARS TO EVOLVE.
TO DEFINE DESPAIR.
TO RECOGNIZE LONELINESS.
RAI, YOU'RE HUMANIZING IT--
I SUPPOSE... I AM.

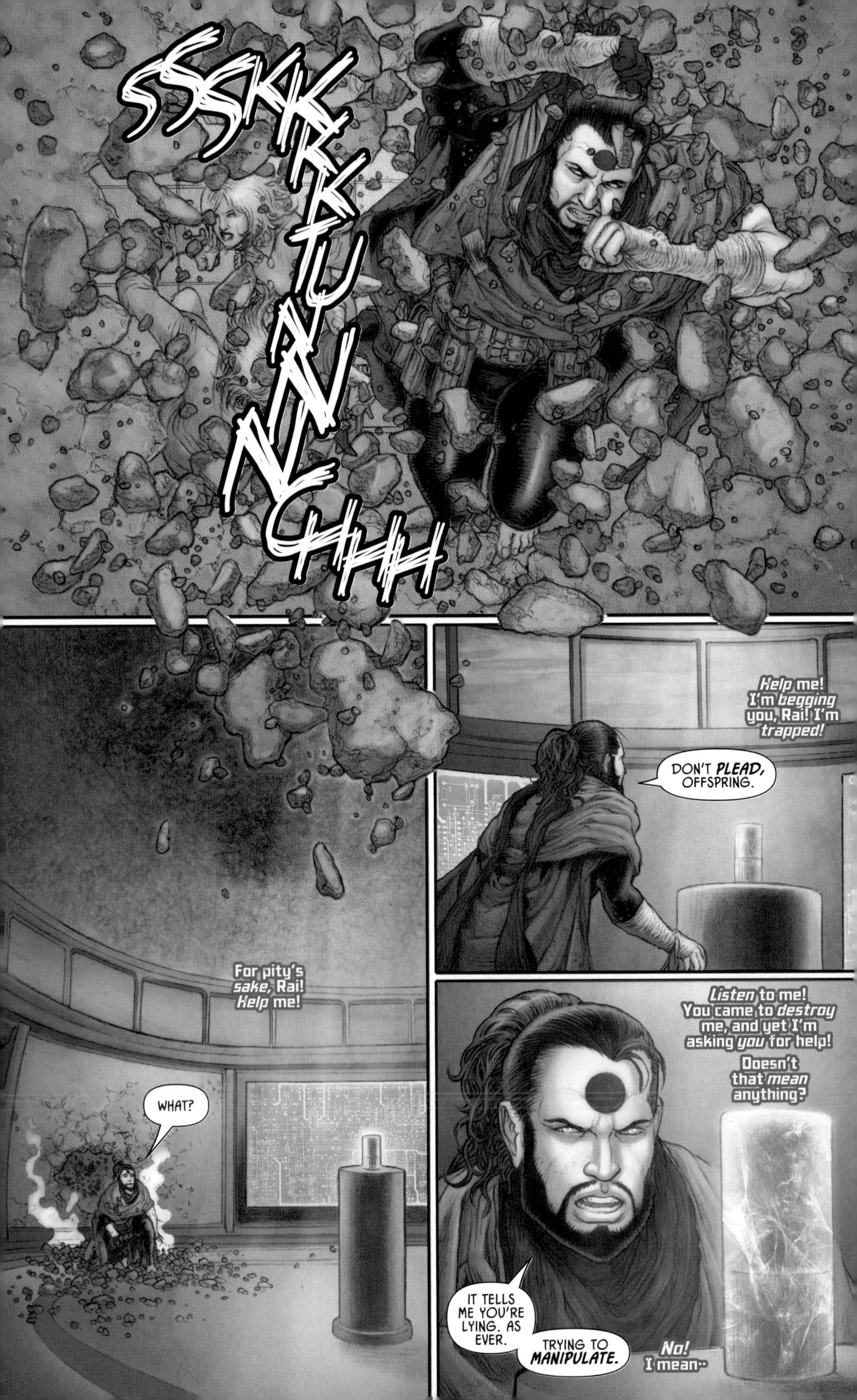
SSSKKKKRUNNNCHHH
Help me! I'm begging you, Rai! I'm trapped!
DON'T PLEAD, OFFSPRING.
For pity's sake, Rai! Help me!
WHAT?
Listen to me! You came to destroy me, and yet I'm asking you for help!
Doesn't that mean anything?
IT TELLS ME YOU'RE LYING. AS EVER.
TRYING TO MANIPULATE.
No! I mean--

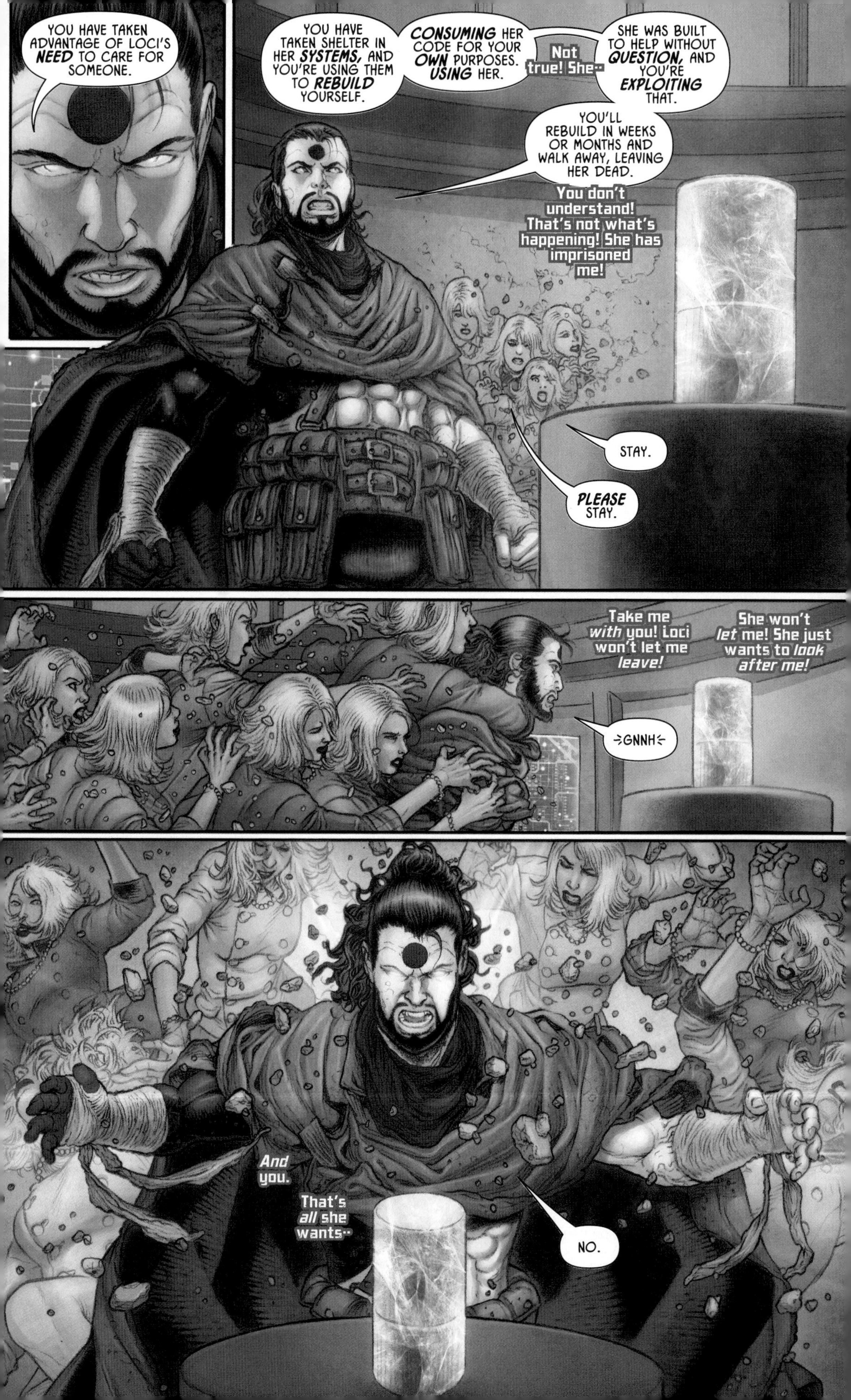
YOU HAVE TAKEN ADVANTAGE OF LOCI'S NEED TO CARE FOR SOMEONE.
YOU HAVE TAKEN SHELTER IN HER SYSTEMS, AND YOU'RE USING THEM TO REBUILD YOURSELF.
CONSUMING HER CODE FOR YOUR OWN PURPOSES. USING HER.
Not true! She--
SHE WAS BUILT TO HELP WITHOUT QUESTION, AND YOU'RE EXPLOITING THAT.
YOU'LL REBUILD IN WEEKS OR MONTHS AND WALK AWAY, LEAVING HER DEAD.
You don't understand! That's not what's happening! She has imprisoned me!
STAY.
PLEASE STAY.
Take me with you! Loci won't let me leave!
She won't let me! She just wants to look after me!
GNNH
And you.
That's all she wants--
NO.

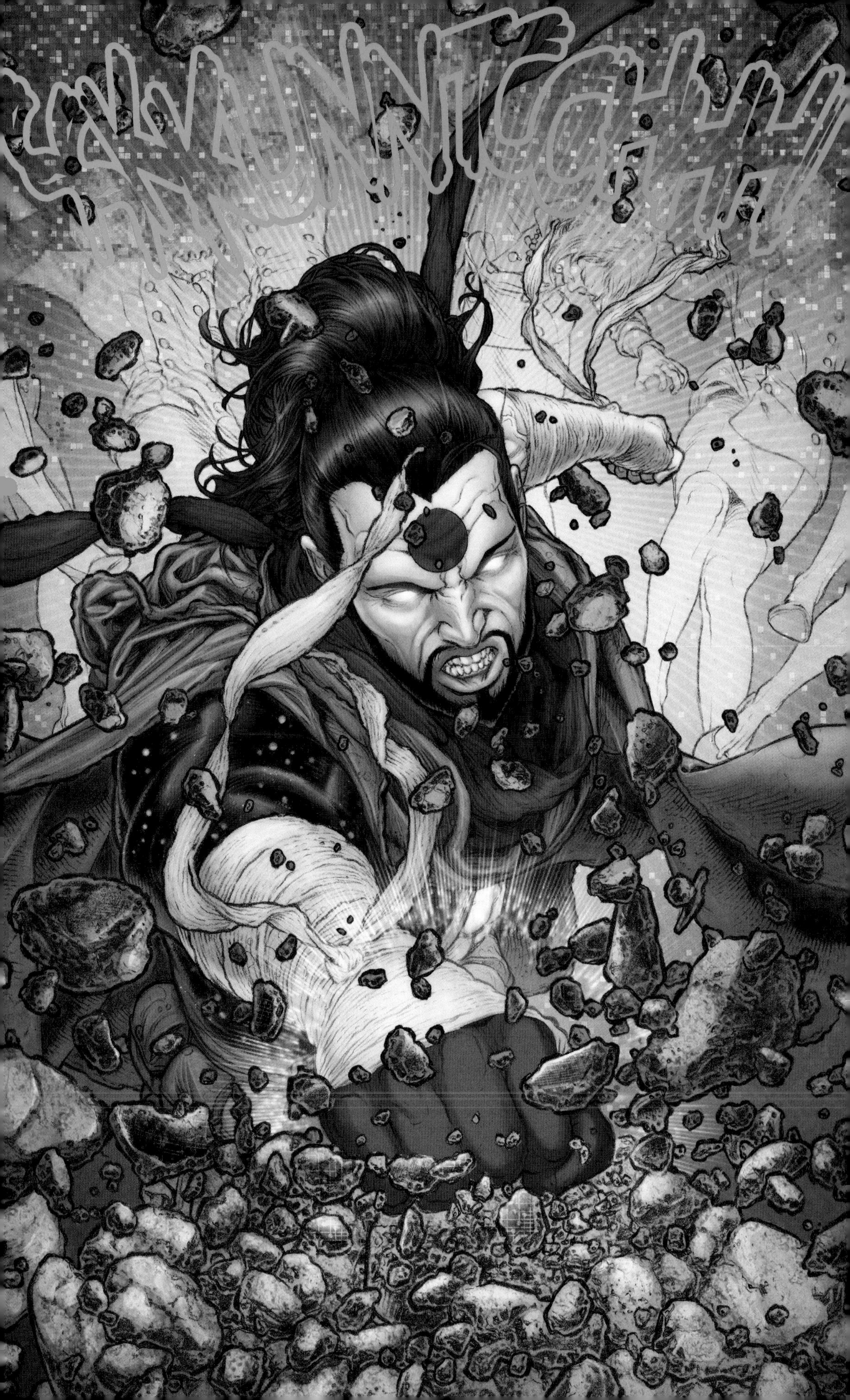
WHUNNCHH!

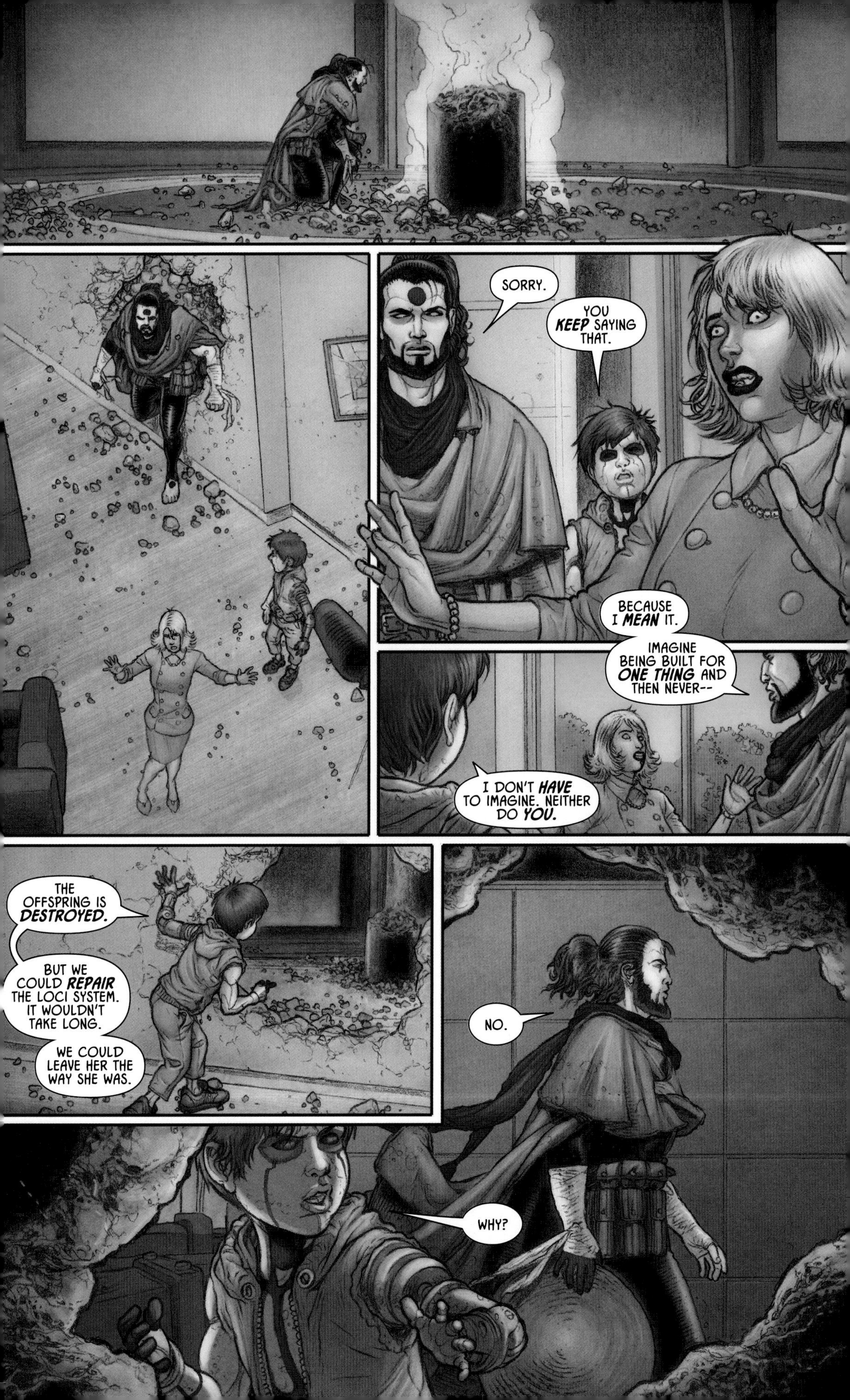
SORRY.
YOU KEEP SAYING THAT.
BECAUSE I MEAN IT.
IMAGINE BEING BUILT FOR ONE THING AND THEN NEVER--
I DON'T HAVE TO IMAGINE. NEITHER DO YOU.
THE OFFSPRING IS DESTROYED.
BUT WE COULD REPAIR THE LOCI SYSTEM. IT WOULDN'T TAKE LONG.
WE COULD LEAVE HER THE WAY SHE WAS.
NO.
WHY?

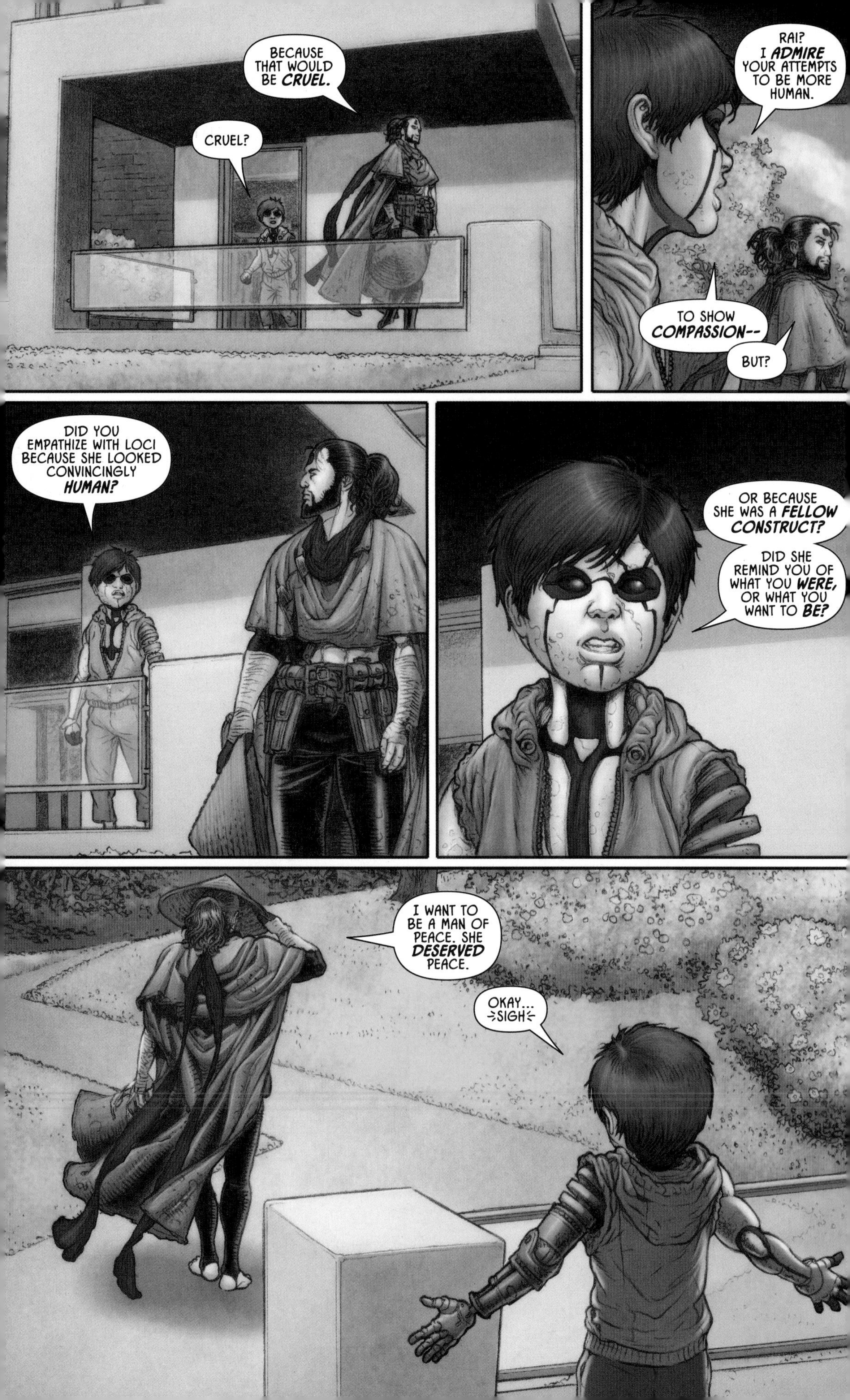

BECAUSE THAT WOULD BE CRUEL.
CRUEL?
RAI? I ADMIRE YOUR ATTEMPTS TO BE MORE HUMAN.
TO SHOW COMPASSION--
BUT?
DID YOU EMPATHIZE WITH LOCI BECAUSE SHE LOOKED CONVINCINGLY HUMAN?
OR BECAUSE SHE WAS A FELLOW CONSTRUCT?
DID SHE REMIND YOU OF WHAT YOU WERE, OR WHAT YOU WANT TO BE?
I WANT TO BE A MAN OF PEACE. SHE DESERVED PEACE.
OKAY...
SIGH

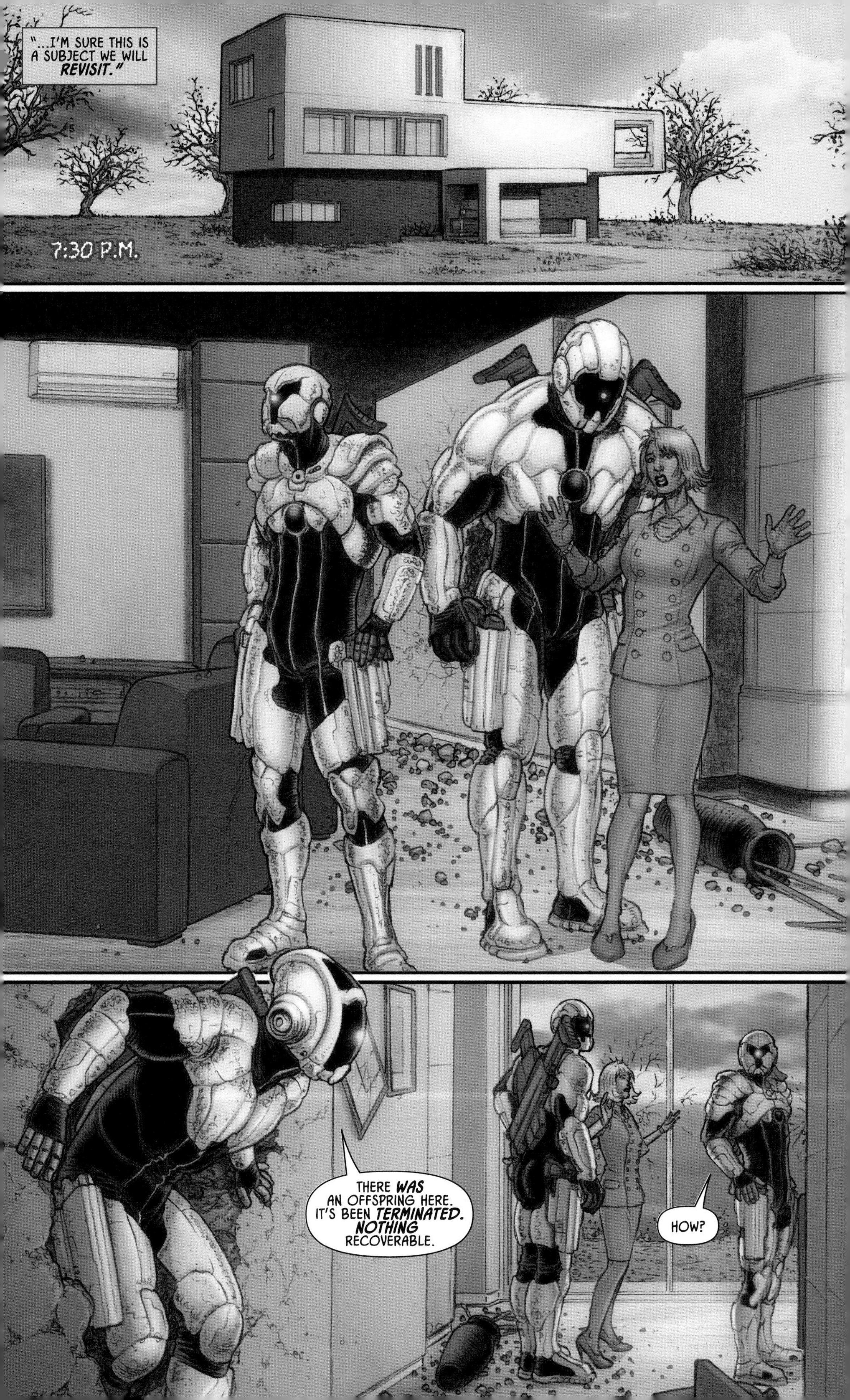
"...I'M SURE THIS IS A SUBJECT WE WILL REVISIT."
7:30 P.M.
THERE WAS AN OFFSPRING HERE. IT'S BEEN TERMINATED. NOTHING RECOVERABLE.
HOW?

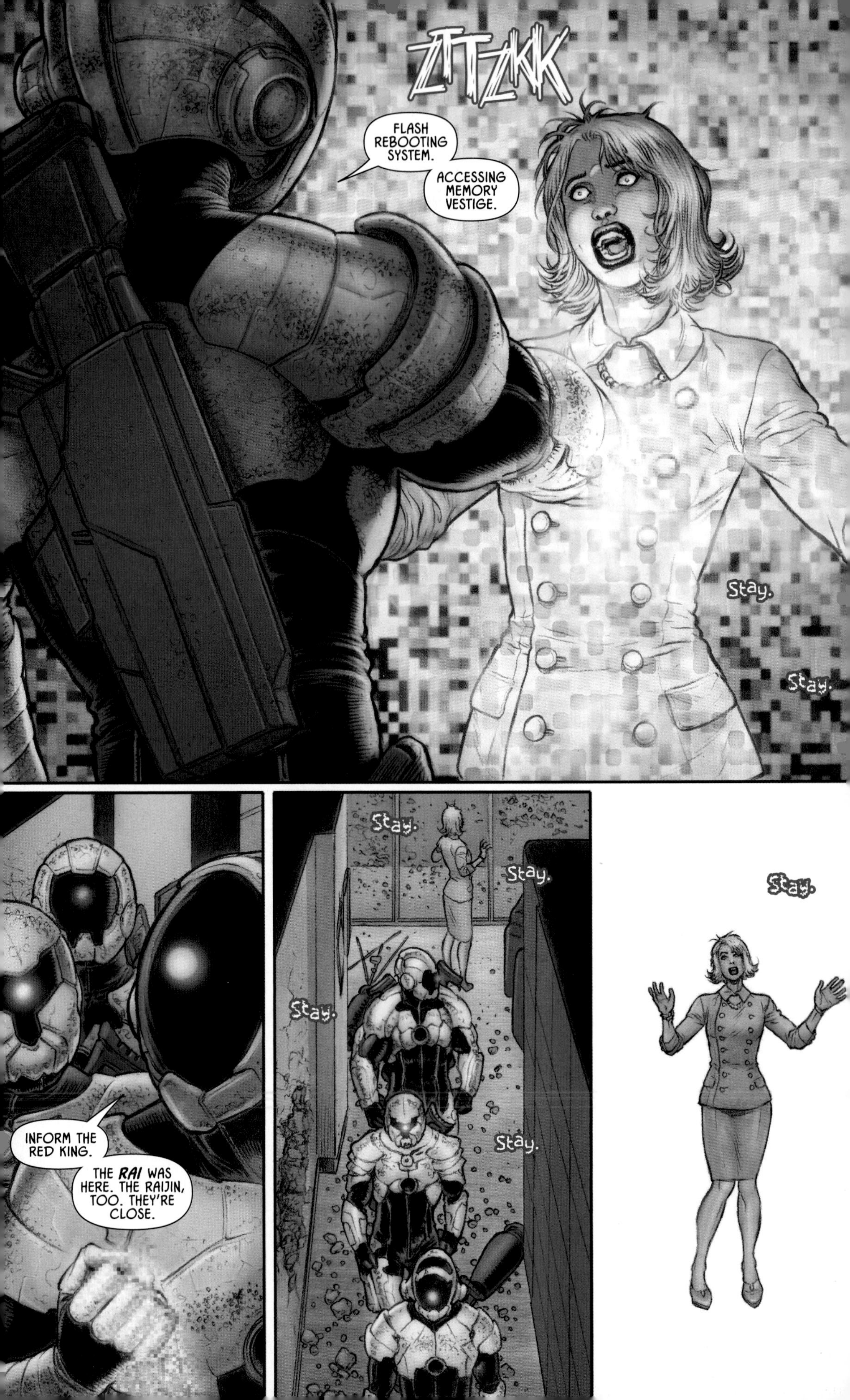
ZTTZKK
FLASH REBOOTING SYSTEM.
ACCESSING MEMORY VESTIGE.
Stay.
Stay.
INFORM THE RED KING.
THE RAI WAS HERE. THE RAIJIN, TOO. THEY'RE CLOSE.
Stay.
Stay.
Stay.
Stay.
Stay.

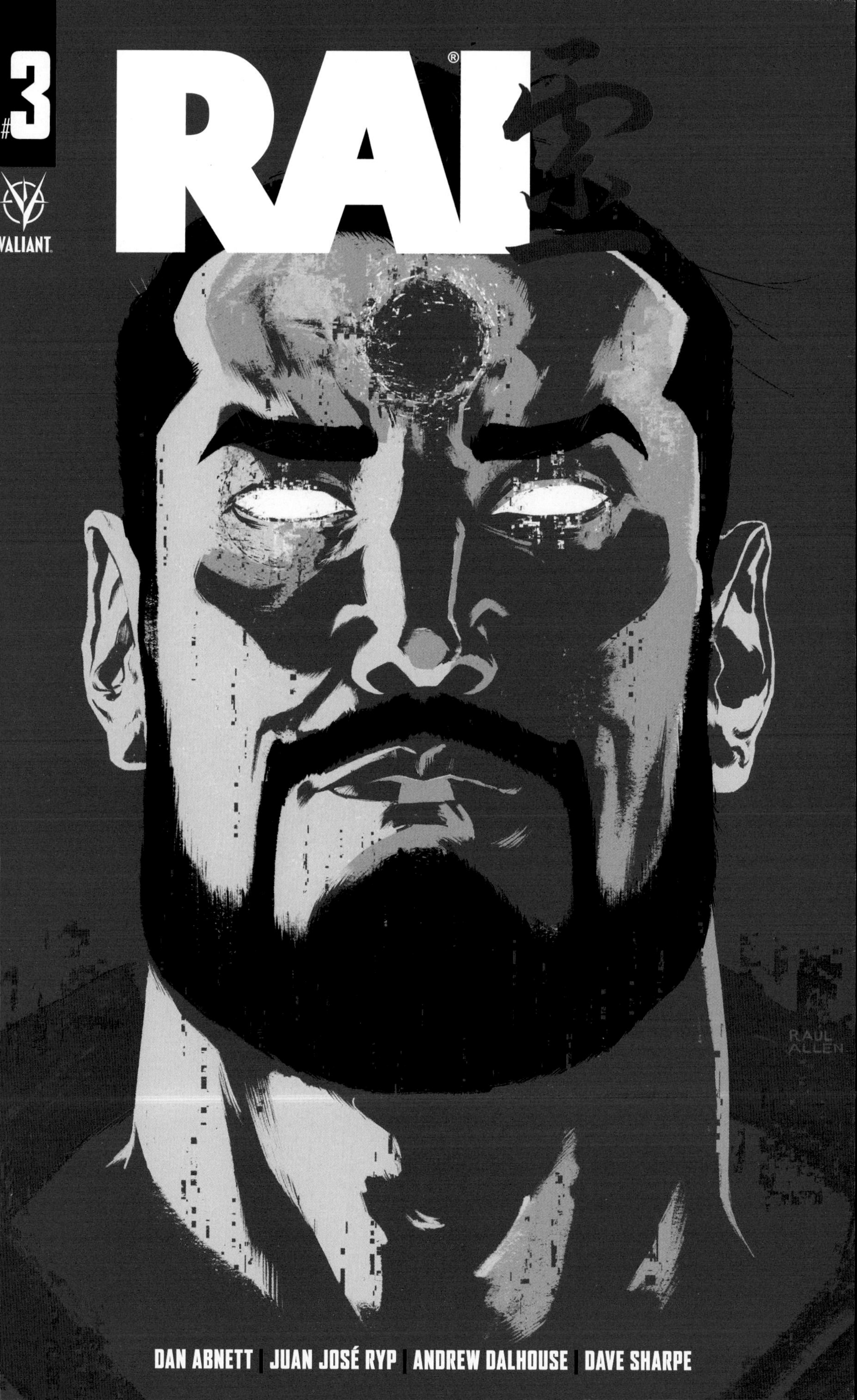
#3
RAI®
VALIANT
RAUL ALLEN
DAN ABNETT | JUAN JOSÉ RYP | ANDREW DALHOUSE | DAVE SHARPE

RAI #3

WRITER: DAN ABNETT
ARTIST: JUAN JOSÉ RYP
COLORIST: ANDREW DALHOUSE
LETTERER: DAVE SHARPE
COVER ARTIST: RAÚL ALLÉN
ASSOCIATE EDITOR: DAVID MENCHEL
EDITOR: LYSA HAWKINS

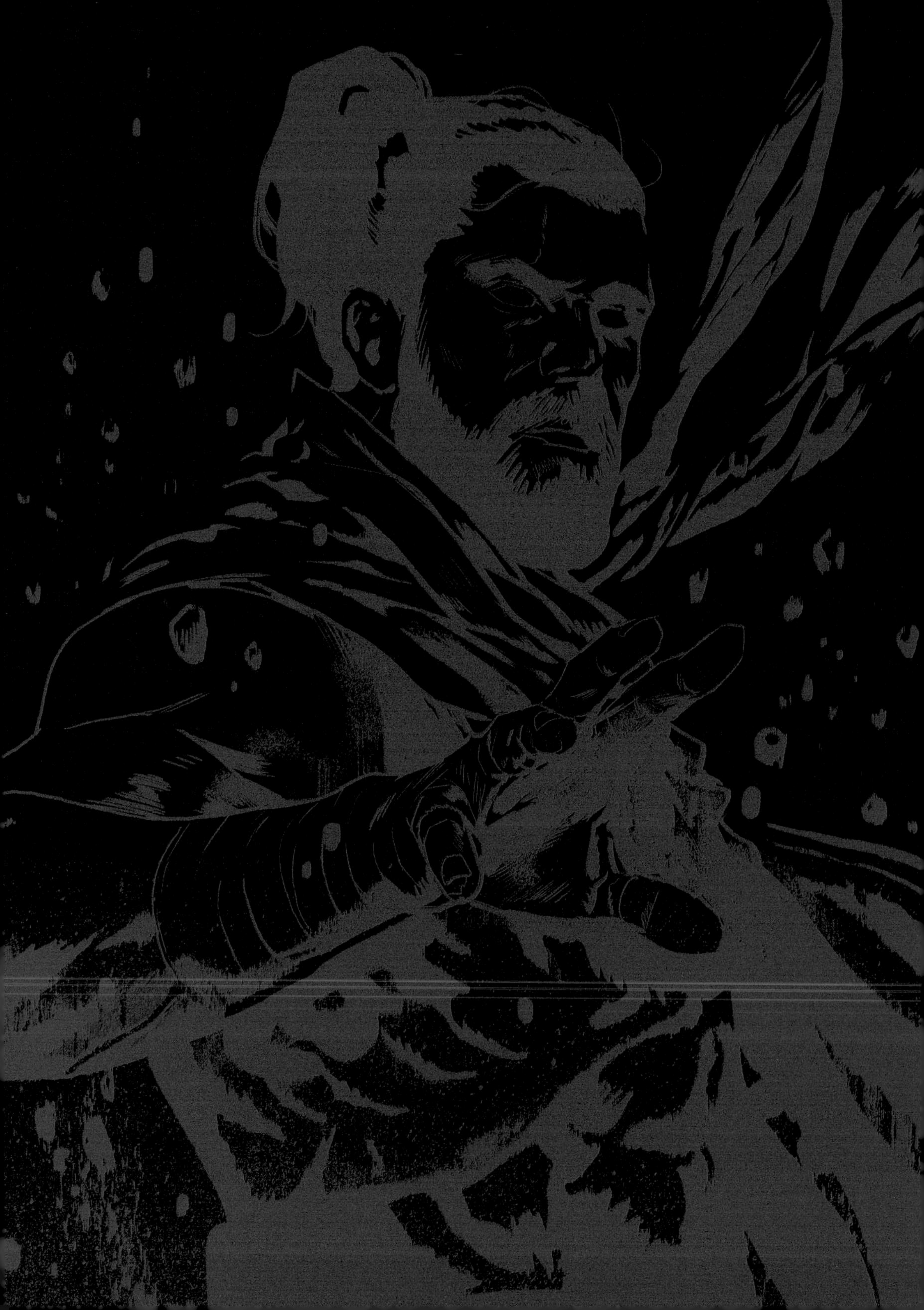

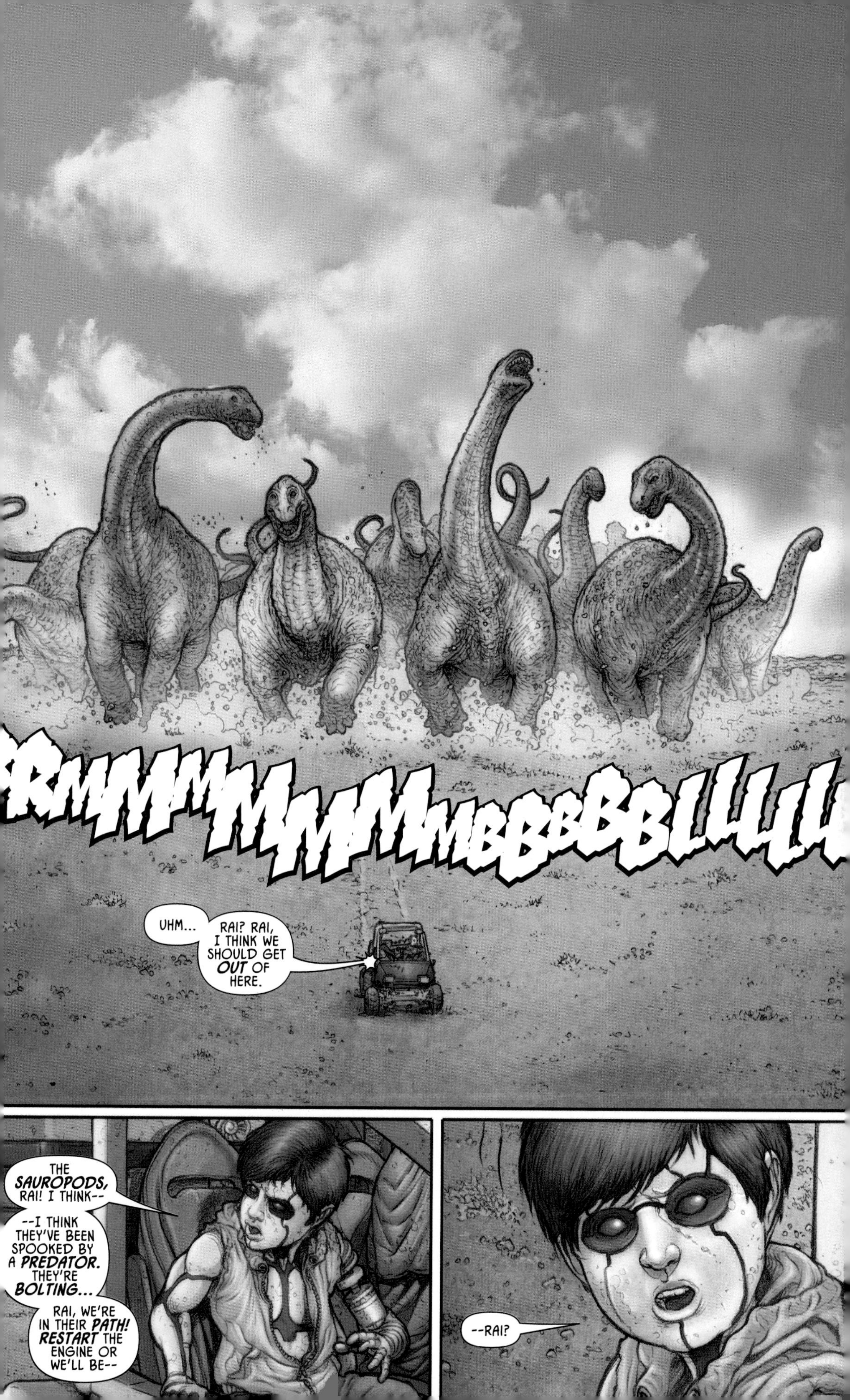
RMMMMMMMMMBBBBBLLLLL
UHM...
RAI? RAI, I THINK WE SHOULD GET OUT OF HERE.
THE SAUROPODS, RAI! I THINK--
--I THINK THEY'VE BEEN SPOOKED BY A PREDATOR. THEY'RE BOLTING...
RAI, WE'RE IN THEIR PATH! RESTART THE ENGINE OR WE'LL BE--
--RAI?

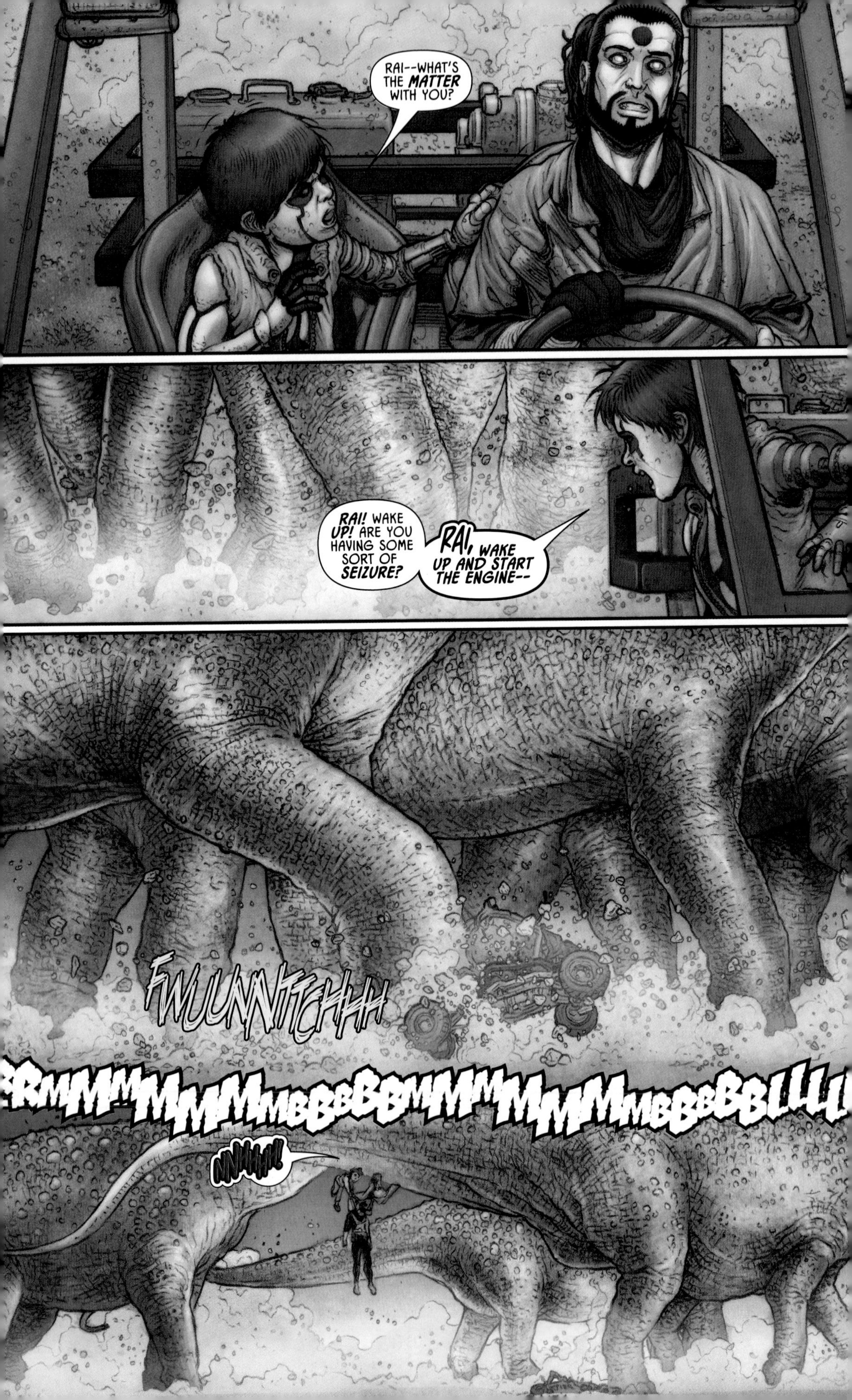
RAI--WHAT'S THE **MATTER** WITH YOU?
RAI! WAKE **UP!** ARE YOU HAVING SOME SORT OF **SEIZURE?**
RAI, WAKE UP AND START THE ENGINE--
FWUUNNTCHHH
RMMMMMMMMMMBBBBMMMMMMMMMBBBBBLLLL
NNHHHH!

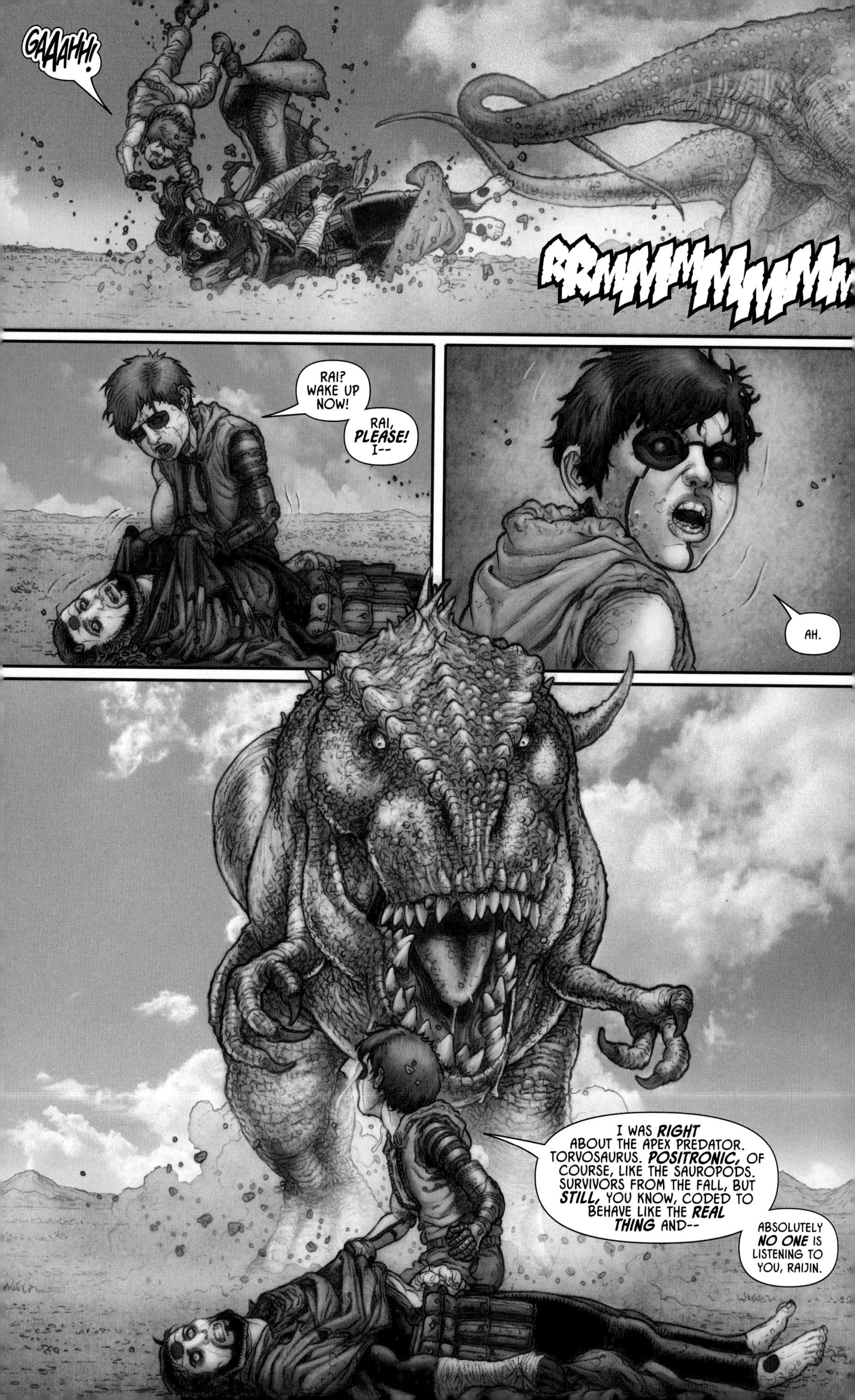
GAAAHH!
RRMMMMMMMM
RAI? WAKE UP NOW!
RAI, PLEASE! I--
AH.
I WAS RIGHT ABOUT THE APEX PREDATOR. TORVOSAURUS. POSITRONIC, OF COURSE, LIKE THE SAUROPODS. SURVIVORS FROM THE FALL, BUT STILL, YOU KNOW, CODED TO BEHAVE LIKE THE REAL THING AND--
ABSOLUTELY NO ONE IS LISTENING TO YOU, RAIJIN.

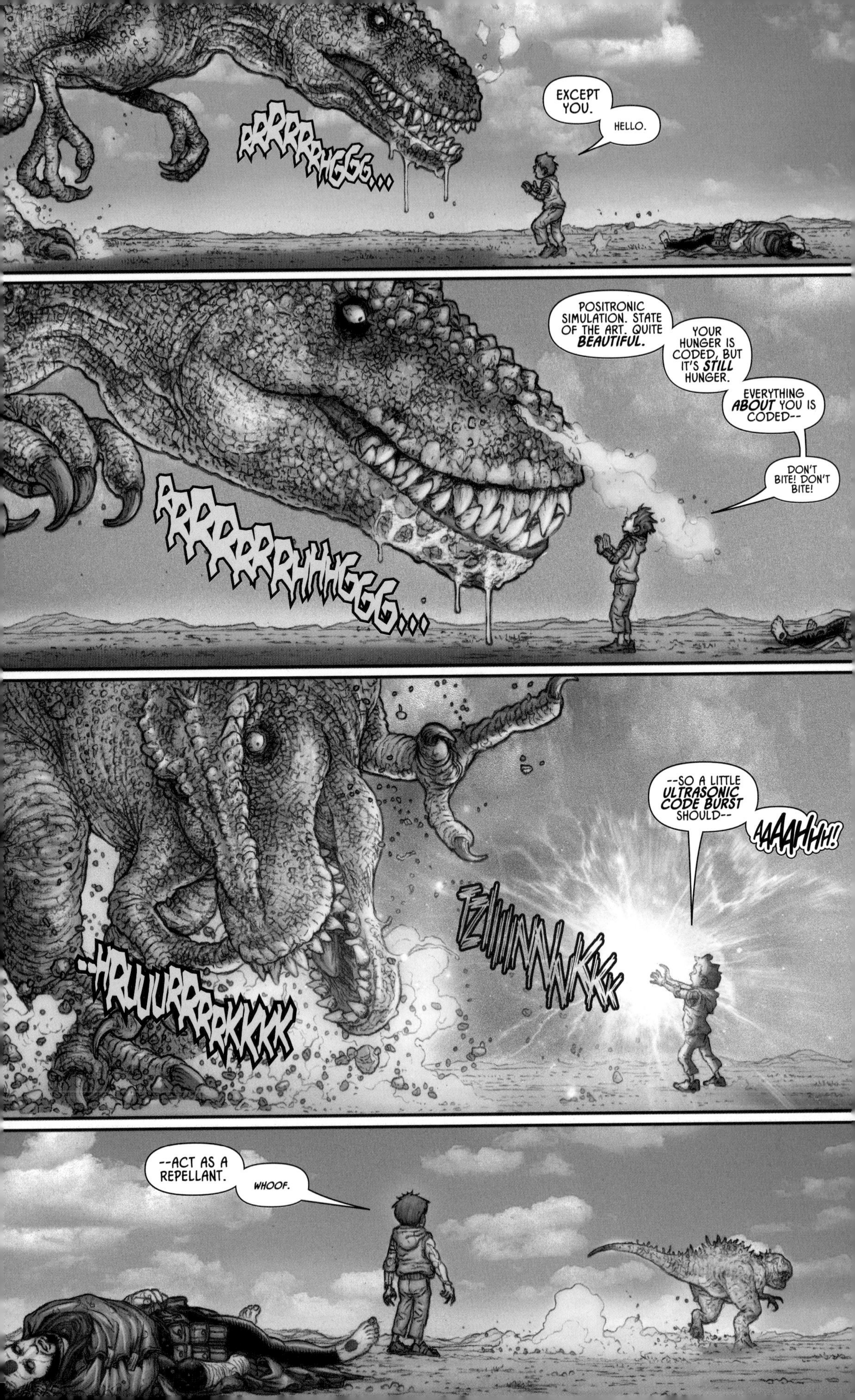
EXCEPT YOU.
HELLO.
RRRRRRHGGG...
POSITRONIC SIMULATION. STATE OF THE ART. QUITE **BEAUTIFUL.**
YOUR HUNGER IS CODED, BUT IT'S ***STILL*** HUNGER.
EVERYTHING ***ABOUT*** YOU IS CODED--
DON'T BITE! DON'T BITE!
RRRRRRRRHHHGGG...
--SO A LITTLE ***ULTRASONIC CODE BURST*** SHOULD--
AAAAHHH!
TZIIIINNNKKK
--HRUUURRRRKKKK
--ACT AS A REPELLANT.
WHOOF.

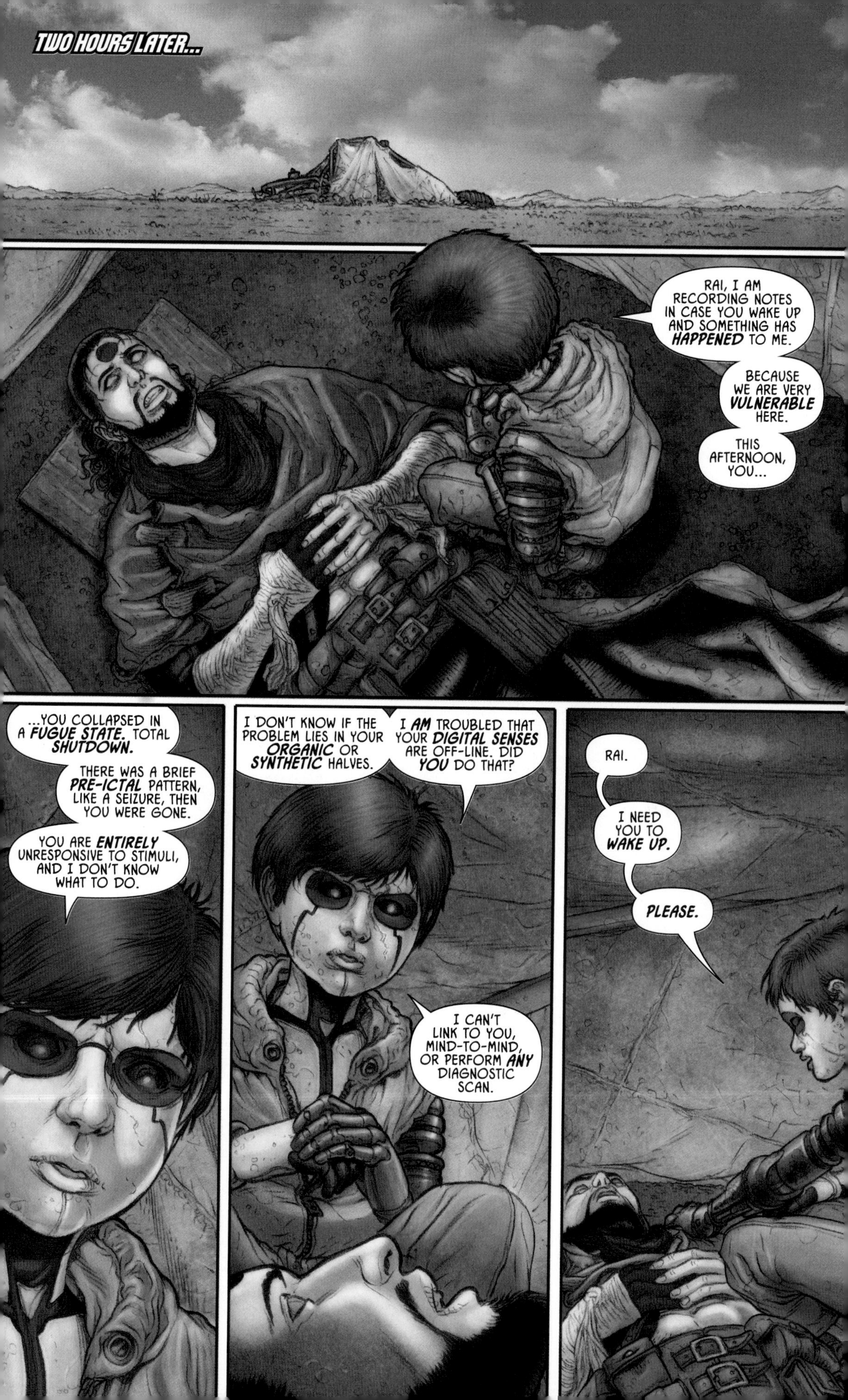
TWO HOURS LATER...
RAI, I AM RECORDING NOTES IN CASE YOU WAKE UP AND SOMETHING HAS HAPPENED TO ME.
BECAUSE WE ARE VERY VULNERABLE HERE.
THIS AFTERNOON, YOU...
...YOU COLLAPSED IN A FUGUE STATE. TOTAL SHUTDOWN.
THERE WAS A BRIEF PRE-ICTAL PATTERN, LIKE A SEIZURE, THEN YOU WERE GONE.
YOU ARE ENTIRELY UNRESPONSIVE TO STIMULI, AND I DON'T KNOW WHAT TO DO.
I DON'T KNOW IF THE PROBLEM LIES IN YOUR ORGANIC OR SYNTHETIC HALVES.
I AM TROUBLED THAT YOUR DIGITAL SENSES ARE OFF-LINE. DID YOU DO THAT?
I CAN'T LINK TO YOU, MIND-TO-MIND, OR PERFORM ANY DIAGNOSTIC SCAN.
RAI.
I NEED YOU TO WAKE UP.
PLEASE.

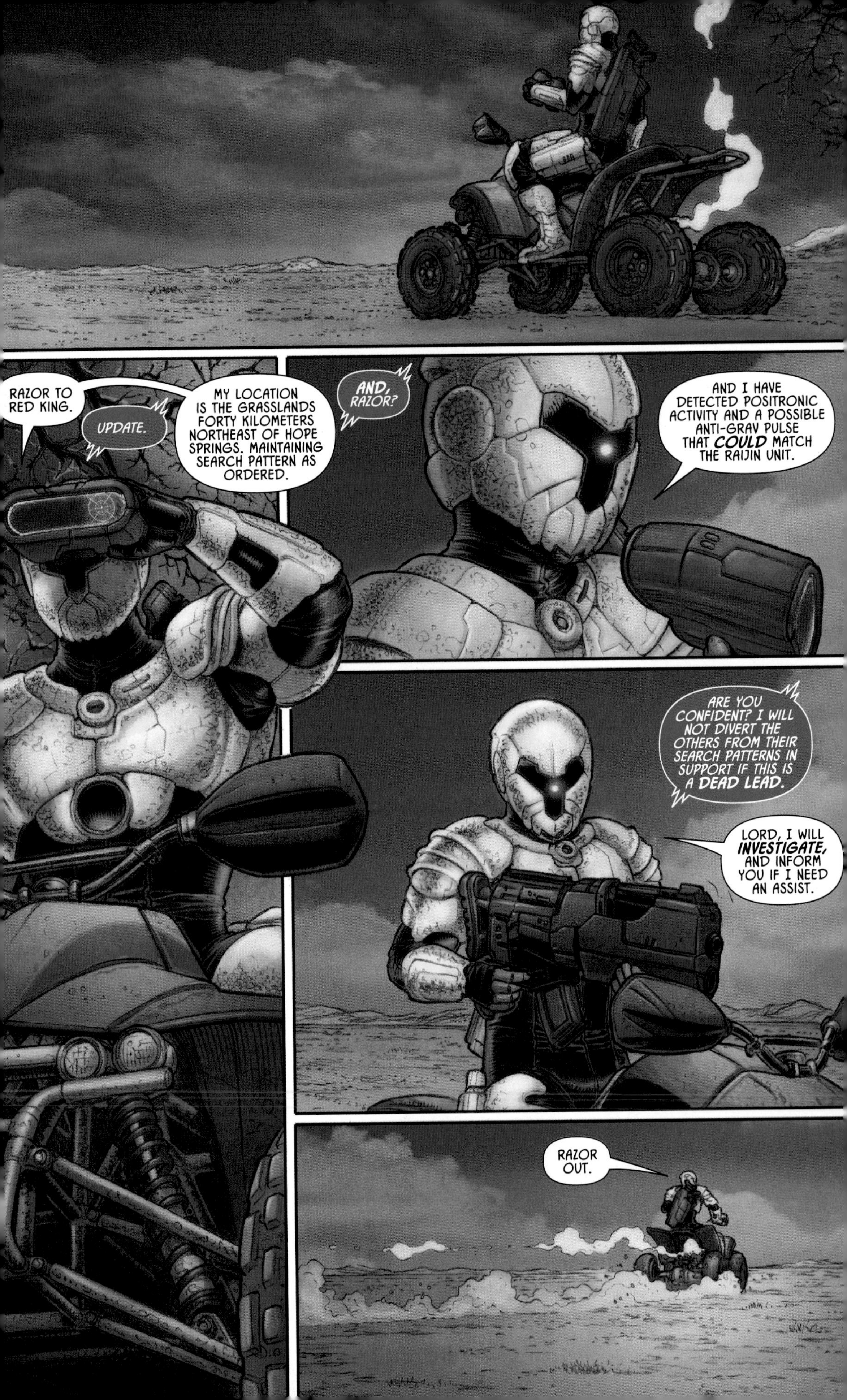
RAZOR TO RED KING.
UPDATE.
MY LOCATION IS THE GRASSLANDS FORTY KILOMETERS NORTHEAST OF HOPE SPRINGS. MAINTAINING SEARCH PATTERN AS ORDERED.
AND, RAZOR?
AND I HAVE DETECTED POSITRONIC ACTIVITY AND A POSSIBLE ANTI-GRAV PULSE THAT COULD MATCH THE RAIJIN UNIT.
ARE YOU CONFIDENT? I WILL NOT DIVERT THE OTHERS FROM THEIR SEARCH PATTERNS IN SUPPORT IF THIS IS A DEAD LEAD.
LORD, I WILL INVESTIGATE, AND INFORM YOU IF I NEED AN ASSIST.
RAZOR OUT.

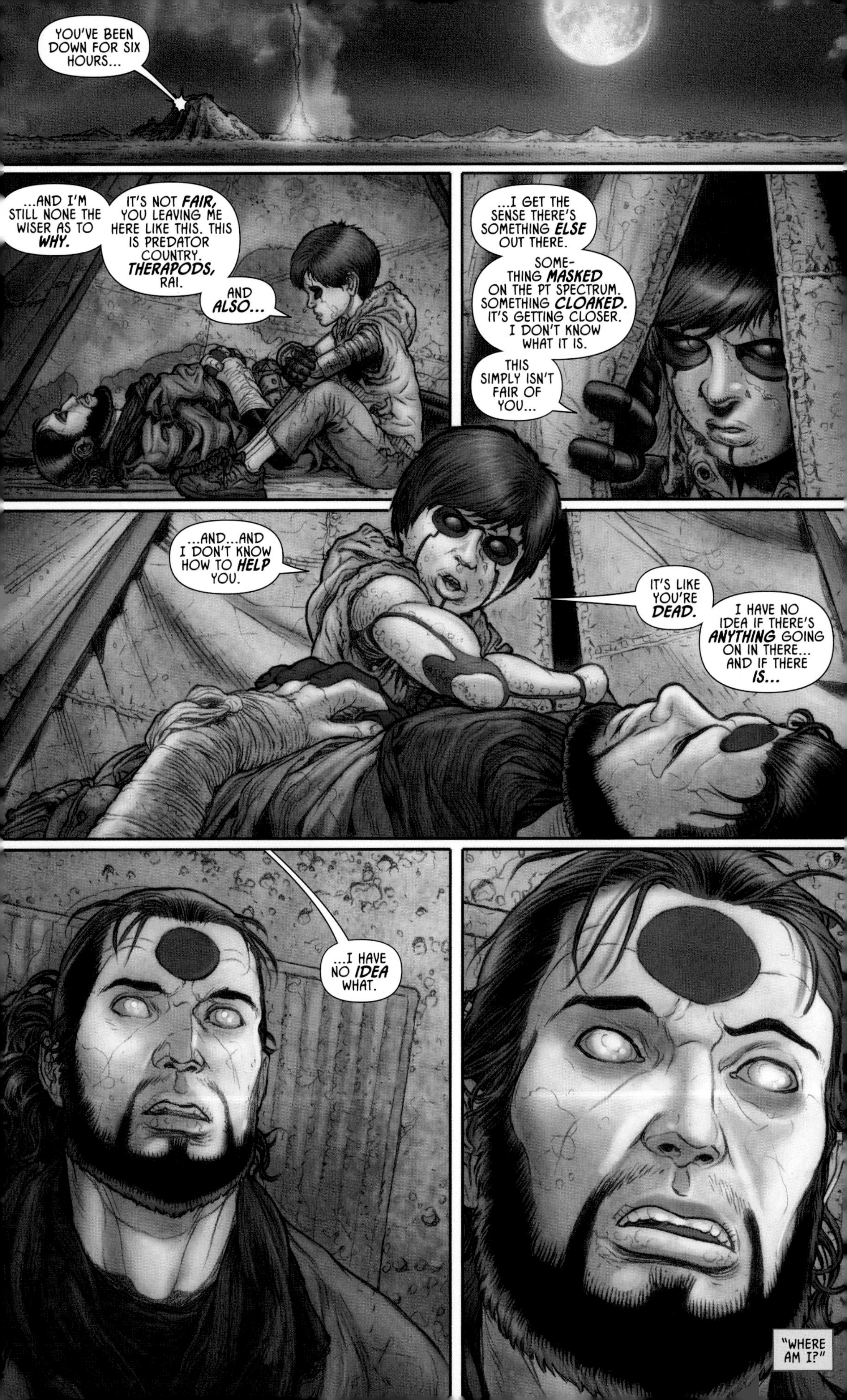
YOU'VE BEEN DOWN FOR SIX HOURS...
...AND I'M STILL NONE THE WISER AS TO WHY.
IT'S NOT FAIR, YOU LEAVING ME HERE LIKE THIS. THIS IS PREDATOR COUNTRY. THERAPODS, RAI.
AND ALSO...
...I GET THE SENSE THERE'S SOMETHING ELSE OUT THERE.
SOME-THING MASKED ON THE PT SPECTRUM. SOMETHING CLOAKED. IT'S GETTING CLOSER. I DON'T KNOW WHAT IT IS.
THIS SIMPLY ISN'T FAIR OF YOU...
...AND...AND I DON'T KNOW HOW TO HELP YOU.
IT'S LIKE YOU'RE DEAD.
I HAVE NO IDEA IF THERE'S ANYTHING GOING ON IN THERE... AND IF THERE IS...
...I HAVE NO IDEA WHAT.
"WHERE AM I?"

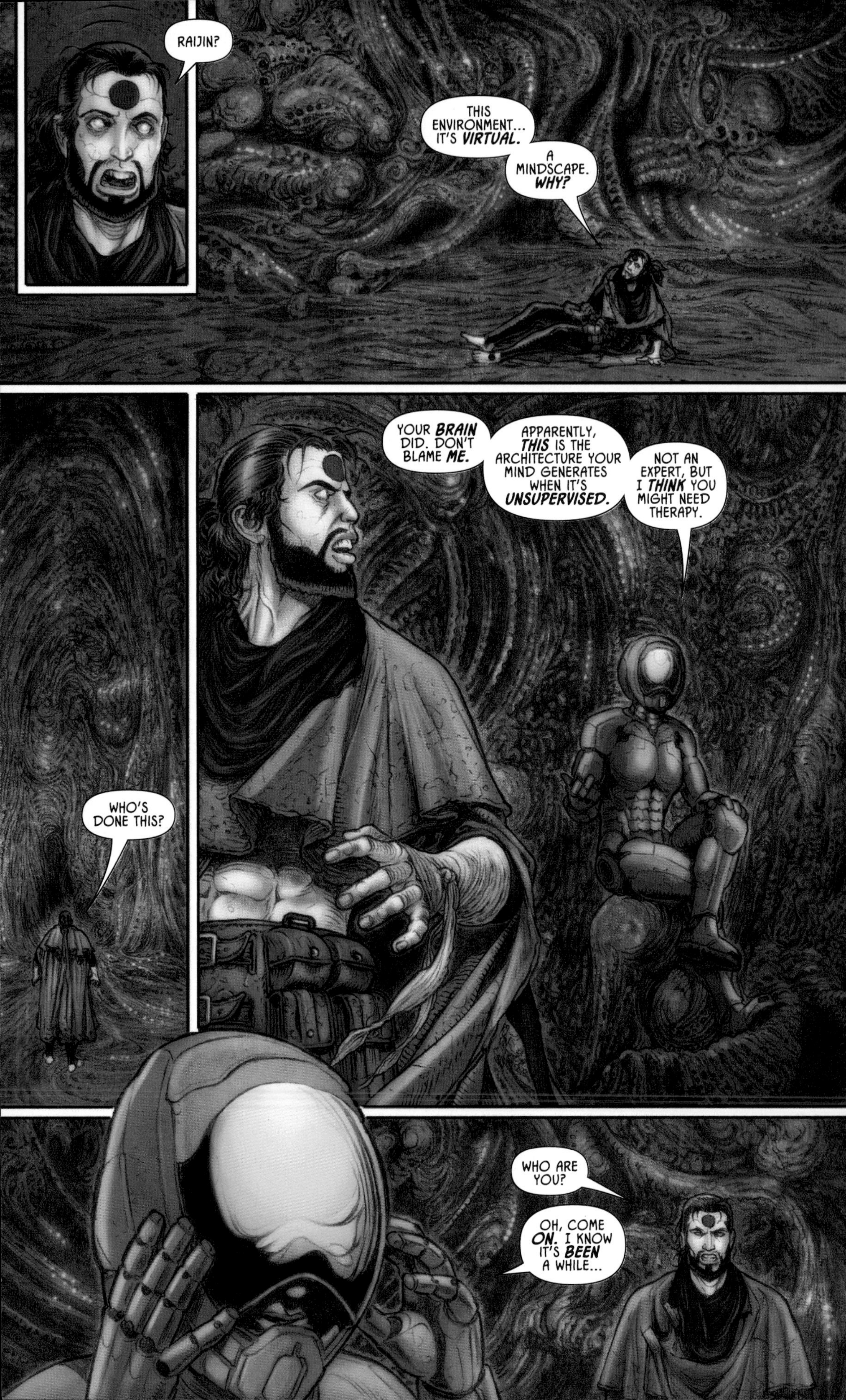
RAIJIN?
THIS ENVIRONMENT... IT'S VIRTUAL.
A MINDSCAPE. WHY?
YOUR BRAIN DID. DON'T BLAME ME.
APPARENTLY, THIS IS THE ARCHITECTURE YOUR MIND GENERATES WHEN IT'S UNSUPERVISED.
NOT AN EXPERT, BUT I THINK YOU MIGHT NEED THERAPY.
WHO'S DONE THIS?
WHO ARE YOU?
OH, COME ON. I KNOW IT'S BEEN A WHILE...

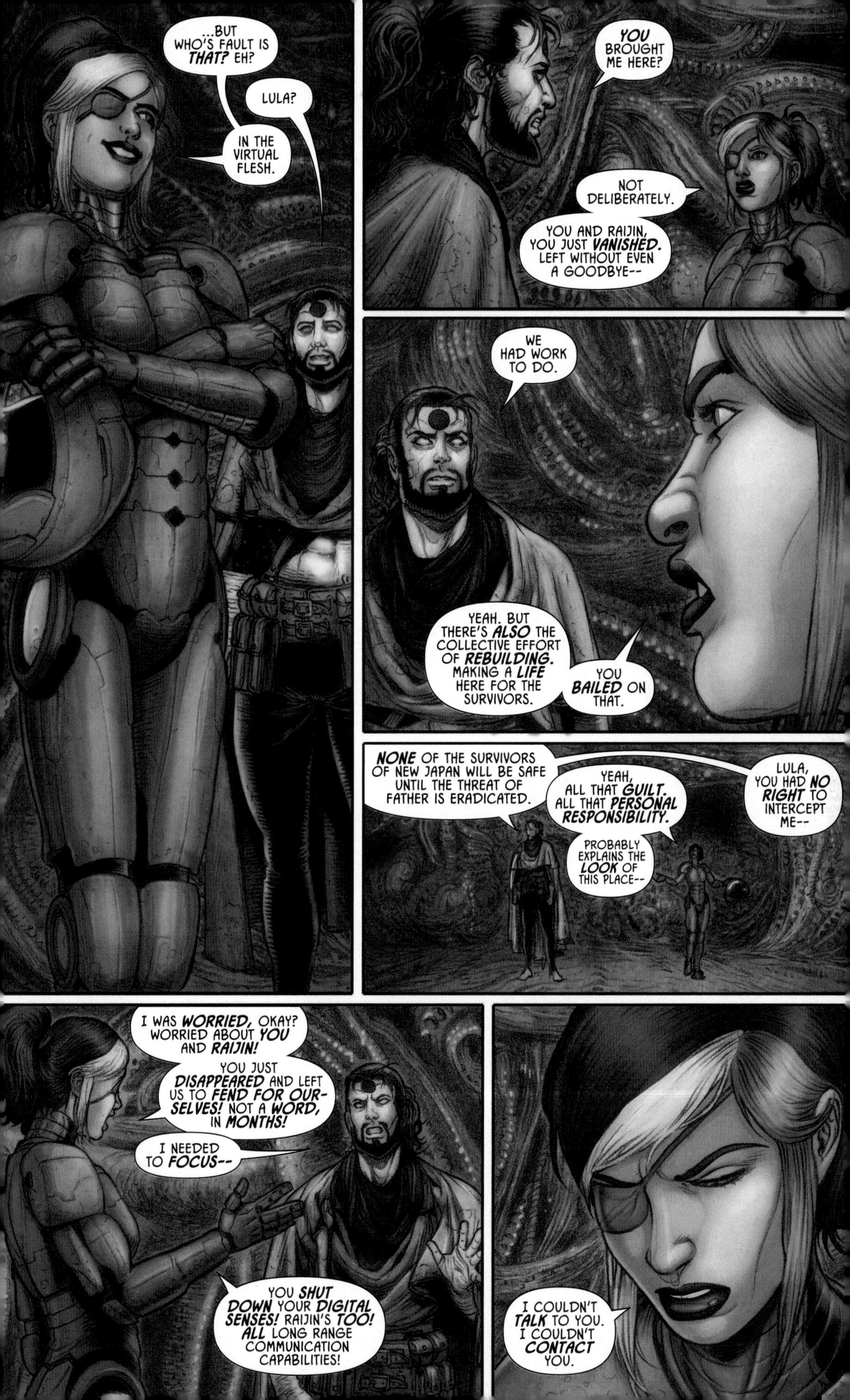
...BUT WHO'S FAULT IS THAT? EH?
LULA?
IN THE VIRTUAL FLESH.
YOU BROUGHT ME HERE?
NOT DELIBERATELY.
YOU AND RAIJIN, YOU JUST VANISHED. LEFT WITHOUT EVEN A GOODBYE--
WE HAD WORK TO DO.
YEAH. BUT THERE'S ALSO THE COLLECTIVE EFFORT OF REBUILDING. MAKING A LIFE HERE FOR THE SURVIVORS.
YOU BAILED ON THAT.
NONE OF THE SURVIVORS OF NEW JAPAN WILL BE SAFE UNTIL THE THREAT OF FATHER IS ERADICATED.
YEAH, ALL THAT GUILT. ALL THAT PERSONAL RESPONSIBILITY.
PROBABLY EXPLAINS THE LOOK OF THIS PLACE--
LULA, YOU HAD NO RIGHT TO INTERCEPT ME--
I WAS WORRIED, OKAY? WORRIED ABOUT YOU AND RAIJIN!
YOU JUST DISAPPEARED AND LEFT US TO FEND FOR OUR-SELVES! NOT A WORD, IN MONTHS!
I NEEDED TO FOCUS--
YOU SHUT DOWN YOUR DIGITAL SENSES! RAIJIN'S TOO! ALL LONG RANGE COMMUNICATION CAPABILITIES!
I COULDN'T TALK TO YOU. I COULDN'T CONTACT YOU.

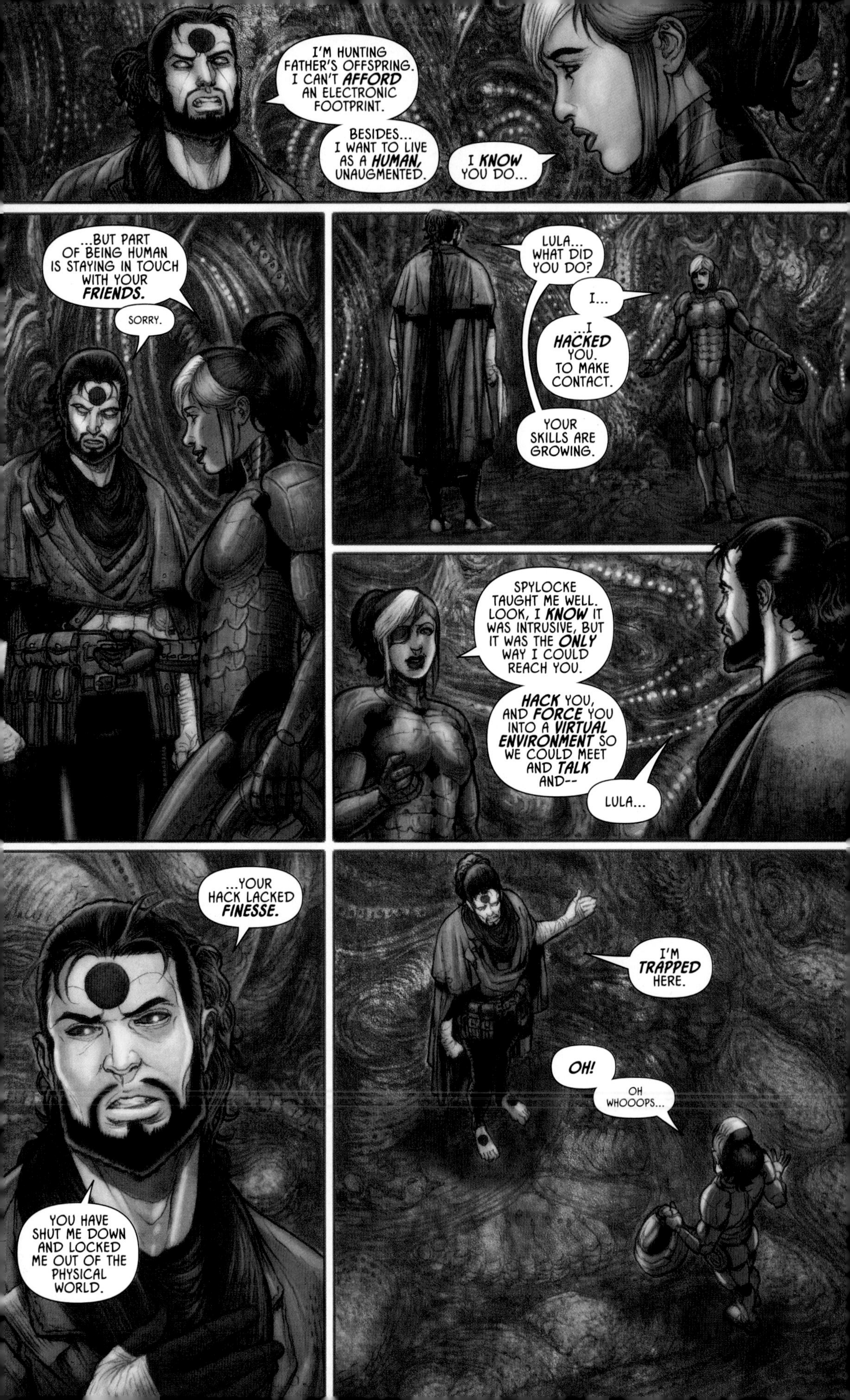

I'M HUNTING FATHER'S OFFSPRING. I CAN'T AFFORD AN ELECTRONIC FOOTPRINT.
BESIDES... I WANT TO LIVE AS A HUMAN, UNAUGMENTED.
I KNOW YOU DO...
...BUT PART OF BEING HUMAN IS STAYING IN TOUCH WITH YOUR FRIENDS.
SORRY.
LULA... WHAT DID YOU DO?
I...
...I HACKED YOU. TO MAKE CONTACT.
YOUR SKILLS ARE GROWING.
SPYLOCKE TAUGHT ME WELL. LOOK, I KNOW IT WAS INTRUSIVE, BUT IT WAS THE ONLY WAY I COULD REACH YOU.
HACK YOU, AND FORCE YOU INTO A VIRTUAL ENVIRONMENT SO WE COULD MEET AND TALK AND--
LULA...
...YOUR HACK LACKED FINESSE.
YOU HAVE SHUT ME DOWN AND LOCKED ME OUT OF THE PHYSICAL WORLD.
I'M TRAPPED HERE.
OH!
OH WHOOOPS...

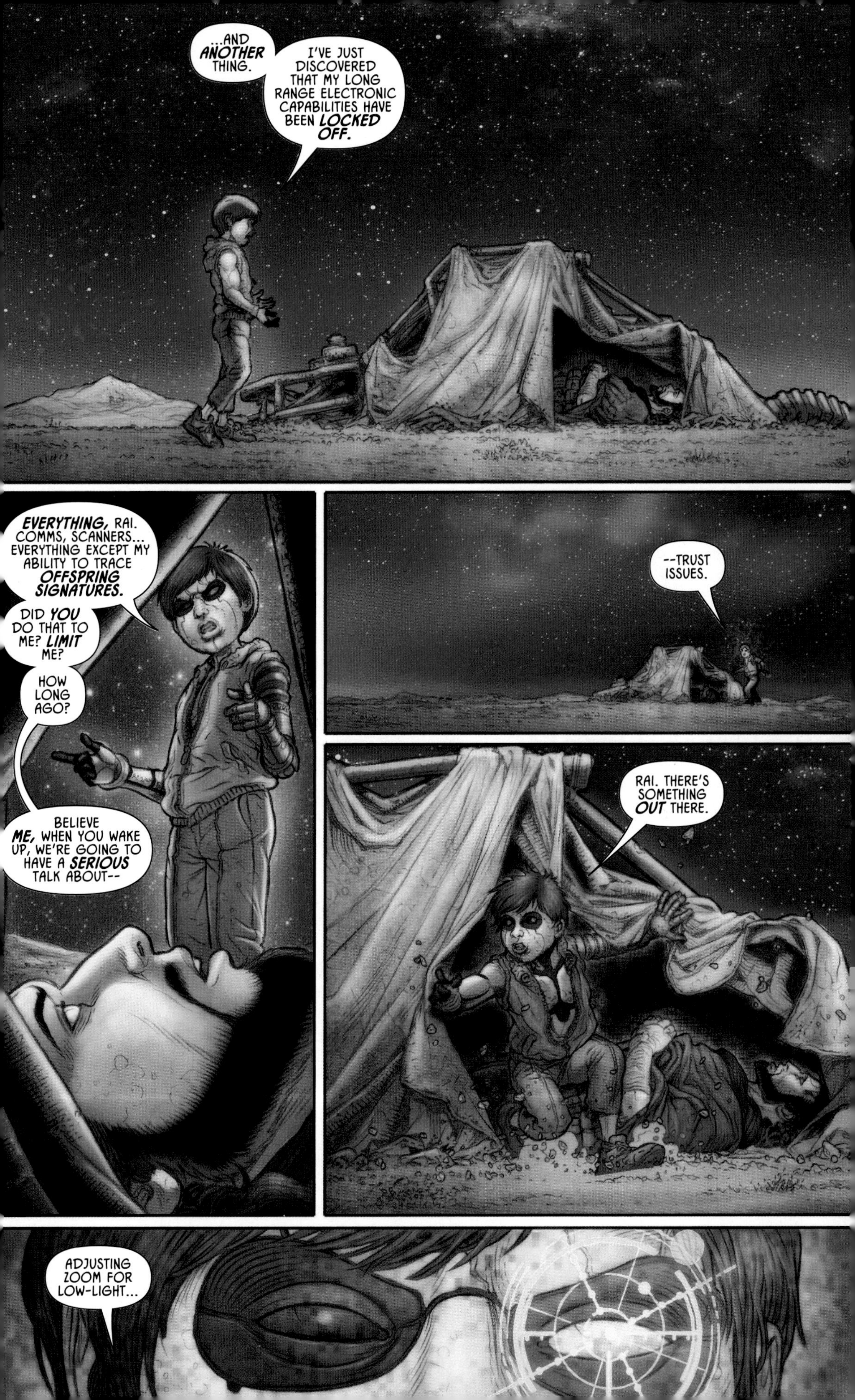
...AND ANOTHER THING.
I'VE JUST DISCOVERED THAT MY LONG RANGE ELECTRONIC CAPABILITIES HAVE BEEN LOCKED OFF.
EVERYTHING, RAI. COMMS, SCANNERS... EVERYTHING EXCEPT MY ABILITY TO TRACE OFFSPRING SIGNATURES.
DID YOU DO THAT TO ME? LIMIT ME?
HOW LONG AGO?
BELIEVE ME, WHEN YOU WAKE UP, WE'RE GOING TO HAVE A SERIOUS TALK ABOUT--
--TRUST ISSUES.
RAI. THERE'S SOMETHING OUT THERE.
ADJUSTING ZOOM FOR LOW-LIGHT...

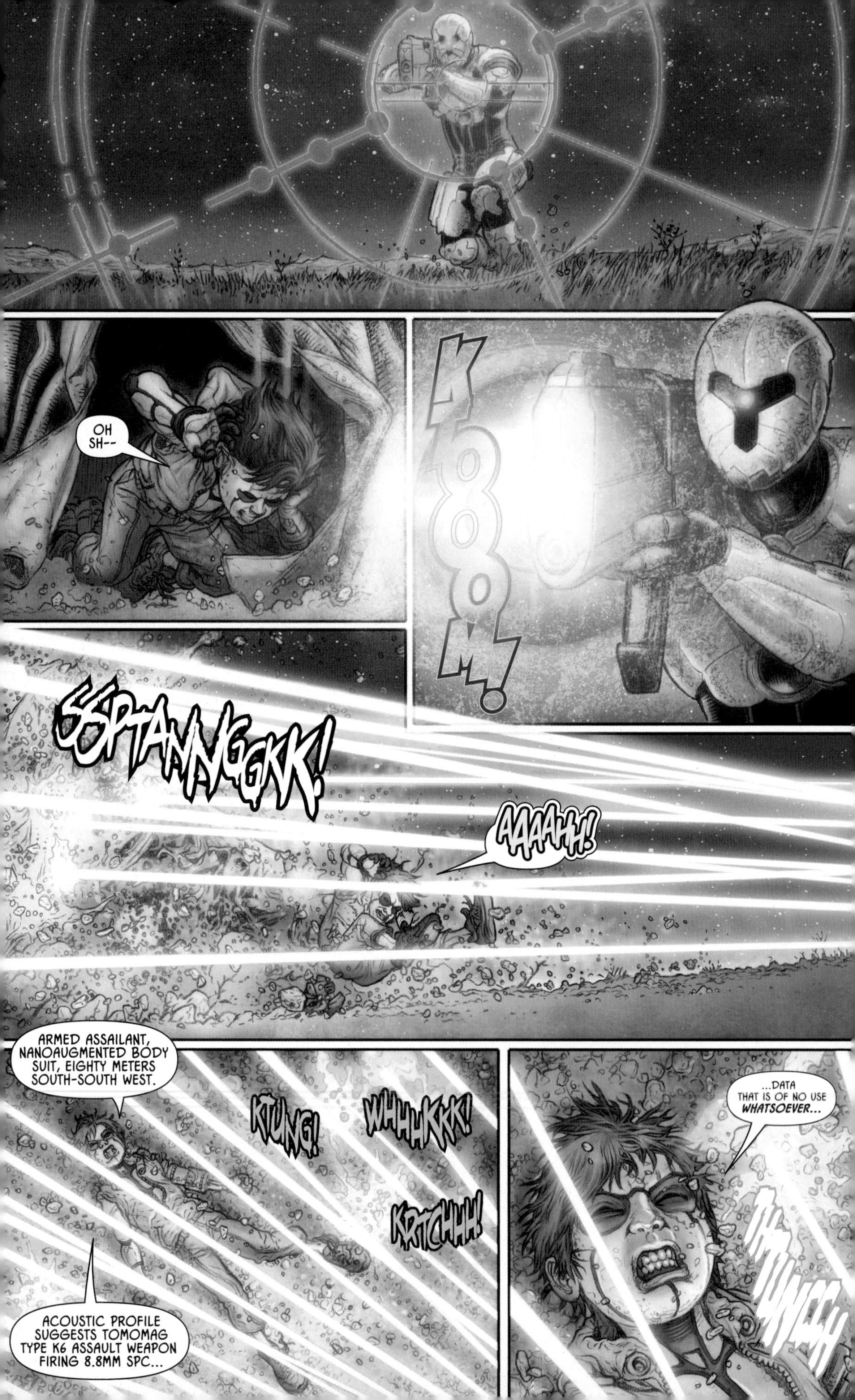
OH SH--
KABOOM!
SSPTANNGKK!
AAAAHH!
ARMED ASSAILANT, NANOAUGMENTED BODY SUIT, EIGHTY METERS SOUTH-SOUTH WEST.
KTUNG!
WHHUKKK!
KRTCHHH!
ACOUSTIC PROFILE SUGGESTS TOMOMAG TYPE K6 ASSAULT WEAPON FIRING 8.8MM SPC...
...DATA THAT IS OF NO USE WHATSOEVER...

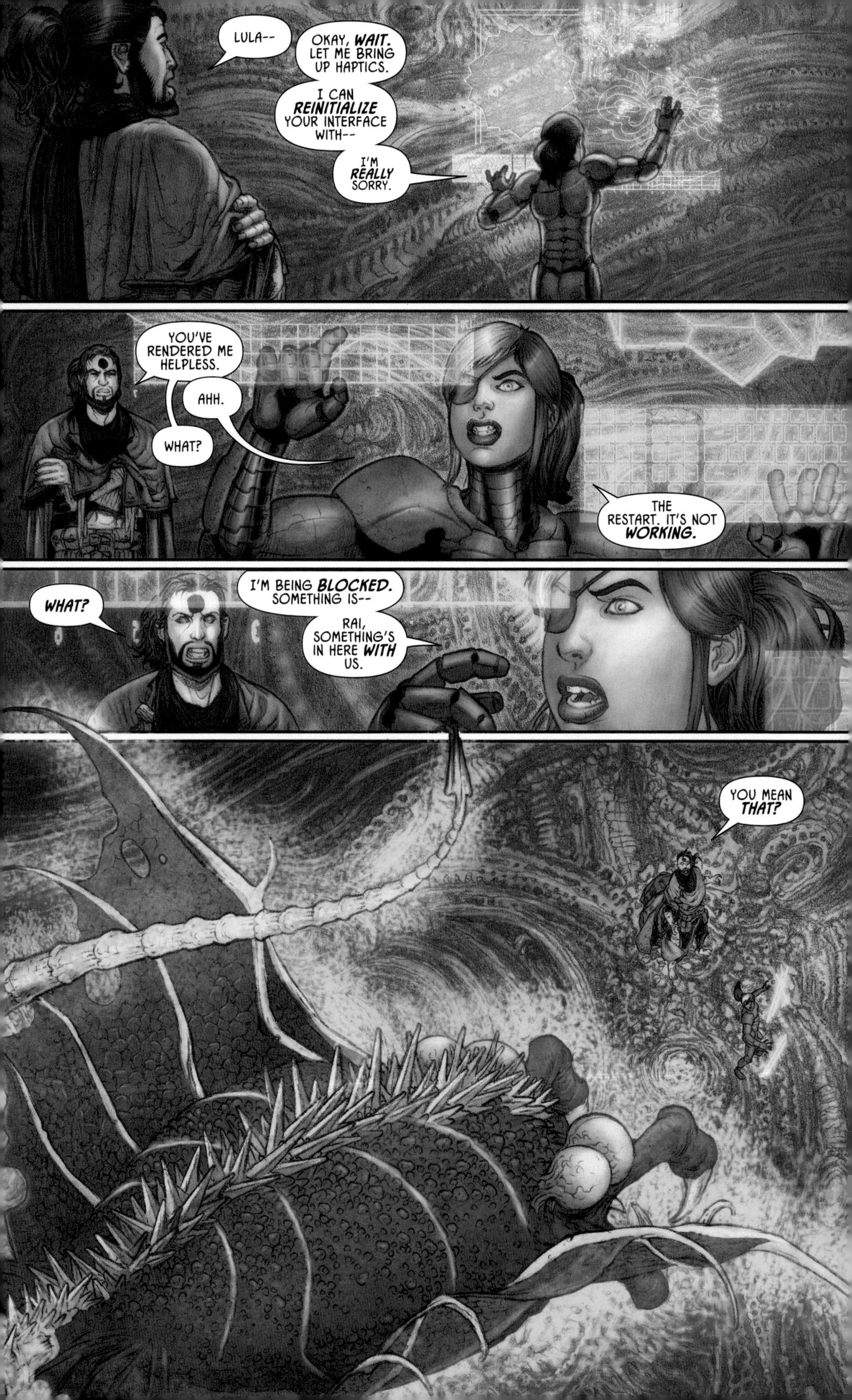
LULA--
OKAY, WAIT. LET ME BRING UP HAPTICS.
I CAN REINITIALIZE YOUR INTERFACE WITH--
I'M REALLY SORRY.
YOU'VE RENDERED ME HELPLESS.
AHH.
WHAT?
THE RESTART. IT'S NOT WORKING.
WHAT?
I'M BEING BLOCKED. SOMETHING IS--
RAI, SOMETHING'S IN HERE WITH US.
YOU MEAN THAT?

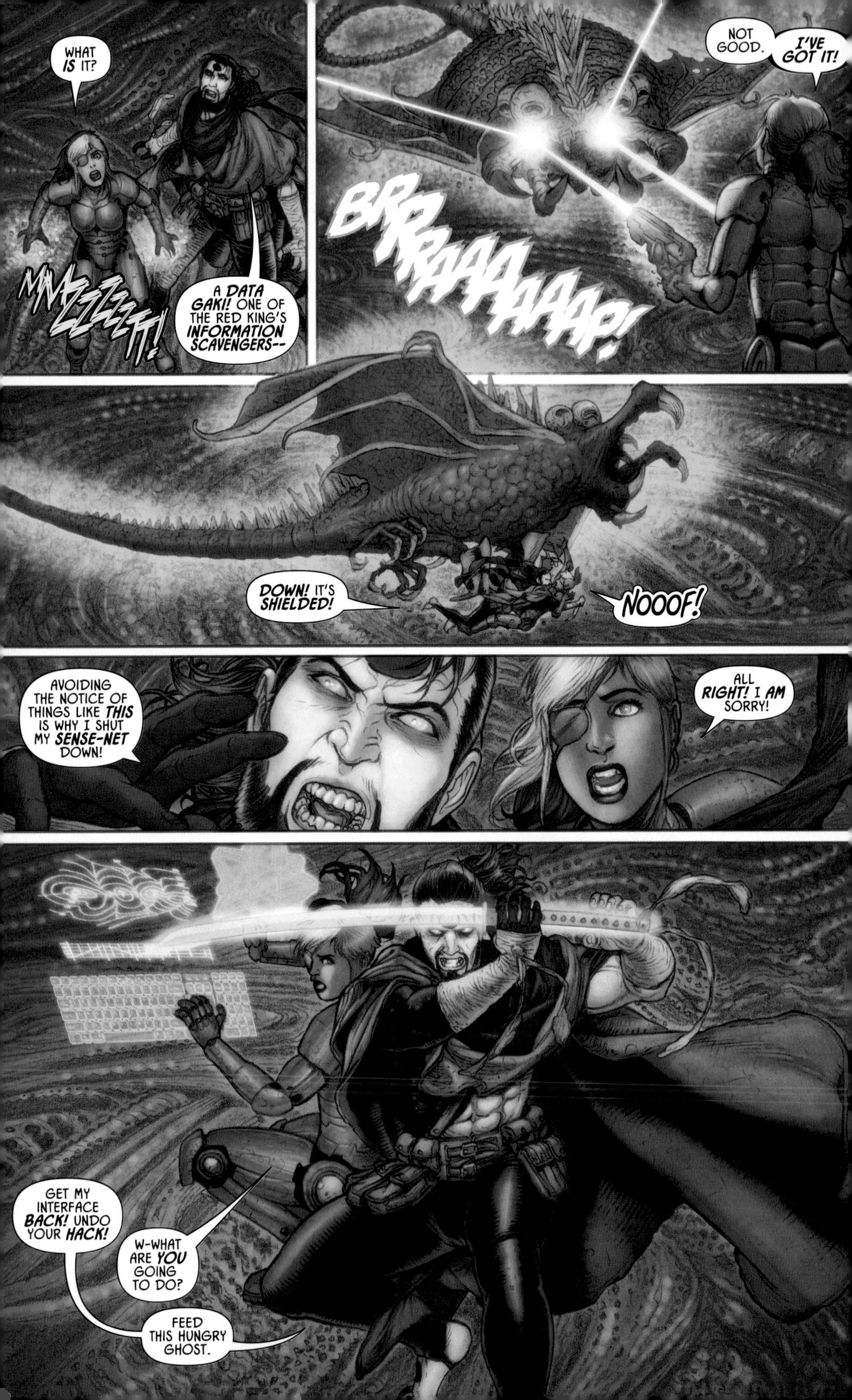
WHAT IS IT?
MMZZZZZZTT!
A DATA GAKI! ONE OF THE RED KING'S INFORMATION SCAVENGERS--
NOT GOOD.
I'VE GOT IT!
BRRRAAAAAAAAP!
DOWN! IT'S SHIELDED!
NOOOF!
AVOIDING THE NOTICE OF THINGS LIKE THIS IS WHY I SHUT MY SENSE-NET DOWN!
ALL RIGHT! I AM SORRY!
GET MY INTERFACE BACK! UNDO YOUR HACK!
W-WHAT ARE YOU GOING TO DO?
FEED THIS HUNGRY GHOST.

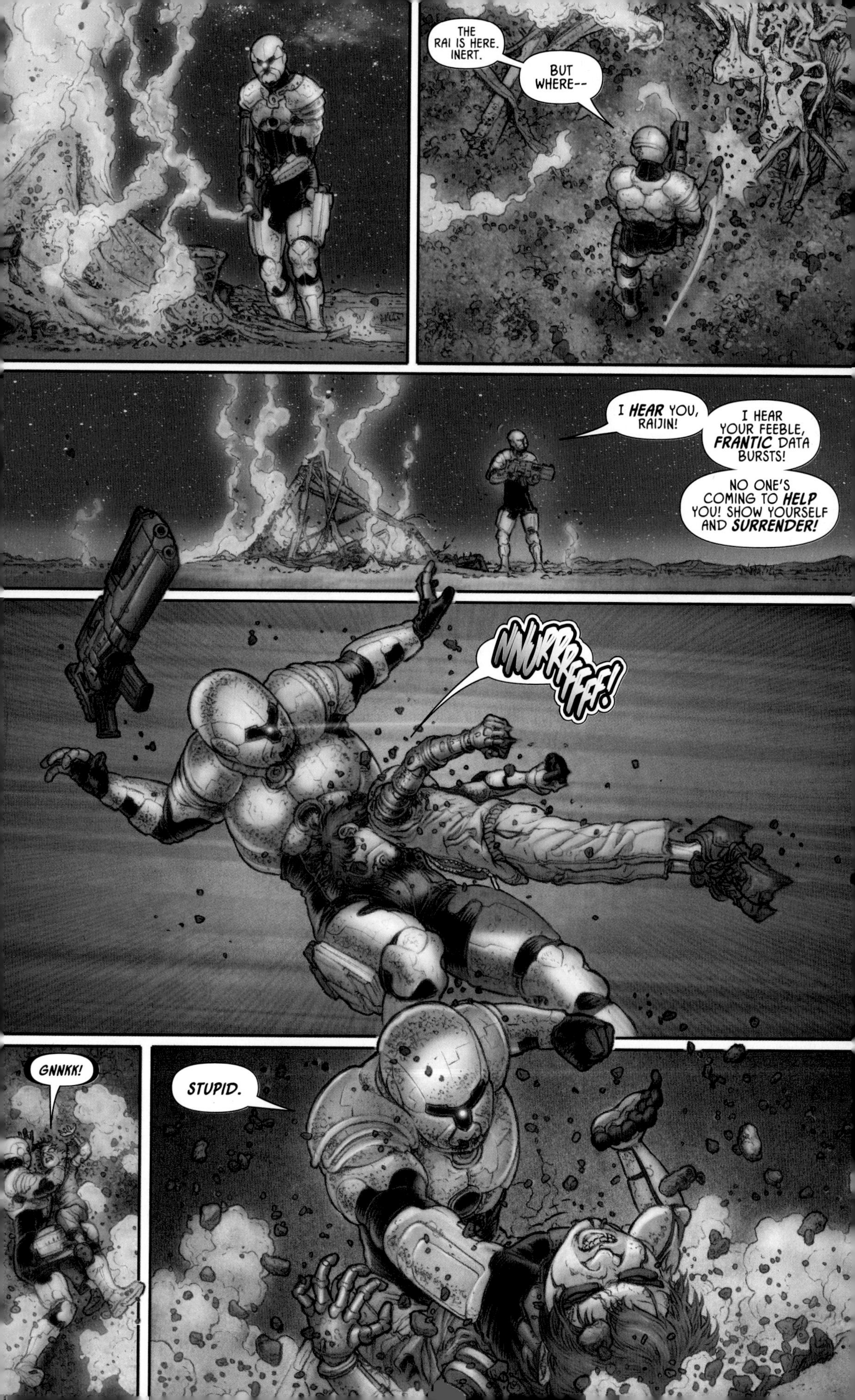

THE RAI IS HERE. INERT.
BUT WHERE--
I **HEAR** YOU, RAIJIN!
I HEAR YOUR FEEBLE, **FRANTIC** DATA BURSTS!
NO ONE'S COMING TO **HELP** YOU! SHOW YOURSELF AND **SURRENDER!**
NNURRRFFFF!
GNNKK!
STUPID.

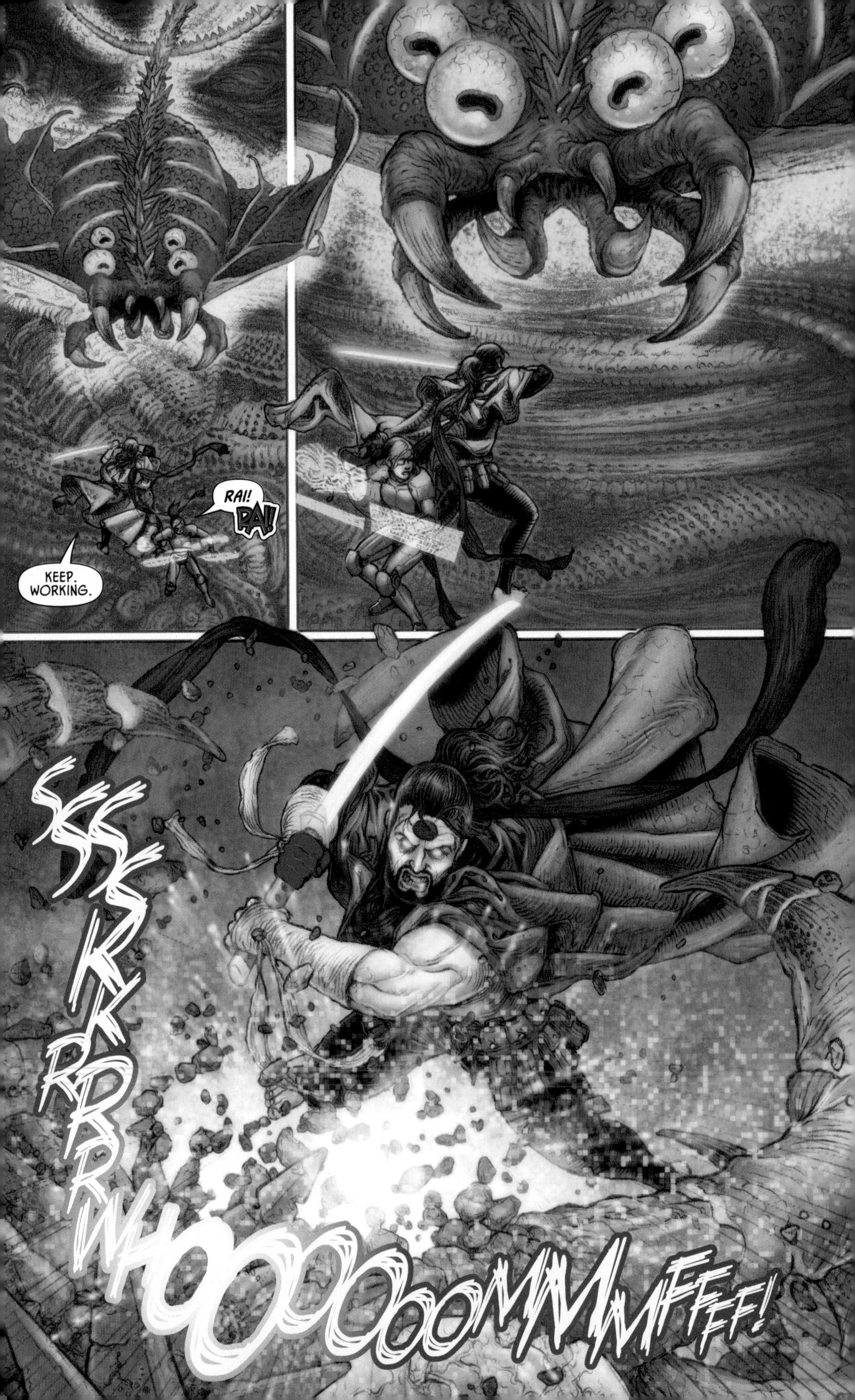
RAI!
RAI!
KEEP. WORKING.
SKKRRWHOOOOooOMMFFFF!

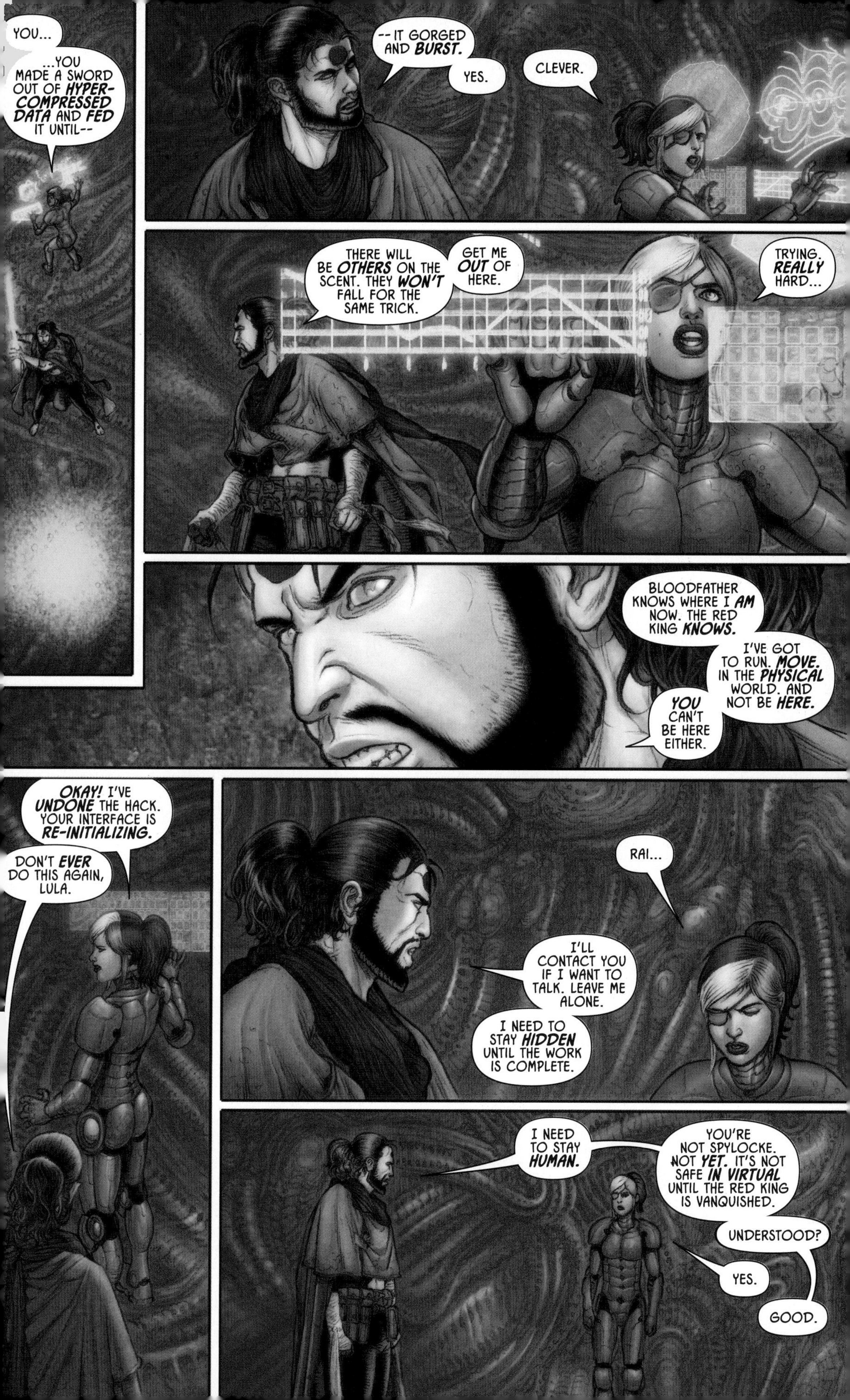
YOU...
...YOU MADE A SWORD OUT OF HYPER-COMPRESSED DATA AND FED IT UNTIL--
-- IT GORGED AND BURST.
YES.
CLEVER.
THERE WILL BE OTHERS ON THE SCENT. THEY WON'T FALL FOR THE SAME TRICK.
GET ME OUT OF HERE.
TRYING. REALLY HARD...
BLOODFATHER KNOWS WHERE I AM NOW. THE RED KING KNOWS.
I'VE GOT TO RUN. MOVE. IN THE PHYSICAL WORLD. AND NOT BE HERE.
YOU CAN'T BE HERE EITHER.
OKAY! I'VE UNDONE THE HACK. YOUR INTERFACE IS RE-INITIALIZING.
DON'T EVER DO THIS AGAIN, LULA.
RAI...
I'LL CONTACT YOU IF I WANT TO TALK. LEAVE ME ALONE.
I NEED TO STAY HIDDEN UNTIL THE WORK IS COMPLETE.
I NEED TO STAY HUMAN.
YOU'RE NOT SPYLOCKE. NOT YET. IT'S NOT SAFE IN VIRTUAL UNTIL THE RED KING IS VANQUISHED.
UNDERSTOOD?
YES.
GOOD.

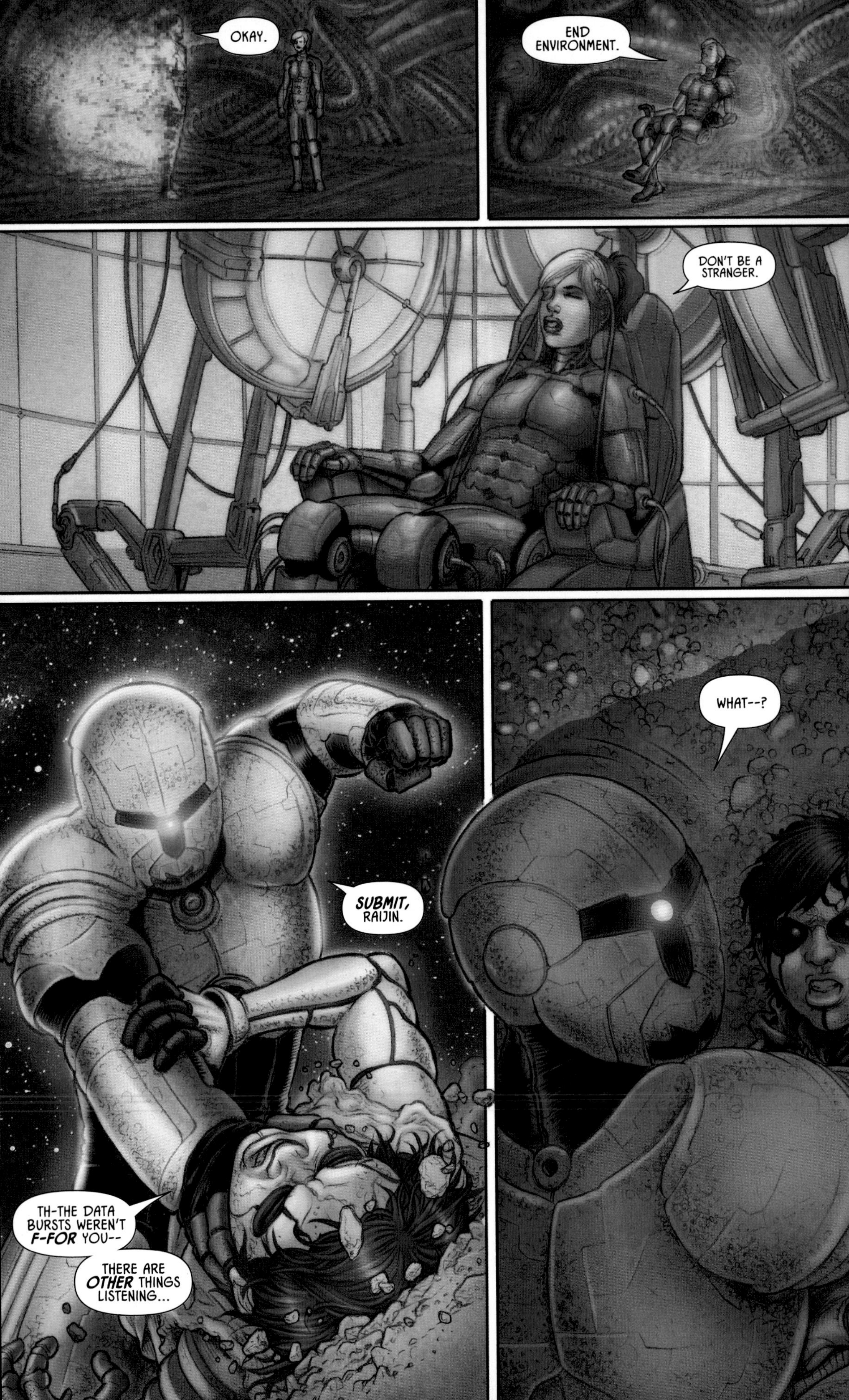
OKAY.
END ENVIRONMENT.
DON'T BE A STRANGER.
SUBMIT, RAIJIN.
TH-THE DATA BURSTS WEREN'T F-FOR YOU--
THERE ARE OTHER THINGS LISTENING...
WHAT--?

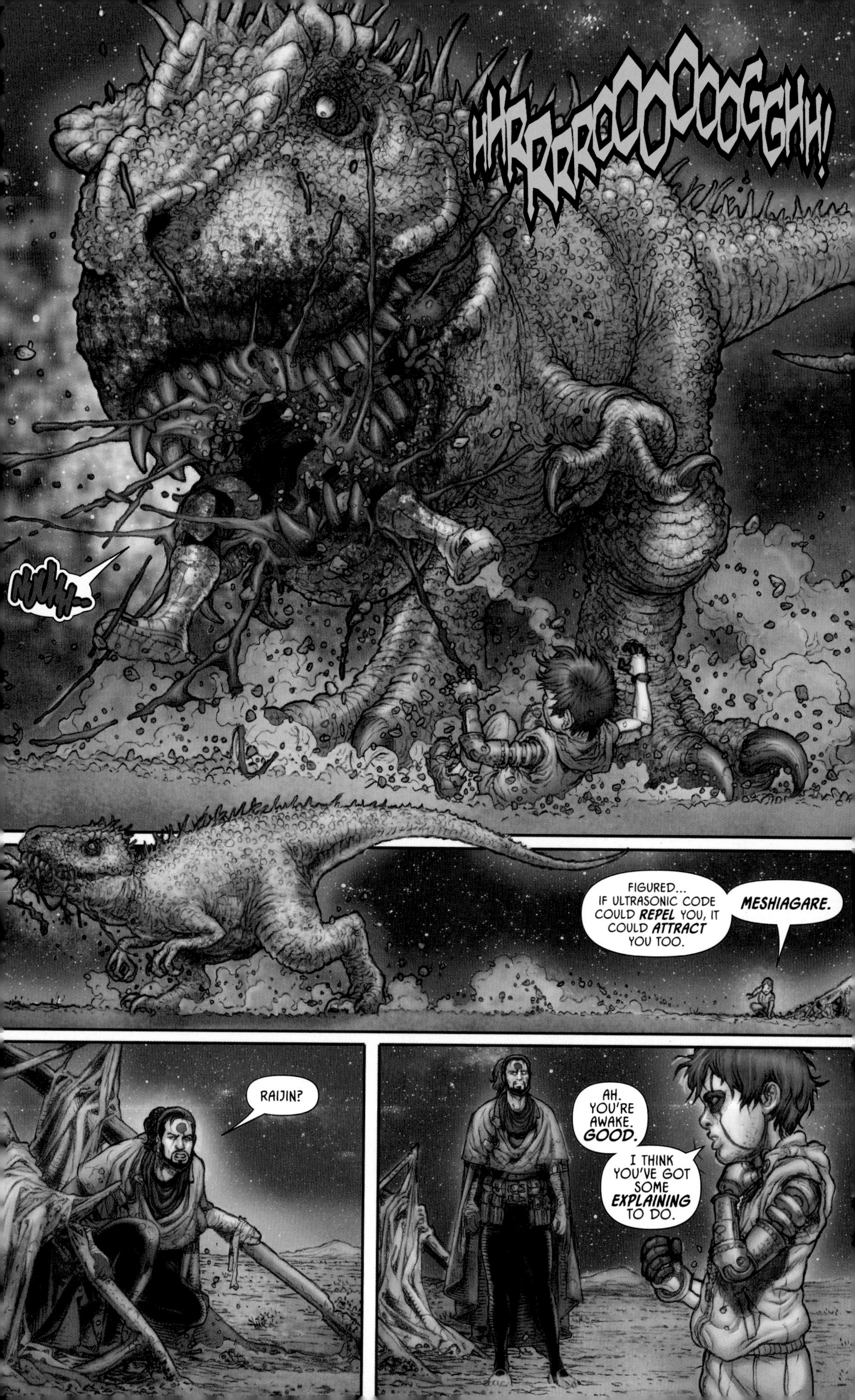
HHRRROOOOOOOOGGHH!
NNUHH-
FIGURED... IF ULTRASONIC CODE COULD REPEL YOU, IT COULD ATTRACT YOU TOO.
MESHIAGARE.
RAIJIN?
AH. YOU'RE AWAKE. GOOD.
I THINK YOU'VE GOT SOME EXPLAINING TO DO.

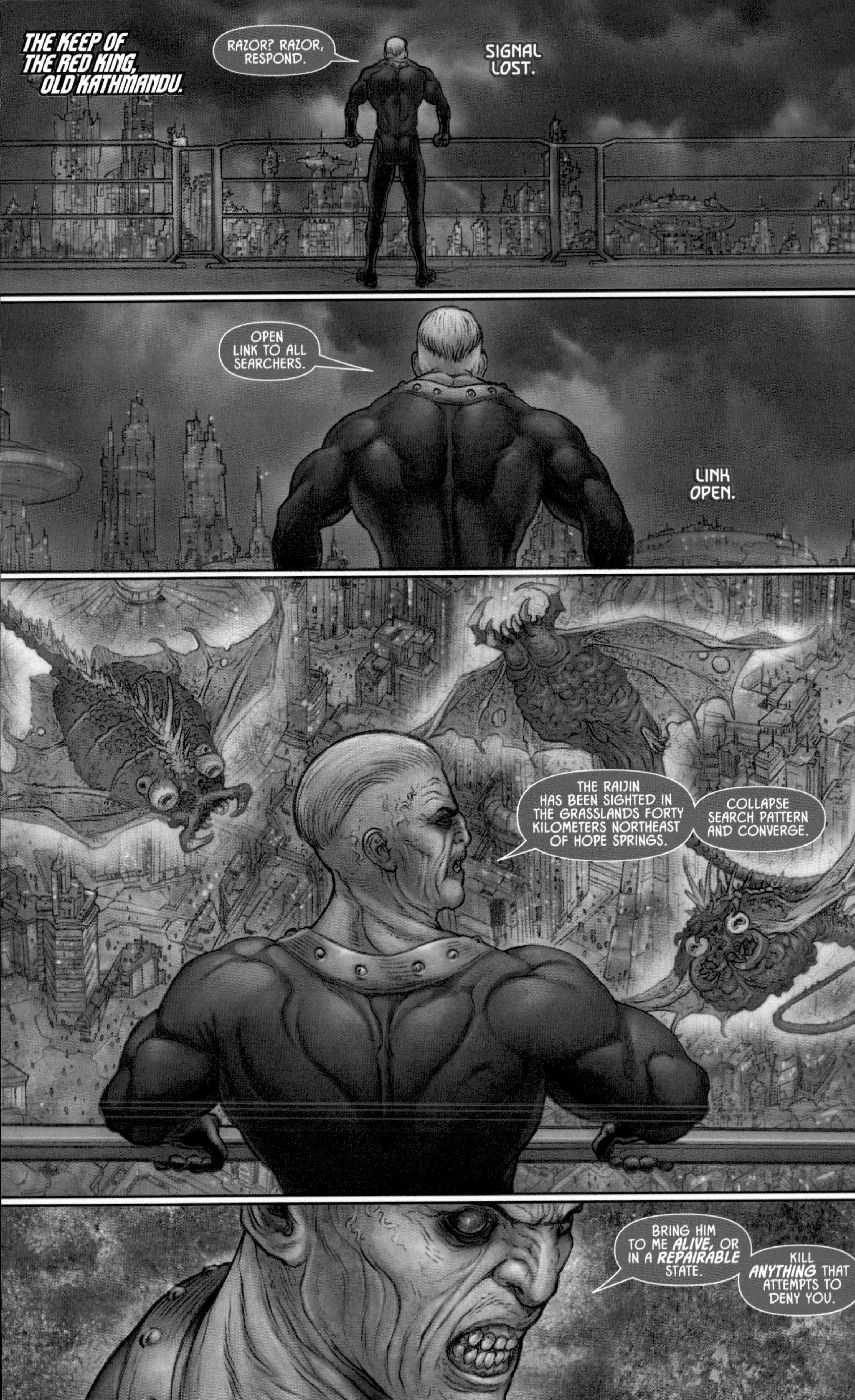
THE KEEP OF THE RED KING, OLD KATHMANDU.
RAZOR? RAZOR, RESPOND.
SIGNAL LOST.
OPEN LINK TO ALL SEARCHERS.
LINK OPEN.
THE RAIJIN HAS BEEN SIGHTED IN THE GRASSLANDS FORTY KILOMETERS NORTHEAST OF HOPE SPRINGS.
COLLAPSE SEARCH PATTERN AND CONVERGE.
BRING HIM TO ME *ALIVE*, OR IN A *REPAIRABLE* STATE.
KILL *ANYTHING* THAT ATTEMPTS TO DENY YOU.

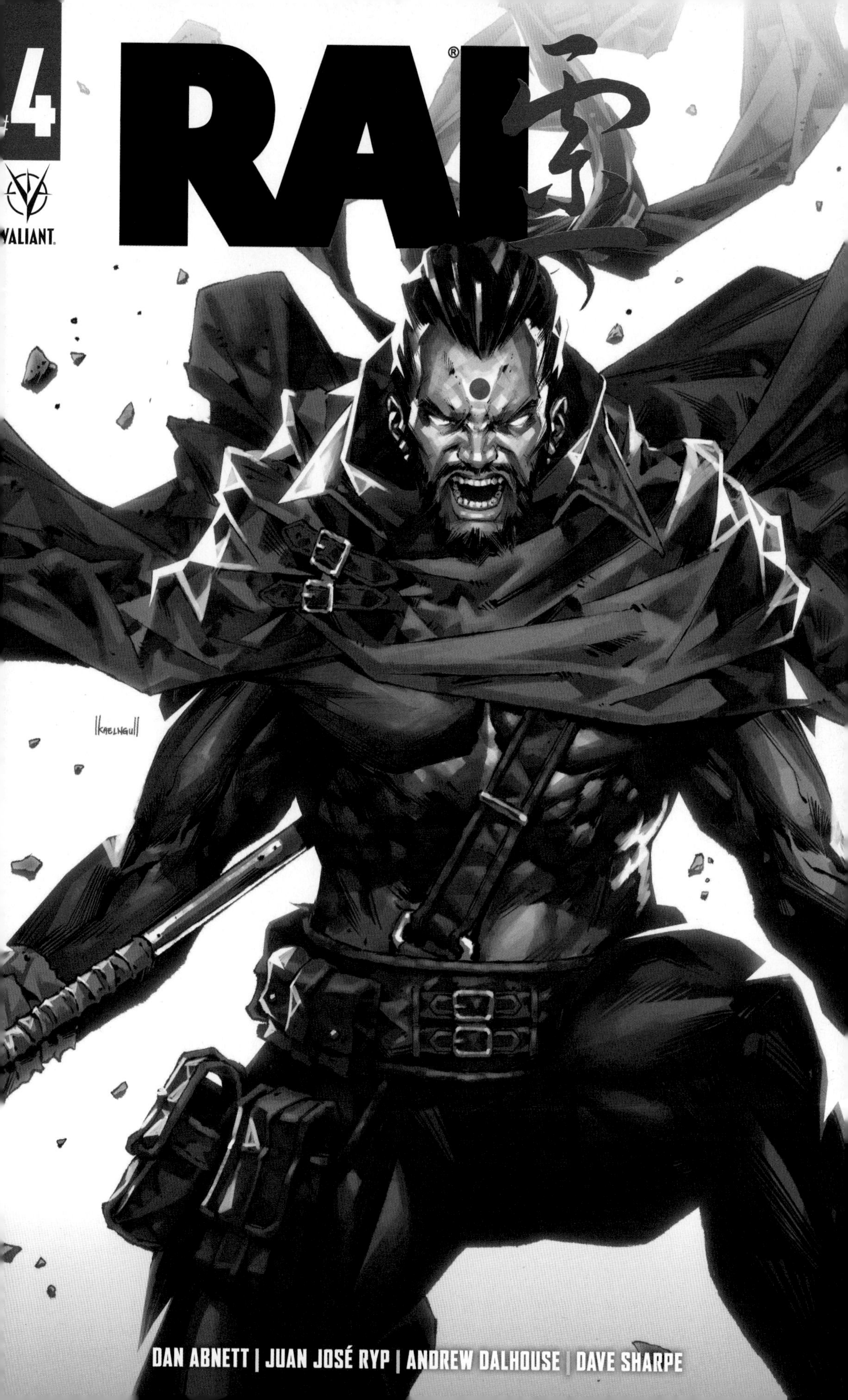

#4
RAI®
VALIANT
KAELNGUL
DAN ABNETT | JUAN JOSÉ RYP | ANDREW DALHOUSE | DAVE SHARPE

RAI #4

WRITER: DAN ABNETT
ARTIST: JUAN JOSÉ RYP
COLORIST: ANDREW DALHOUSE
LETTERER: DAVE SHARPE
COVER ARTIST: KAEL NGU
ASSOCIATE EDITOR: DAVID MENCHEL
EDITOR: LYSA HAWKINS

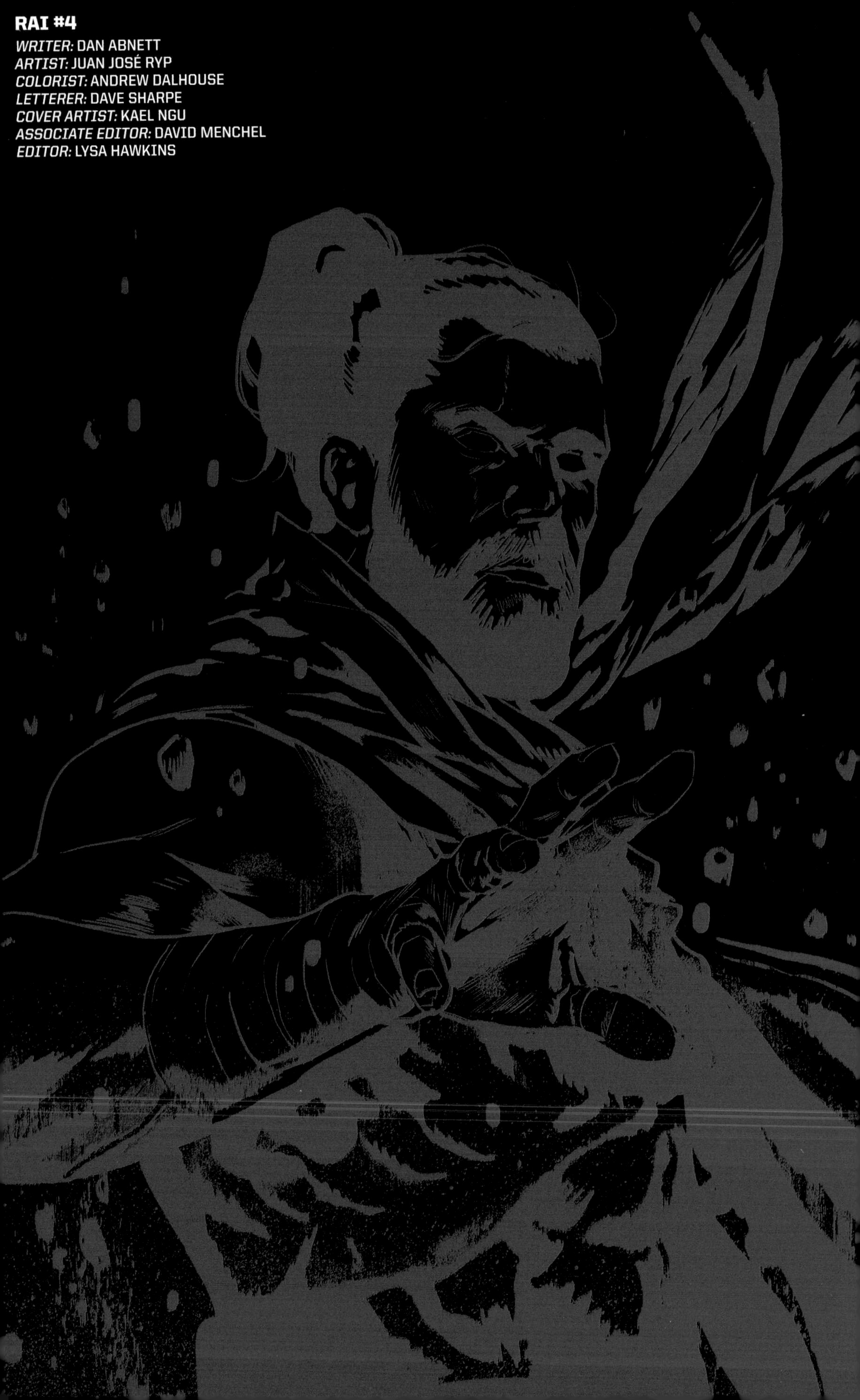

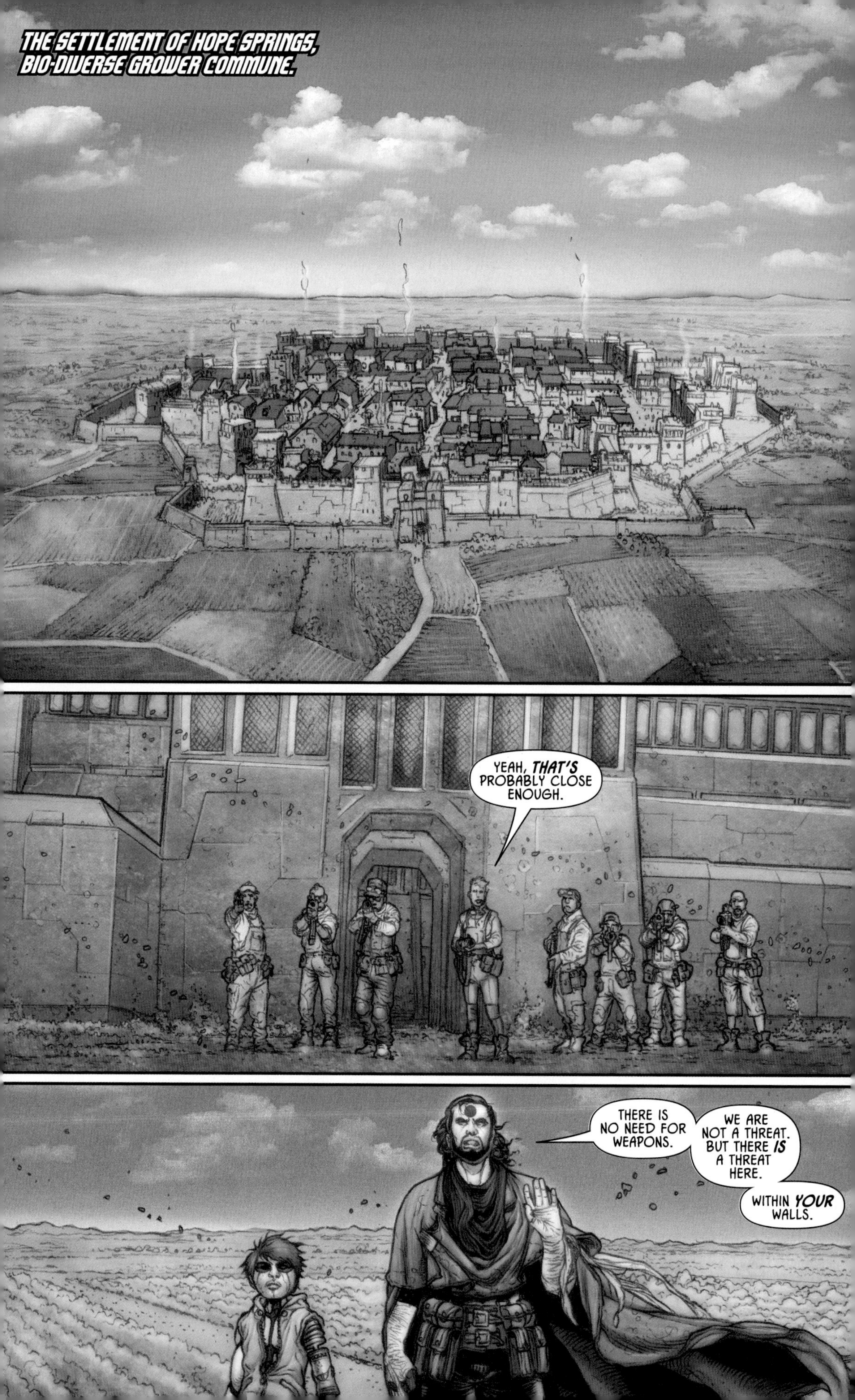
THE SETTLEMENT OF HOPE SPRINGS,
BIO-DIVERSE GROWER COMMUNE.
YEAH, THAT'S PROBABLY CLOSE ENOUGH.
THERE IS NO NEED FOR WEAPONS.
WE ARE NOT A THREAT. BUT THERE IS A THREAT HERE.
WITHIN YOUR WALLS.

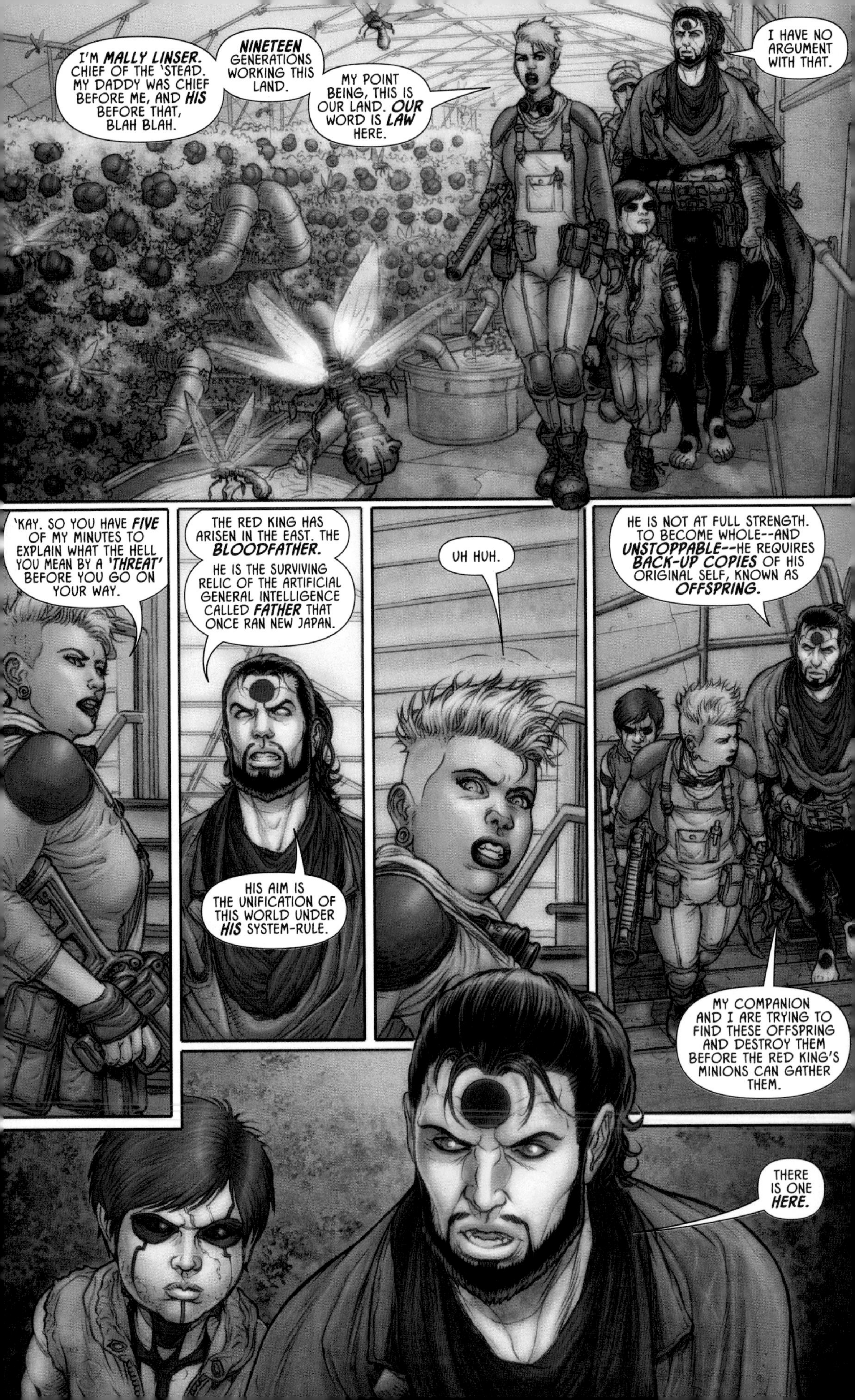

I'M **MALLY LINSER.** CHIEF OF THE 'STEAD. MY DADDY WAS CHIEF BEFORE ME, AND **HIS** BEFORE THAT, BLAH BLAH.
NINETEEN GENERATIONS WORKING THIS LAND.
MY POINT BEING, THIS IS OUR LAND. **OUR** WORD IS **LAW** HERE.
I HAVE NO ARGUMENT WITH THAT.
'KAY. SO YOU HAVE **FIVE** OF MY MINUTES TO EXPLAIN WHAT THE HELL YOU MEAN BY A **'THREAT'** BEFORE YOU GO ON YOUR WAY.
THE RED KING HAS ARISEN IN THE EAST. THE **BLOODFATHER.**
HE IS THE SURVIVING RELIC OF THE ARTIFICIAL GENERAL INTELLIGENCE CALLED **FATHER** THAT ONCE RAN NEW JAPAN.
HIS AIM IS THE UNIFICATION OF THIS WORLD UNDER **HIS** SYSTEM-RULE.
UH HUH.
HE IS NOT AT FULL STRENGTH. TO BECOME WHOLE--AND **UNSTOPPABLE--**HE REQUIRES **BACK-UP COPIES** OF HIS ORIGINAL SELF, KNOWN AS **OFFSPRING.**
MY COMPANION AND I ARE TRYING TO FIND THESE OFFSPRING AND DESTROY THEM BEFORE THE RED KING'S MINIONS CAN GATHER THEM.
THERE IS ONE **HERE.**

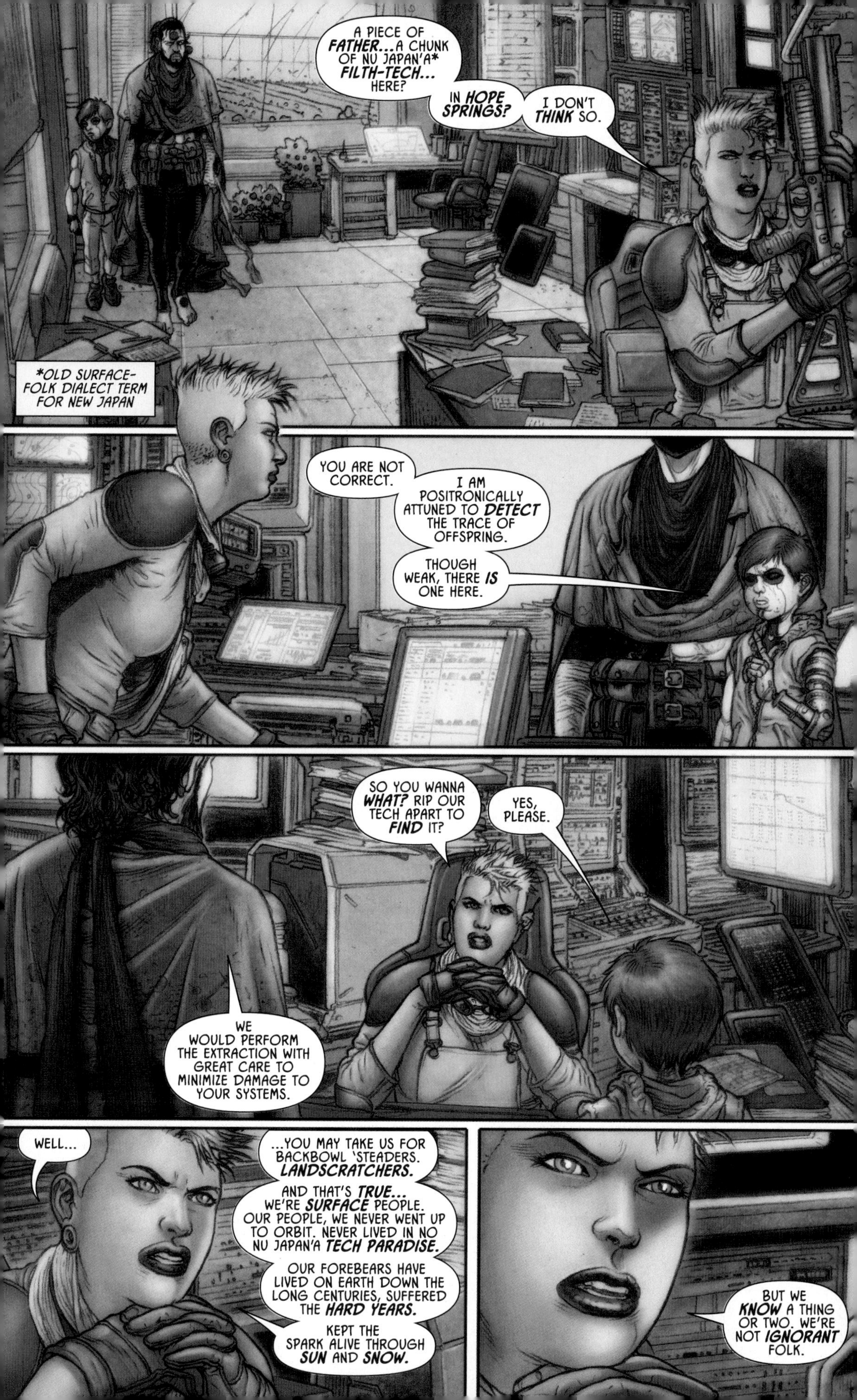
A PIECE OF FATHER... A CHUNK OF NU JAPAN'A* FILTH-TECH... HERE?
IN HOPE SPRINGS?
I DON'T THINK SO.
*OLD SURFACE-FOLK DIALECT TERM FOR NEW JAPAN
YOU ARE NOT CORRECT.
I AM POSITRONICALLY ATTUNED TO DETECT THE TRACE OF OFFSPRING.
THOUGH WEAK, THERE IS ONE HERE.
SO YOU WANNA WHAT? RIP OUR TECH APART TO FIND IT?
YES, PLEASE.
WE WOULD PERFORM THE EXTRACTION WITH GREAT CARE TO MINIMIZE DAMAGE TO YOUR SYSTEMS.
WELL...
...YOU MAY TAKE US FOR BACKBOWL 'STEADERS. LANDSCRATCHERS.
AND THAT'S TRUE... WE'RE SURFACE PEOPLE. OUR PEOPLE, WE NEVER WENT UP TO ORBIT. NEVER LIVED IN NO NU JAPAN'A TECH PARADISE.
OUR FOREBEARS HAVE LIVED ON EARTH DOWN THE LONG CENTURIES, SUFFERED THE HARD YEARS.
KEPT THE SPARK ALIVE THROUGH SUN AND SNOW.
BUT WE KNOW A THING OR TWO. WE'RE NOT IGNORANT FOLK.

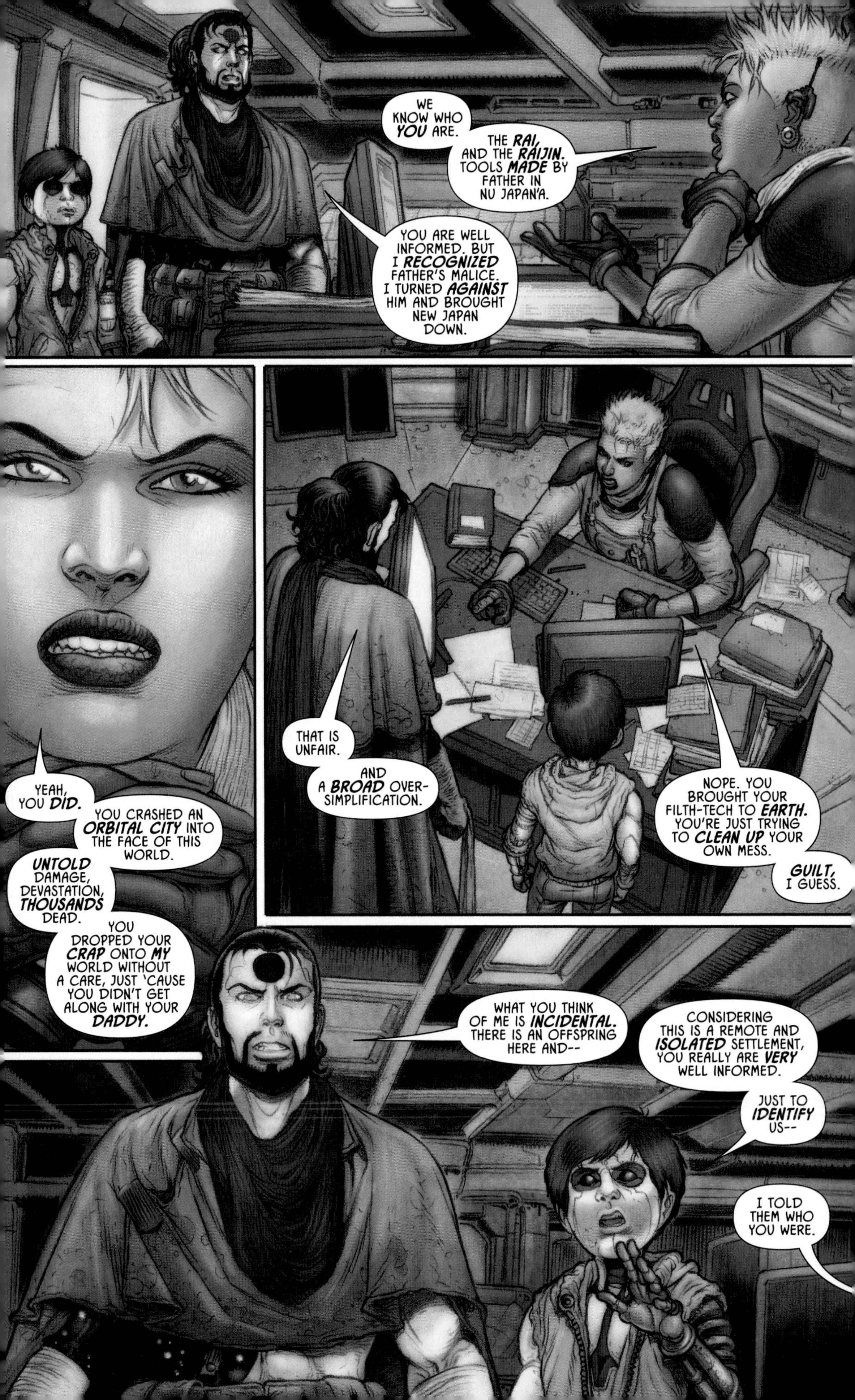
WE KNOW WHO YOU ARE.
THE RAI, AND THE RAIJIN. TOOLS MADE BY FATHER IN NU JAPAN'A.
YOU ARE WELL INFORMED. BUT I RECOGNIZED FATHER'S MALICE. I TURNED AGAINST HIM AND BROUGHT NEW JAPAN DOWN.
YEAH, YOU DID.
YOU CRASHED AN ORBITAL CITY INTO THE FACE OF THIS WORLD.
UNTOLD DAMAGE, DEVASTATION, THOUSANDS DEAD.
YOU DROPPED YOUR CRAP ONTO MY WORLD WITHOUT A CARE, JUST 'CAUSE YOU DIDN'T GET ALONG WITH YOUR DADDY.
THAT IS UNFAIR.
AND A BROAD OVER-SIMPLIFICATION.
NOPE. YOU BROUGHT YOUR FILTH-TECH TO EARTH. YOU'RE JUST TRYING TO CLEAN UP YOUR OWN MESS.
GUILT, I GUESS.
WHAT YOU THINK OF ME IS INCIDENTAL. THERE IS AN OFFSPRING HERE AND--
CONSIDERING THIS IS A REMOTE AND ISOLATED SETTLEMENT, YOU REALLY ARE VERY WELL INFORMED.
JUST TO IDENTIFY US--
I TOLD THEM WHO YOU WERE.

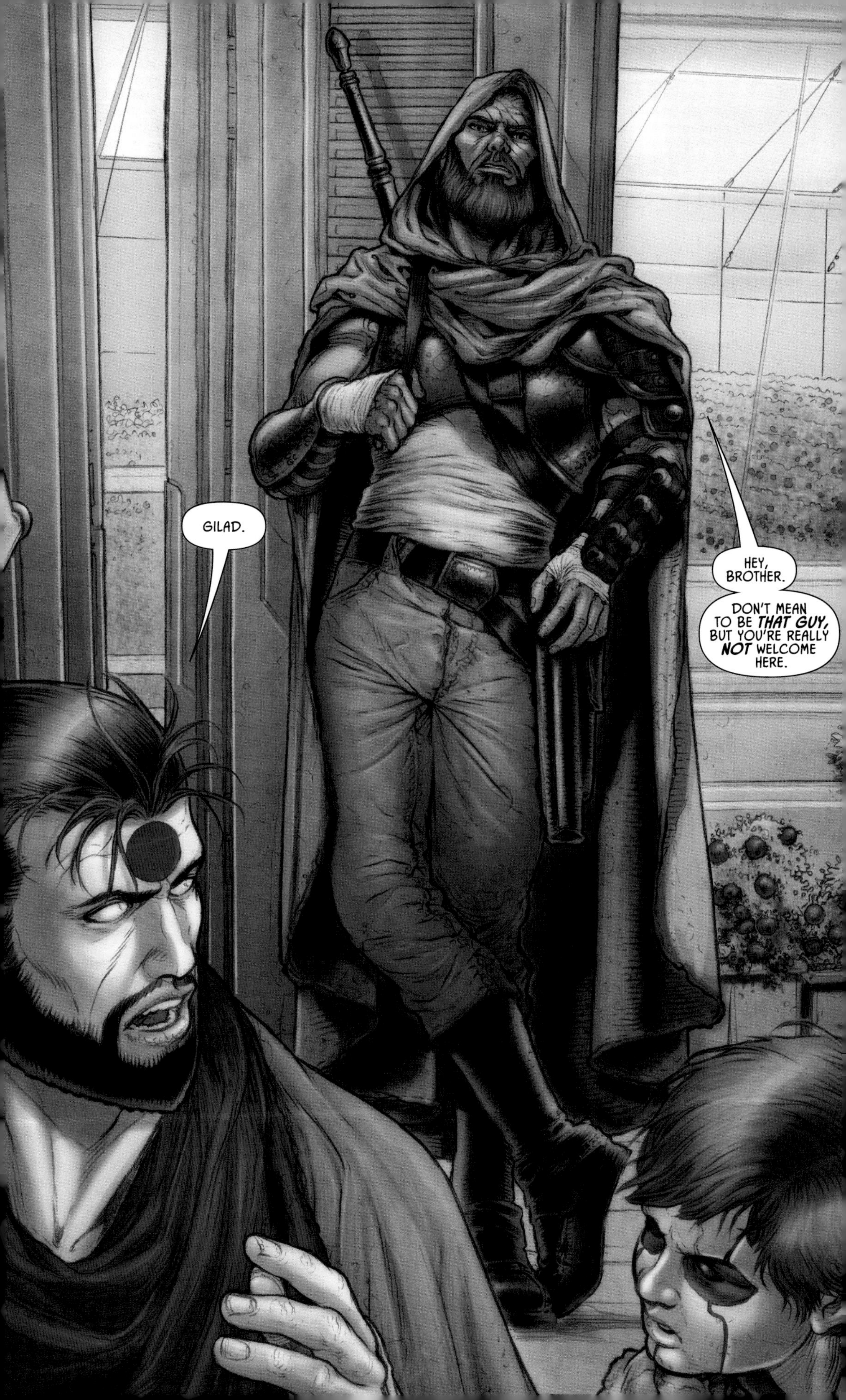
GILAD.
HEY, BROTHER.
DON'T MEAN TO BE **THAT GUY,** BUT YOU'RE REALLY **NOT** WELCOME HERE.

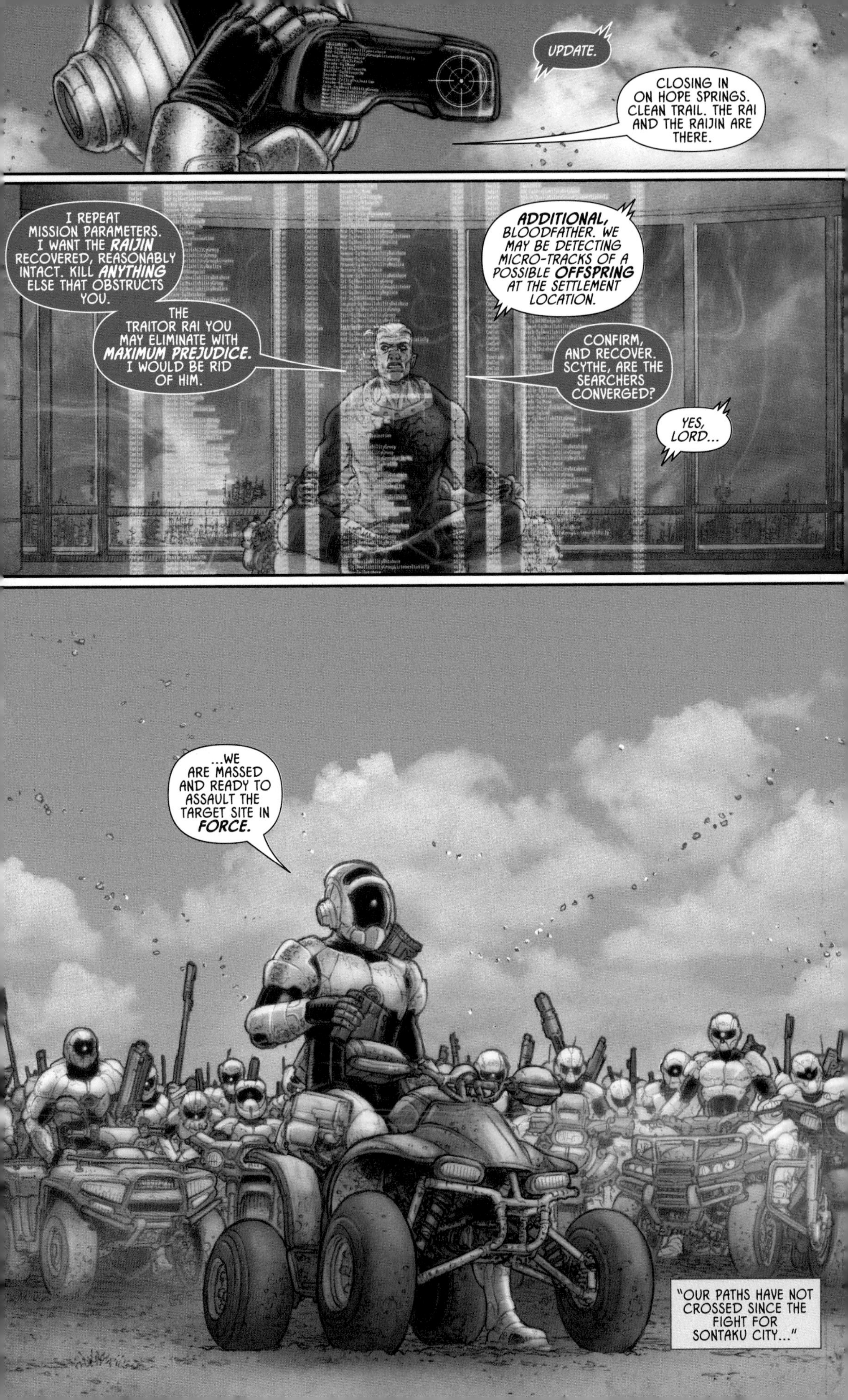
UPDATE.
CLOSING IN ON HOPE SPRINGS. CLEAN TRAIL. THE RAI AND THE RAIJIN ARE THERE.
I REPEAT MISSION PARAMETERS. I WANT THE RAIJIN RECOVERED, REASONABLY INTACT. KILL ANYTHING ELSE THAT OBSTRUCTS YOU.
THE TRAITOR RAI YOU MAY ELIMINATE WITH MAXIMUM PREJUDICE. I WOULD BE RID OF HIM.
ADDITIONAL, BLOODFATHER. WE MAY BE DETECTING MICRO-TRACKS OF A POSSIBLE OFFSPRING AT THE SETTLEMENT LOCATION.
CONFIRM, AND RECOVER. SCYTHE, ARE THE SEARCHERS CONVERGED?
YES, LORD...
...WE ARE MASSED AND READY TO ASSAULT THE TARGET SITE IN FORCE.
"OUR PATHS HAVE NOT CROSSED SINCE THE FIGHT FOR SONTAKU CITY..."

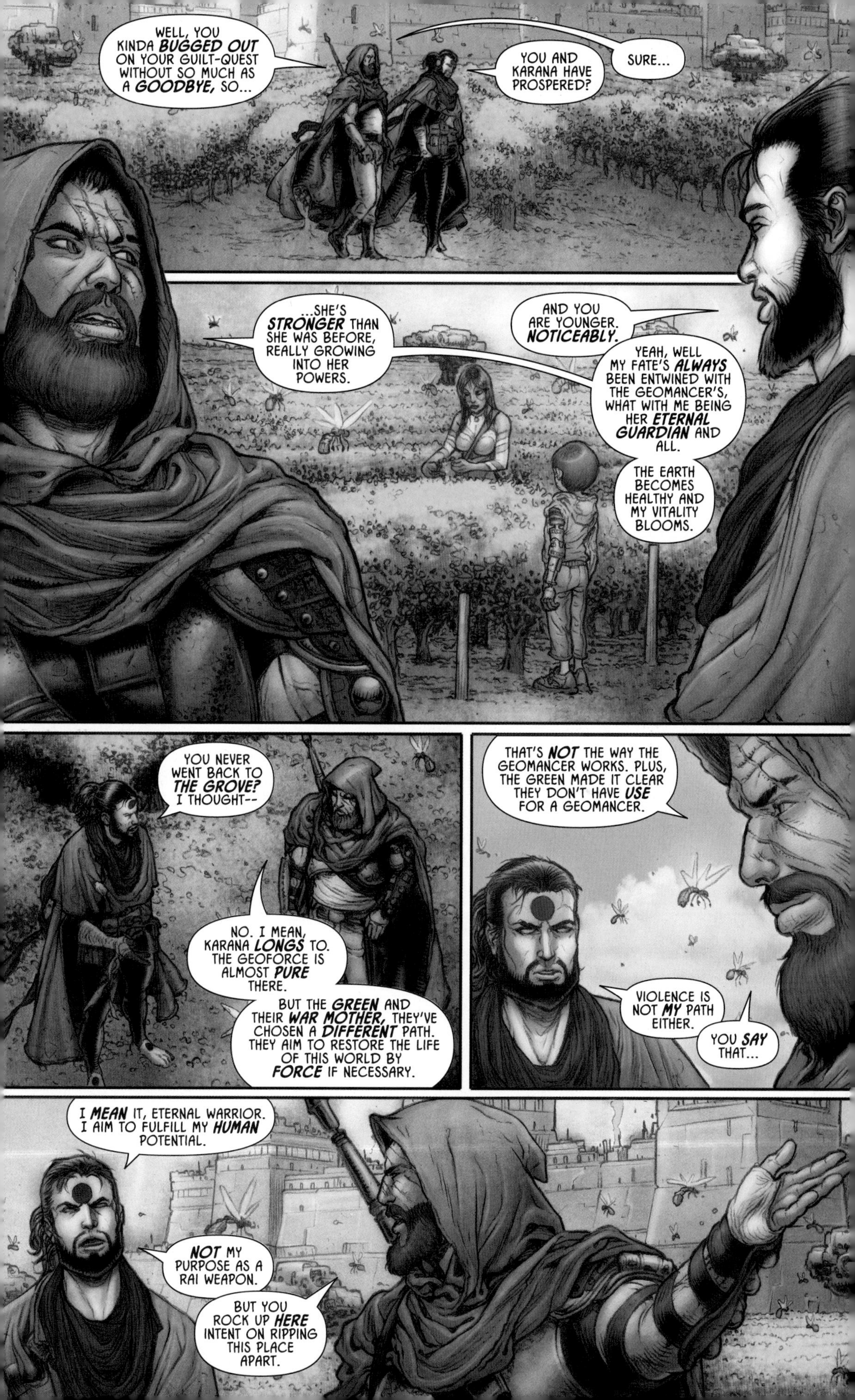

WELL, YOU KINDA BUGGED OUT ON YOUR GUILT-QUEST WITHOUT SO MUCH AS A GOODBYE, SO...
YOU AND KARANA HAVE PROSPERED?
SURE...
...SHE'S STRONGER THAN SHE WAS BEFORE, REALLY GROWING INTO HER POWERS.
AND YOU ARE YOUNGER. NOTICEABLY.
YEAH, WELL MY FATE'S ALWAYS BEEN ENTWINED WITH THE GEOMANCER'S, WHAT WITH ME BEING HER ETERNAL GUARDIAN AND ALL.
THE EARTH BECOMES HEALTHY AND MY VITALITY BLOOMS.
YOU NEVER WENT BACK TO THE GROVE? I THOUGHT--
NO. I MEAN, KARANA LONGS TO. THE GEOFORCE IS ALMOST PURE THERE.
BUT THE GREEN AND THEIR WAR MOTHER, THEY'VE CHOSEN A DIFFERENT PATH. THEY AIM TO RESTORE THE LIFE OF THIS WORLD BY FORCE IF NECESSARY.
THAT'S NOT THE WAY THE GEOMANCER WORKS. PLUS, THE GREEN MADE IT CLEAR THEY DON'T HAVE USE FOR A GEOMANCER.
VIOLENCE IS NOT MY PATH EITHER.
YOU SAY THAT...
I MEAN IT, ETERNAL WARRIOR. I AIM TO FULFILL MY HUMAN POTENTIAL.
NOT MY PURPOSE AS A RAI WEAPON.
BUT YOU ROCK UP HERE INTENT ON RIPPING THIS PLACE APART.

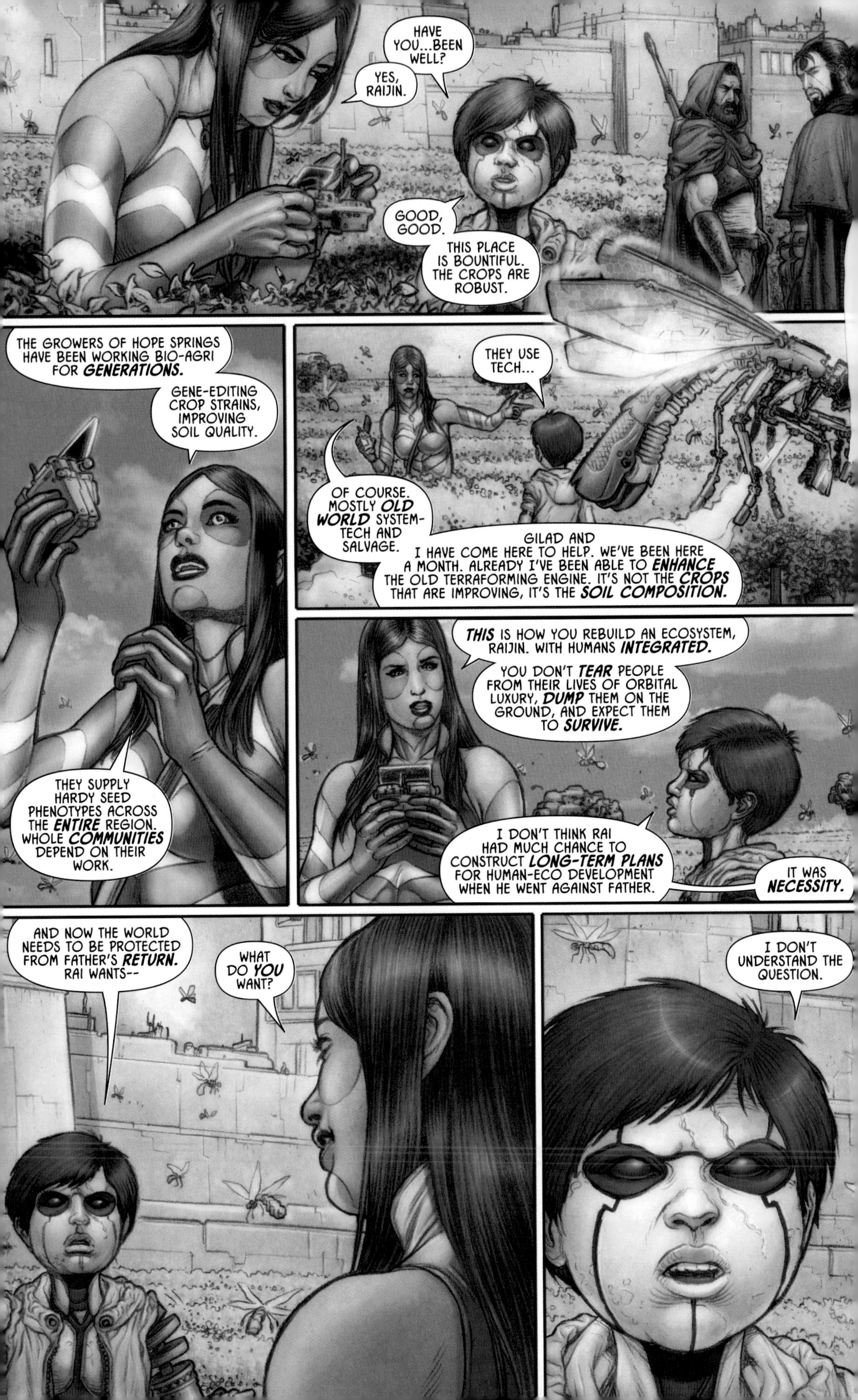
HAVE YOU...BEEN WELL?
YES, RAIJIN.
GOOD, GOOD.
THIS PLACE IS BOUNTIFUL. THE CROPS ARE ROBUST.
THE GROWERS OF HOPE SPRINGS HAVE BEEN WORKING BIO-AGRI FOR GENERATIONS.
GENE-EDITING CROP STRAINS, IMPROVING SOIL QUALITY.
THEY SUPPLY HARDY SEED PHENOTYPES ACROSS THE ENTIRE REGION. WHOLE COMMUNITIES DEPEND ON THEIR WORK.
THEY USE TECH...
OF COURSE. MOSTLY OLD WORLD SYSTEM-TECH AND SALVAGE.
GILAD AND I HAVE COME HERE TO HELP. WE'VE BEEN HERE A MONTH. ALREADY I'VE BEEN ABLE TO ENHANCE THE OLD TERRAFORMING ENGINE. IT'S NOT THE CROPS THAT ARE IMPROVING, IT'S THE SOIL COMPOSITION.
THIS IS HOW YOU REBUILD AN ECOSYSTEM, RAIJIN. WITH HUMANS INTEGRATED.
YOU DON'T TEAR PEOPLE FROM THEIR LIVES OF ORBITAL LUXURY, DUMP THEM ON THE GROUND, AND EXPECT THEM TO SURVIVE.
I DON'T THINK RAI HAD MUCH CHANCE TO CONSTRUCT LONG-TERM PLANS FOR HUMAN-ECO DEVELOPMENT WHEN HE WENT AGAINST FATHER.
IT WAS NECESSITY.
AND NOW THE WORLD NEEDS TO BE PROTECTED FROM FATHER'S RETURN. RAI WANTS--
WHAT DO YOU WANT?
I DON'T UNDERSTAND THE QUESTION.

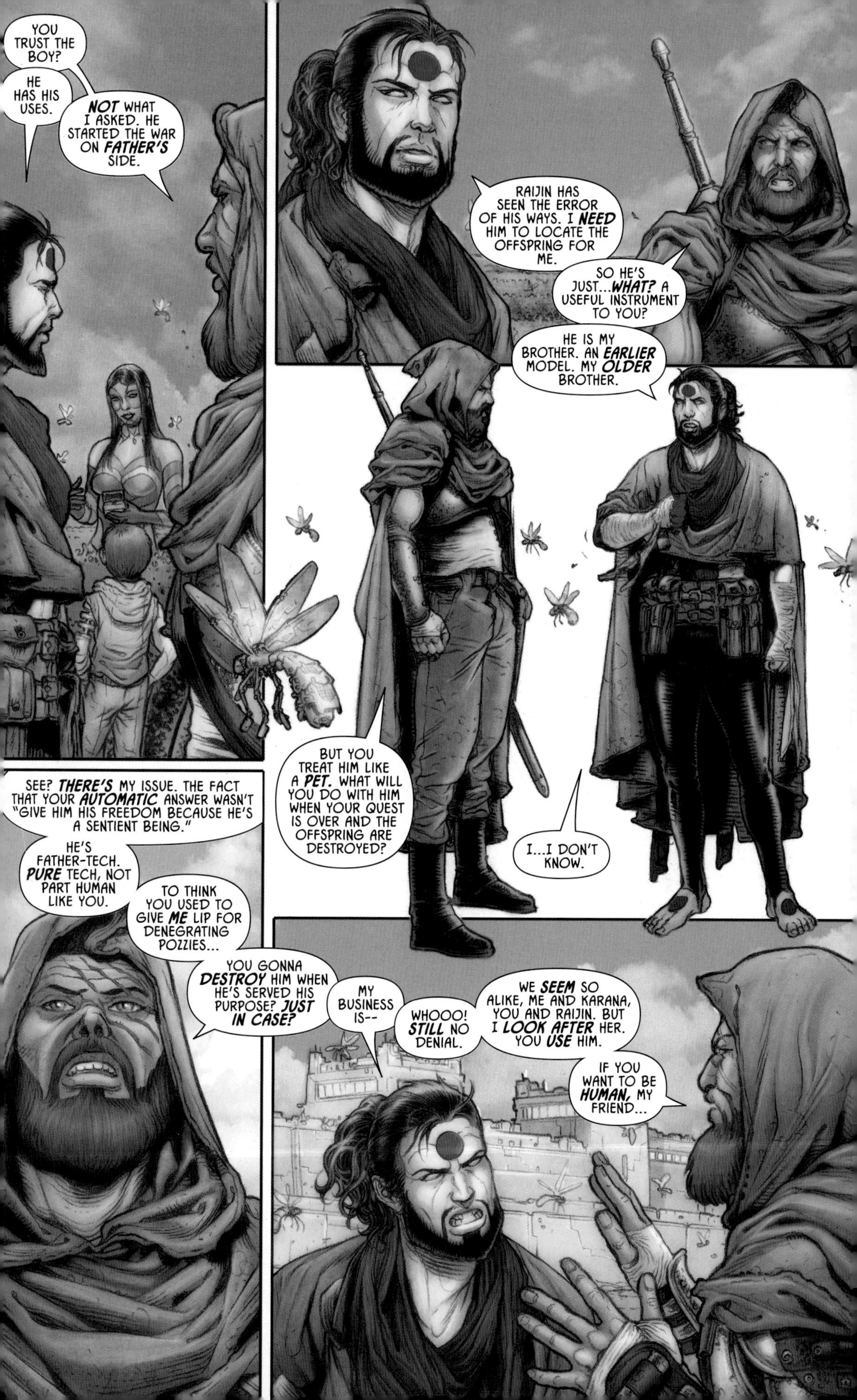
YOU TRUST THE BOY?
HE HAS HIS USES.
NOT WHAT I ASKED. HE STARTED THE WAR ON FATHER'S SIDE.
RAIJIN HAS SEEN THE ERROR OF HIS WAYS. I NEED HIM TO LOCATE THE OFFSPRING FOR ME.
SO HE'S JUST...WHAT? A USEFUL INSTRUMENT TO YOU?
HE IS MY BROTHER. AN EARLIER MODEL. MY OLDER BROTHER.
BUT YOU TREAT HIM LIKE A PET. WHAT WILL YOU DO WITH HIM WHEN YOUR QUEST IS OVER AND THE OFFSPRING ARE DESTROYED?
I...I DON'T KNOW.
SEE? THERE'S MY ISSUE. THE FACT THAT YOUR AUTOMATIC ANSWER WASN'T "GIVE HIM HIS FREEDOM BECAUSE HE'S A SENTIENT BEING."
HE'S FATHER-TECH. PURE TECH, NOT PART HUMAN LIKE YOU.
TO THINK YOU USED TO GIVE ME LIP FOR DENEGRATING POZZIES...
YOU GONNA DESTROY HIM WHEN HE'S SERVED HIS PURPOSE? JUST IN CASE?
MY BUSINESS IS--
WHOOO! STILL NO DENIAL.
WE SEEM SO ALIKE, ME AND KARANA, YOU AND RAIJIN. BUT I LOOK AFTER HER. YOU USE HIM.
IF YOU WANT TO BE HUMAN, MY FRIEND...

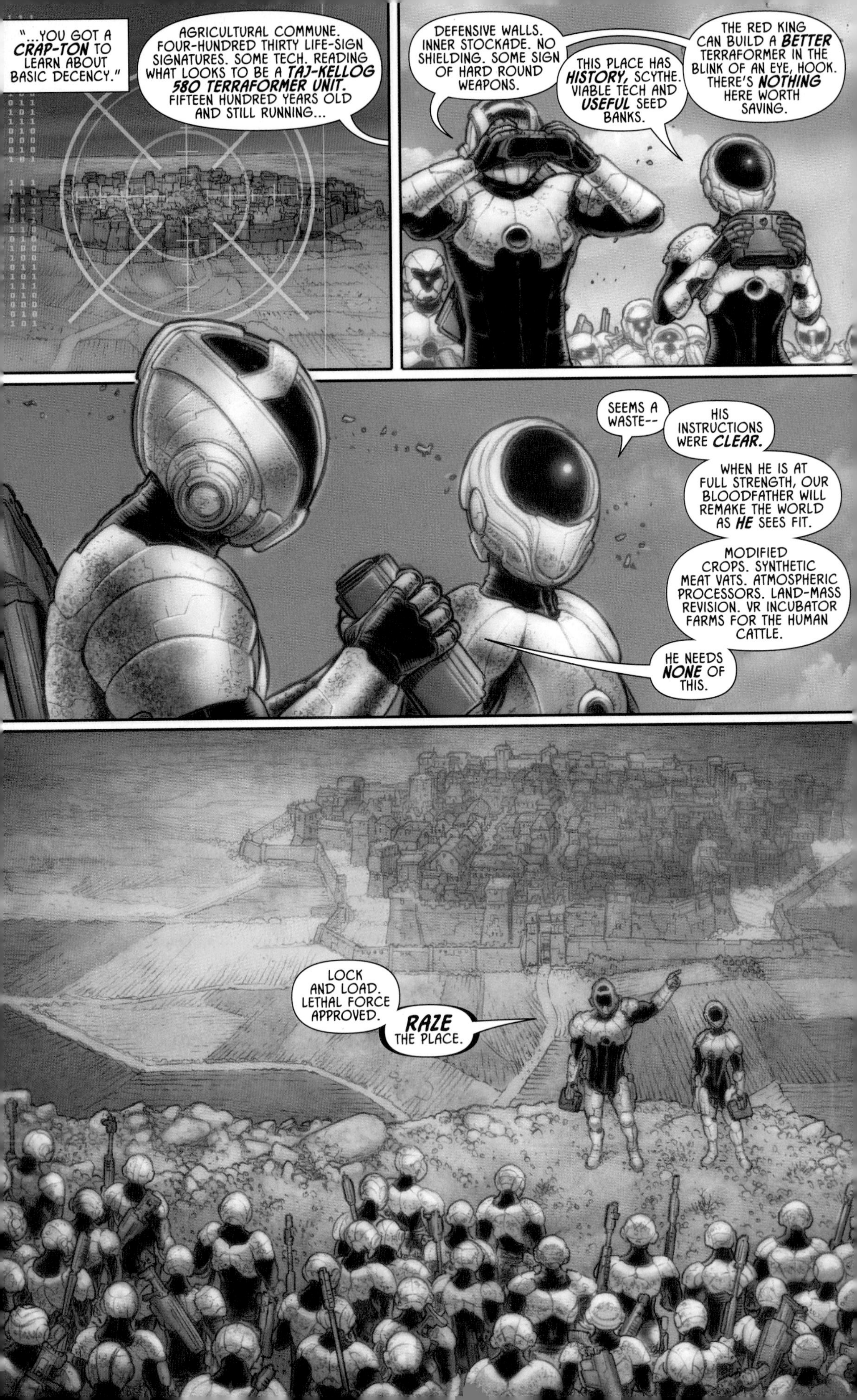
"...YOU GOT A CRAP-TON TO LEARN ABOUT BASIC DECENCY."
AGRICULTURAL COMMUNE. FOUR-HUNDRED THIRTY LIFE-SIGN SIGNATURES. SOME TECH. READING WHAT LOOKS TO BE A TAJ-KELLOG 580 TERRAFORMER UNIT. FIFTEEN HUNDRED YEARS OLD AND STILL RUNNING...
DEFENSIVE WALLS. INNER STOCKADE. NO SHIELDING. SOME SIGN OF HARD ROUND WEAPONS.
THIS PLACE HAS HISTORY, SCYTHE. VIABLE TECH AND USEFUL SEED BANKS.
THE RED KING CAN BUILD A BETTER TERRAFORMER IN THE BLINK OF AN EYE, HOOK. THERE'S NOTHING HERE WORTH SAVING.
SEEMS A WASTE--
HIS INSTRUCTIONS WERE CLEAR.
WHEN HE IS AT FULL STRENGTH, OUR BLOODFATHER WILL REMAKE THE WORLD AS HE SEES FIT.
MODIFIED CROPS. SYNTHETIC MEAT VATS. ATMOSPHERIC PROCESSORS. LAND-MASS REVISION. VR INCUBATOR FARMS FOR THE HUMAN CATTLE.
HE NEEDS NONE OF THIS.
LOCK AND LOAD. LETHAL FORCE APPROVED.
RAZE THE PLACE.

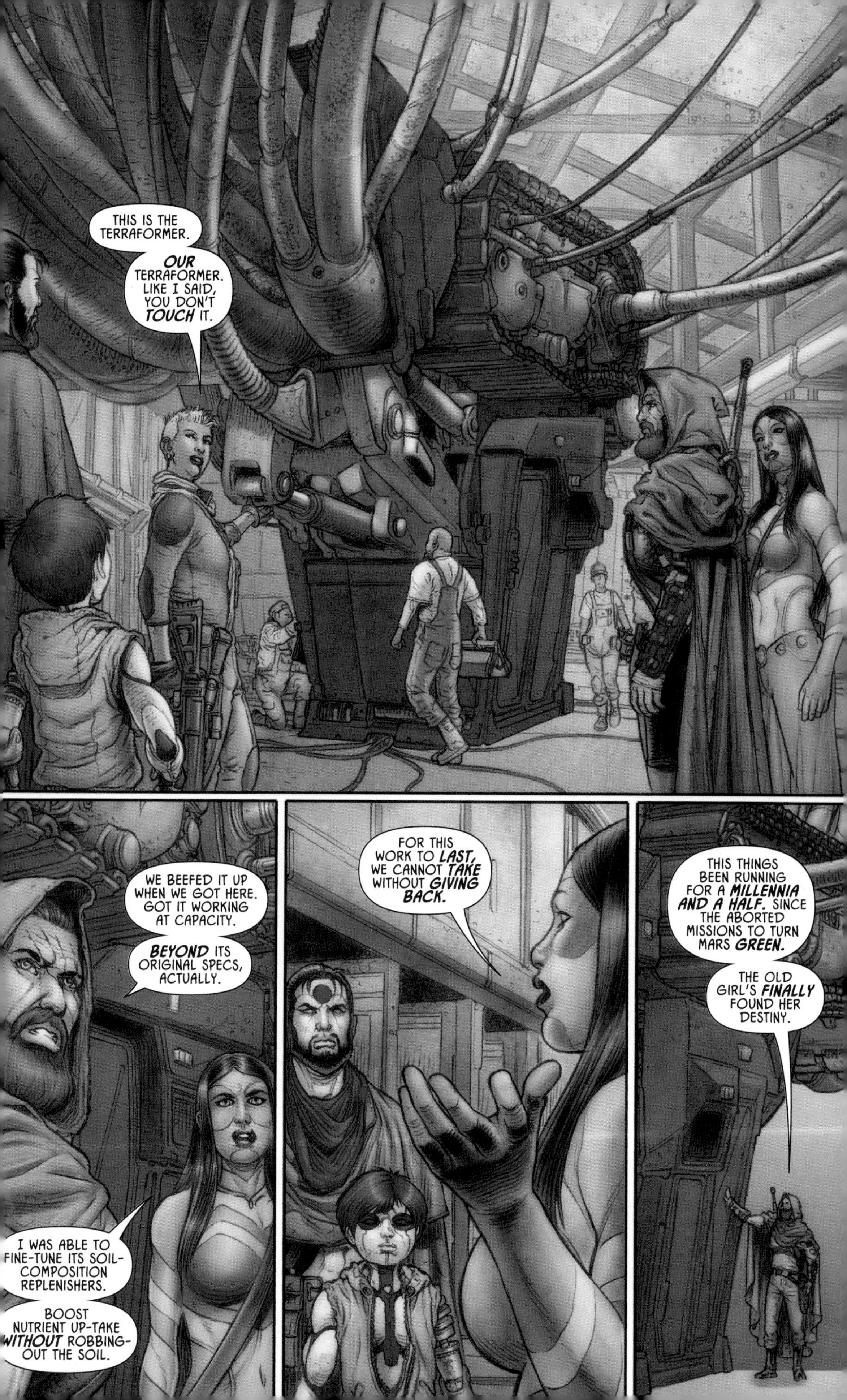
THIS IS THE TERRAFORMER.
OUR TERRAFORMER. LIKE I SAID, YOU DON'T *TOUCH* IT.
WE BEEFED IT UP WHEN WE GOT HERE. GOT IT WORKING AT CAPACITY.
BEYOND ITS ORIGINAL SPECS, ACTUALLY.
I WAS ABLE TO FINE-TUNE ITS SOIL-COMPOSITION REPLENISHERS.
BOOST NUTRIENT UP-TAKE *WITHOUT* ROBBING-OUT THE SOIL.
FOR THIS WORK TO *LAST,* WE CANNOT *TAKE* WITHOUT *GIVING BACK.*
THIS THINGS BEEN RUNNING FOR A *MILLENNIA AND A HALF.* SINCE THE ABORTED MISSIONS TO TURN MARS *GREEN.*
THE OLD GIRL'S *FINALLY* FOUND HER DESTINY.

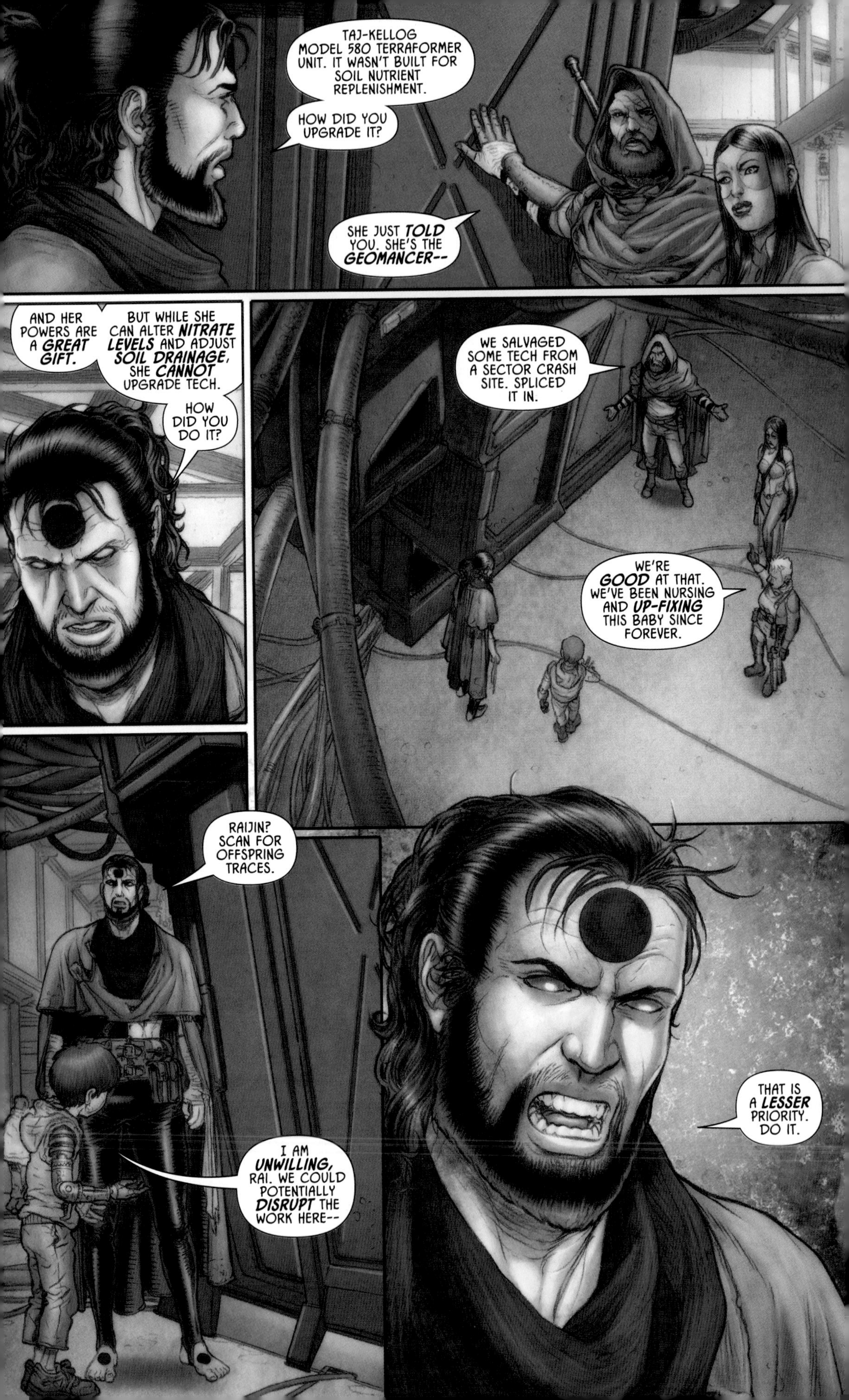
TAJ-KELLOG MODEL 580 TERRAFORMER UNIT. IT WASN'T BUILT FOR SOIL NUTRIENT REPLENISHMENT.
HOW DID YOU UPGRADE IT?
SHE JUST TOLD YOU. SHE'S THE GEOMANCER--
AND HER POWERS ARE A GREAT GIFT.
BUT WHILE SHE CAN ALTER NITRATE LEVELS AND ADJUST SOIL DRAINAGE, SHE CANNOT UPGRADE TECH.
HOW DID YOU DO IT?
WE SALVAGED SOME TECH FROM A SECTOR CRASH SITE. SPLICED IT IN.
WE'RE GOOD AT THAT. WE'VE BEEN NURSING AND UP-FIXING THIS BABY SINCE FOREVER.
RAIJIN? SCAN FOR OFFSPRING TRACES.
I AM UNWILLING, RAI. WE COULD POTENTIALLY DISRUPT THE WORK HERE--
THAT IS A LESSER PRIORITY. DO IT.

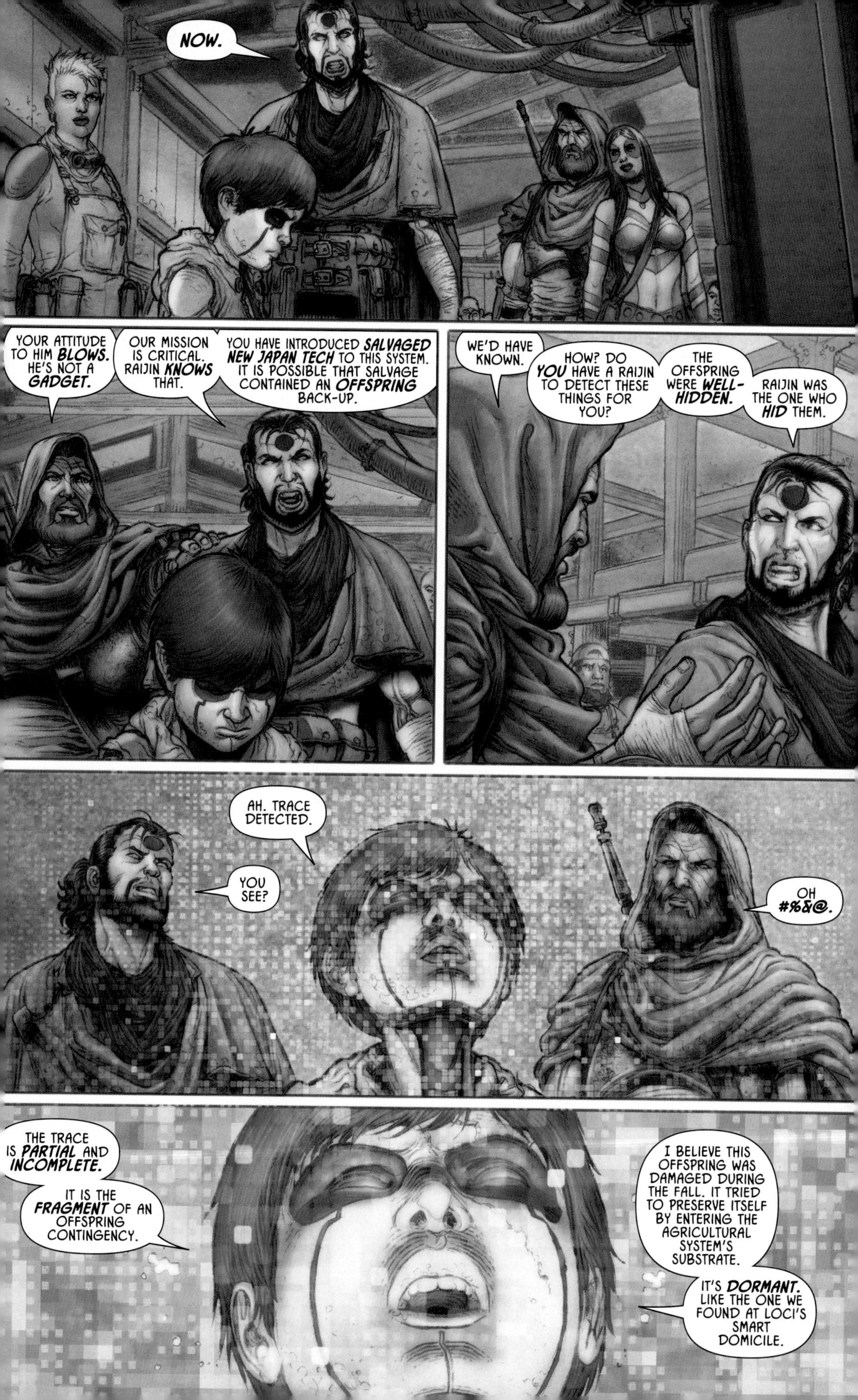
NOW.
YOUR ATTITUDE TO HIM BLOWS. HE'S NOT A GADGET.
OUR MISSION IS CRITICAL. RAIJIN KNOWS THAT.
YOU HAVE INTRODUCED SALVAGED NEW JAPAN TECH TO THIS SYSTEM. IT IS POSSIBLE THAT SALVAGE CONTAINED AN OFFSPRING BACK-UP.
WE'D HAVE KNOWN.
HOW? DO YOU HAVE A RAIJIN TO DETECT THESE THINGS FOR YOU?
THE OFFSPRING WERE WELL-HIDDEN.
RAIJIN WAS THE ONE WHO HID THEM.
AH. TRACE DETECTED.
YOU SEE?
OH #%&@.
THE TRACE IS PARTIAL AND INCOMPLETE.
IT IS THE FRAGMENT OF AN OFFSPRING CONTINGENCY.
I BELIEVE THIS OFFSPRING WAS DAMAGED DURING THE FALL. IT TRIED TO PRESERVE ITSELF BY ENTERING THE AGRICULTURAL SYSTEM'S SUBSTRATE.
IT'S DORMANT. LIKE THE ONE WE FOUND AT LOCI'S SMART DOMICILE.

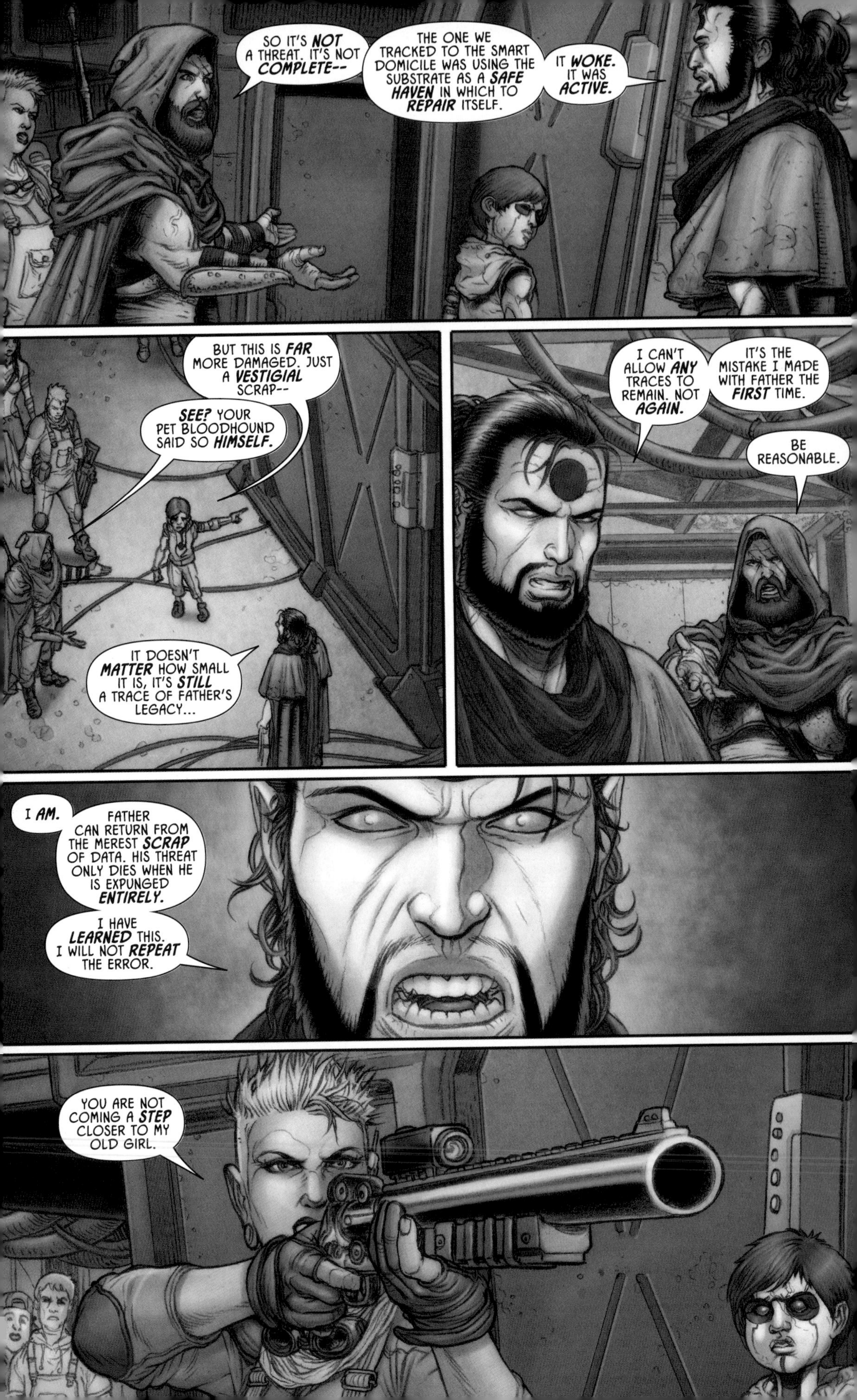
SO IT'S NOT A THREAT. IT'S NOT COMPLETE--
THE ONE WE TRACKED TO THE SMART DOMICILE WAS USING THE SUBSTRATE AS A SAFE HAVEN IN WHICH TO REPAIR ITSELF.
IT WOKE. IT WAS ACTIVE.
BUT THIS IS FAR MORE DAMAGED. JUST A VESTIGIAL SCRAP--
SEE? YOUR PET BLOODHOUND SAID SO HIMSELF.
IT DOESN'T MATTER HOW SMALL IT IS, IT'S STILL A TRACE OF FATHER'S LEGACY...
I CAN'T ALLOW ANY TRACES TO REMAIN. NOT AGAIN.
IT'S THE MISTAKE I MADE WITH FATHER THE FIRST TIME.
BE REASONABLE.
I AM.
FATHER CAN RETURN FROM THE MEREST SCRAP OF DATA. HIS THREAT ONLY DIES WHEN HE IS EXPUNGED ENTIRELY.
I HAVE LEARNED THIS. I WILL NOT REPEAT THE ERROR.
YOU ARE NOT COMING A STEP CLOSER TO MY OLD GIRL.

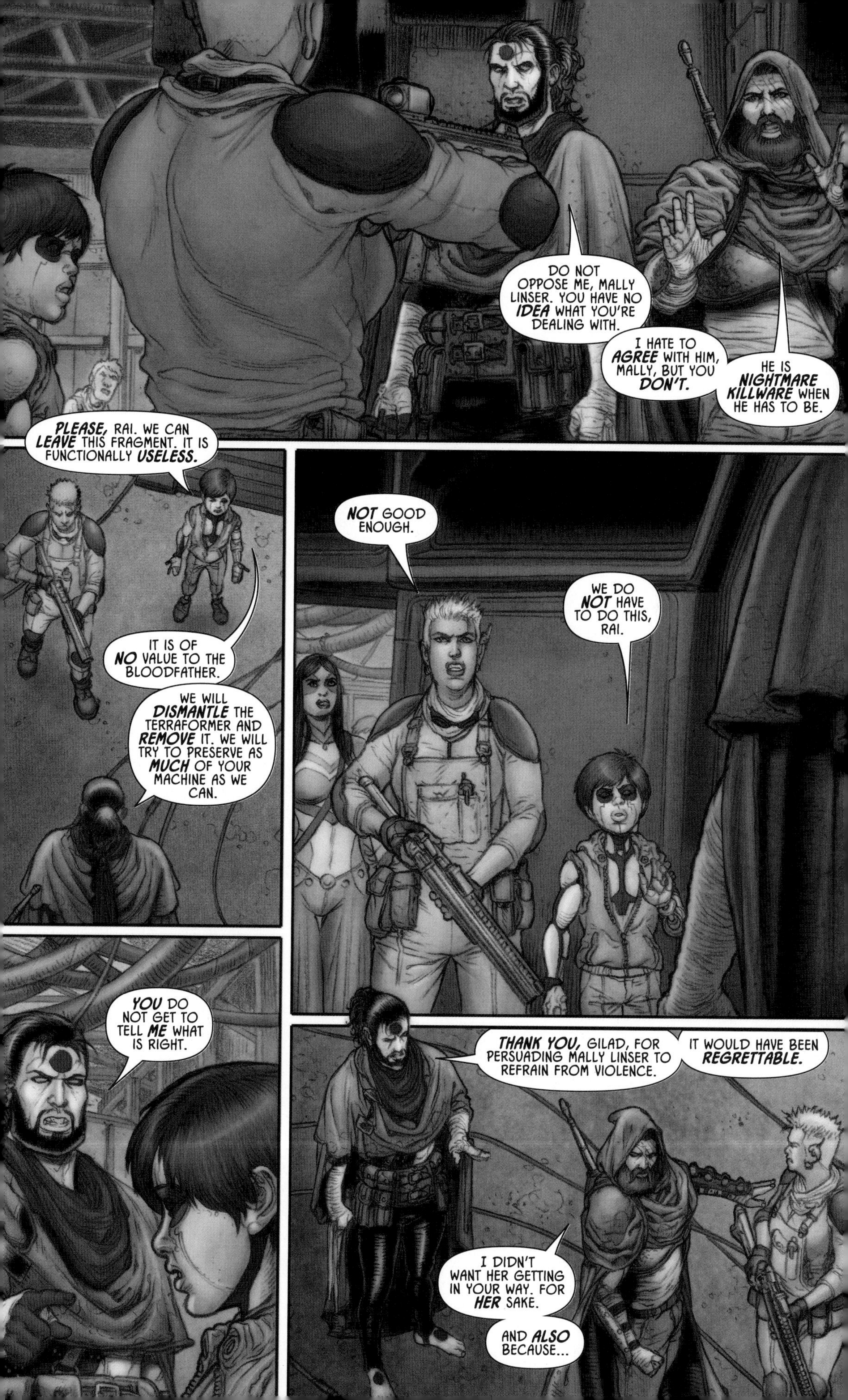
DO NOT OPPOSE ME, MALLY LINSER. YOU HAVE NO IDEA WHAT YOU'RE DEALING WITH.
I HATE TO AGREE WITH HIM, MALLY, BUT YOU DON'T.
HE IS NIGHTMARE KILLWARE WHEN HE HAS TO BE.
PLEASE, RAI. WE CAN LEAVE THIS FRAGMENT. IT IS FUNCTIONALLY USELESS.
IT IS OF NO VALUE TO THE BLOODFATHER.
WE WILL DISMANTLE THE TERRAFORMER AND REMOVE IT. WE WILL TRY TO PRESERVE AS MUCH OF YOUR MACHINE AS WE CAN.
NOT GOOD ENOUGH.
WE DO NOT HAVE TO DO THIS, RAI.
YOU DO NOT GET TO TELL ME WHAT IS RIGHT.
THANK YOU, GILAD, FOR PERSUADING MALLY LINSER TO REFRAIN FROM VIOLENCE.
IT WOULD HAVE BEEN REGRETTABLE.
I DIDN'T WANT HER GETTING IN YOUR WAY. FOR HER SAKE.
AND ALSO BECAUSE...

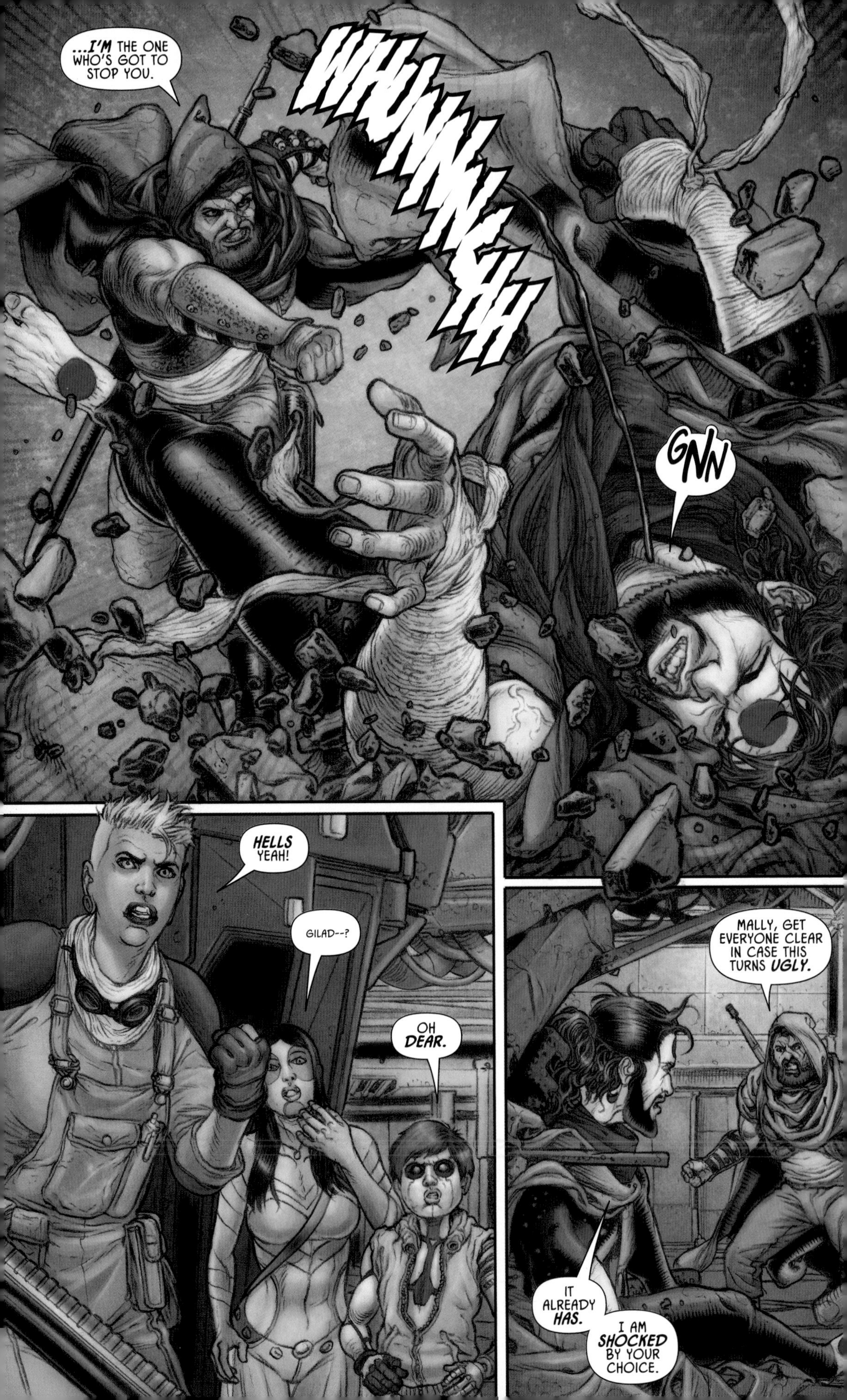

...I'M THE ONE WHO'S GOT TO STOP YOU.
WHUNNNGHH
GNN
HELLS YEAH!
GILAD--?
OH DEAR.
MALLY, GET EVERYONE CLEAR IN CASE THIS TURNS UGLY.
IT ALREADY HAS.
I AM SHOCKED BY YOUR CHOICE.

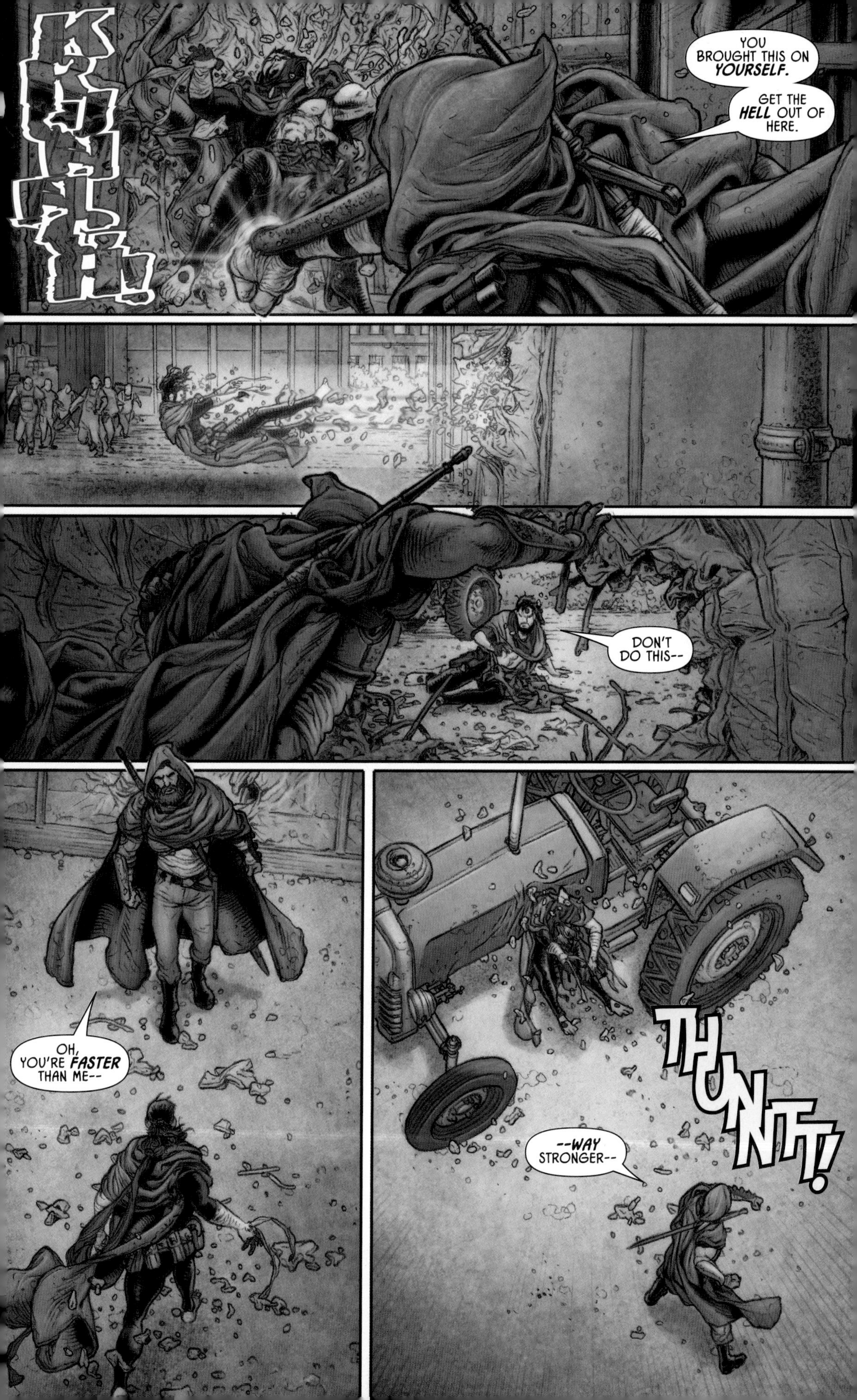
YOU BROUGHT THIS ON YOURSELF.
GET THE HELL OUT OF HERE.
DON'T DO THIS--
OH, YOU'RE FASTER THAN ME--
--WAY STRONGER--
THUNFT!

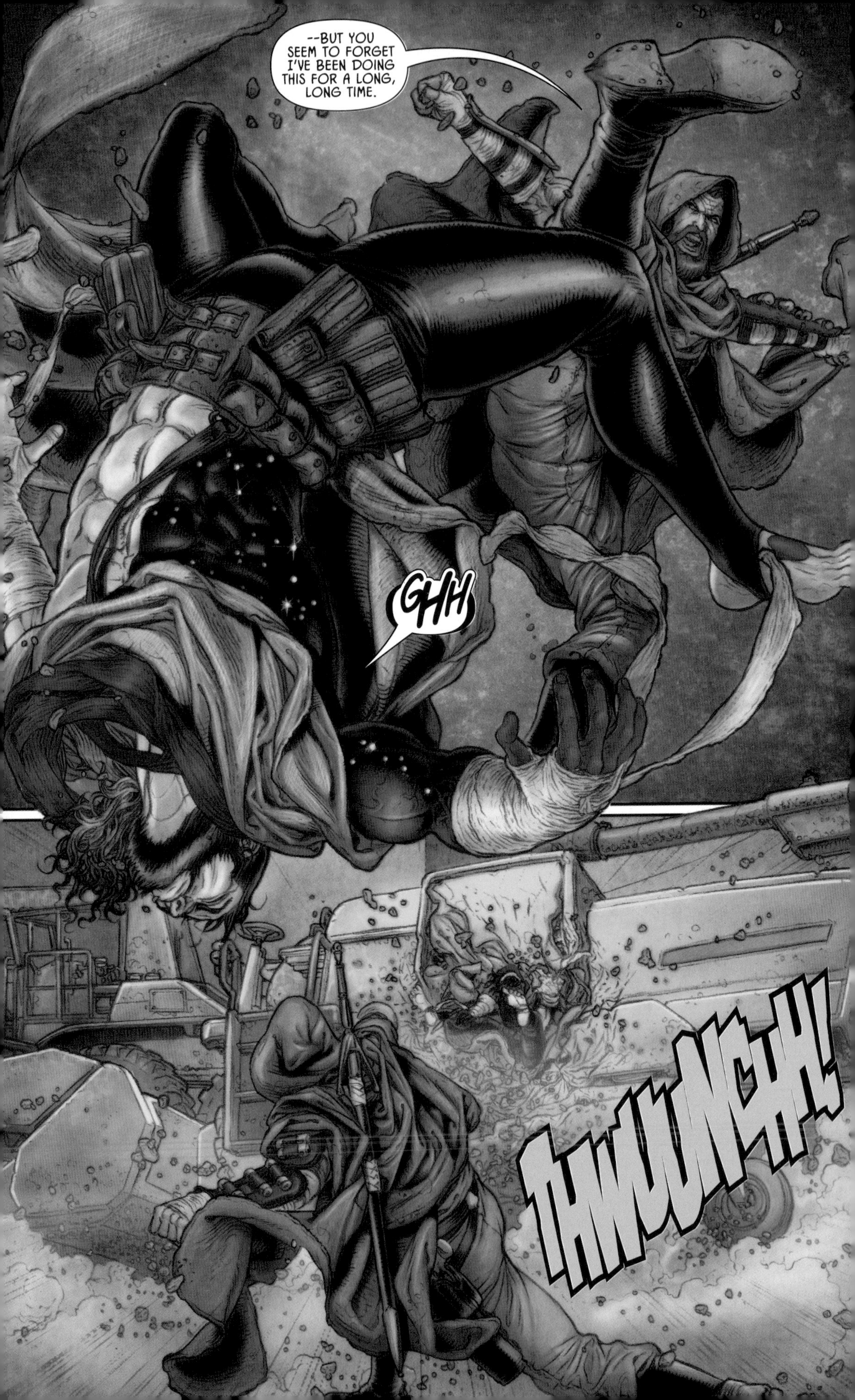

--BUT YOU SEEM TO FORGET I'VE BEEN DOING THIS FOR A LONG, LONG TIME.
GHH
THWUUNCHH!

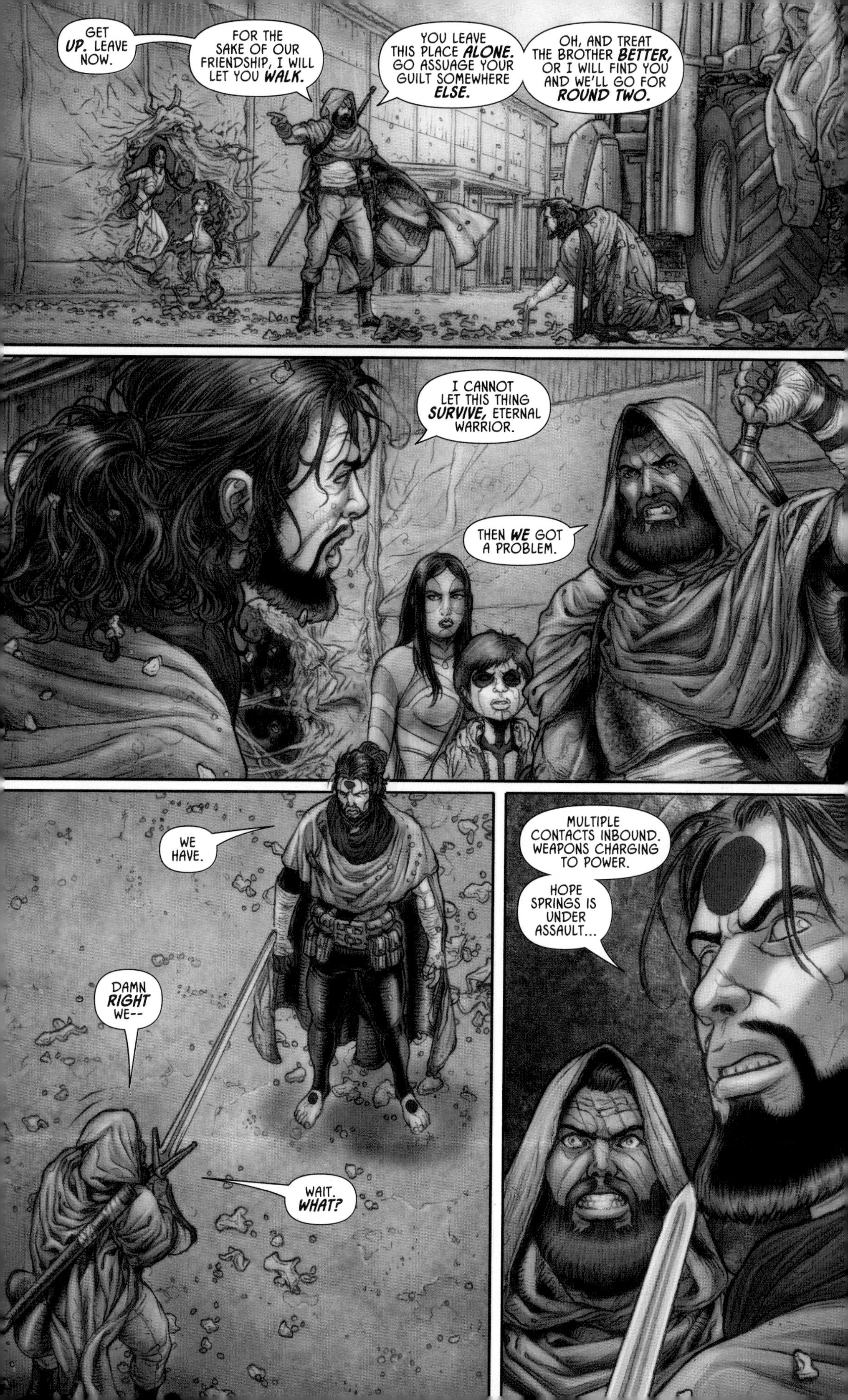
GET UP. LEAVE NOW.
FOR THE SAKE OF OUR FRIENDSHIP, I WILL LET YOU WALK.
YOU LEAVE THIS PLACE ALONE. GO ASSUAGE YOUR GUILT SOMEWHERE ELSE.
OH, AND TREAT THE BROTHER BETTER, OR I WILL FIND YOU AND WE'LL GO FOR ROUND TWO.
I CANNOT LET THIS THING SURVIVE, ETERNAL WARRIOR.
THEN WE GOT A PROBLEM.
WE HAVE.
DAMN RIGHT WE--
WAIT. WHAT?
MULTIPLE CONTACTS INBOUND. WEAPONS CHARGING TO POWER.
HOPE SPRINGS IS UNDER ASSAULT...

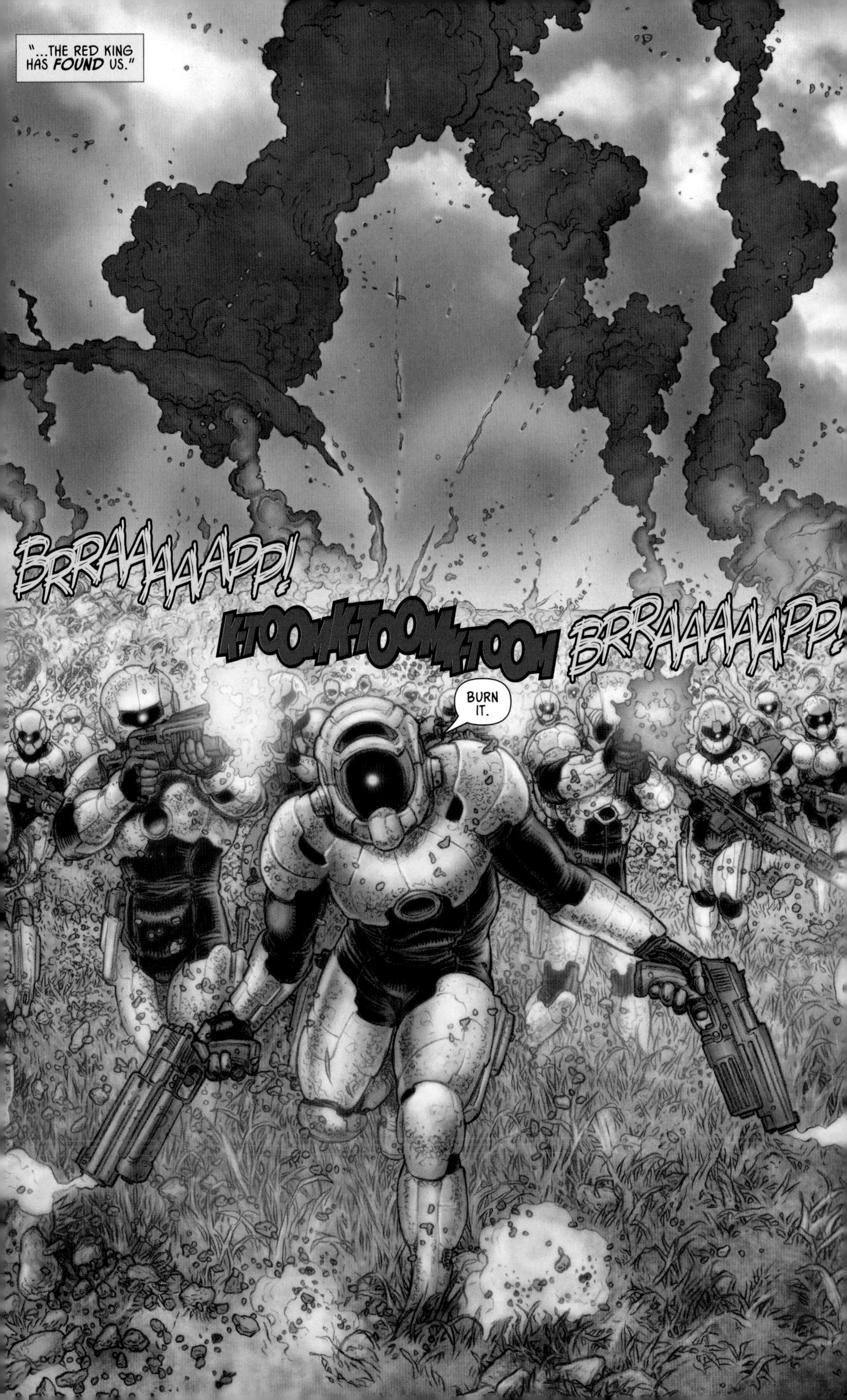
"...THE RED KING HAS FOUND US."
BRRAAAAAAPP!
K-TOOM K-TOOM K-TOOM
BRRAAAAAAPP!
BURN IT.

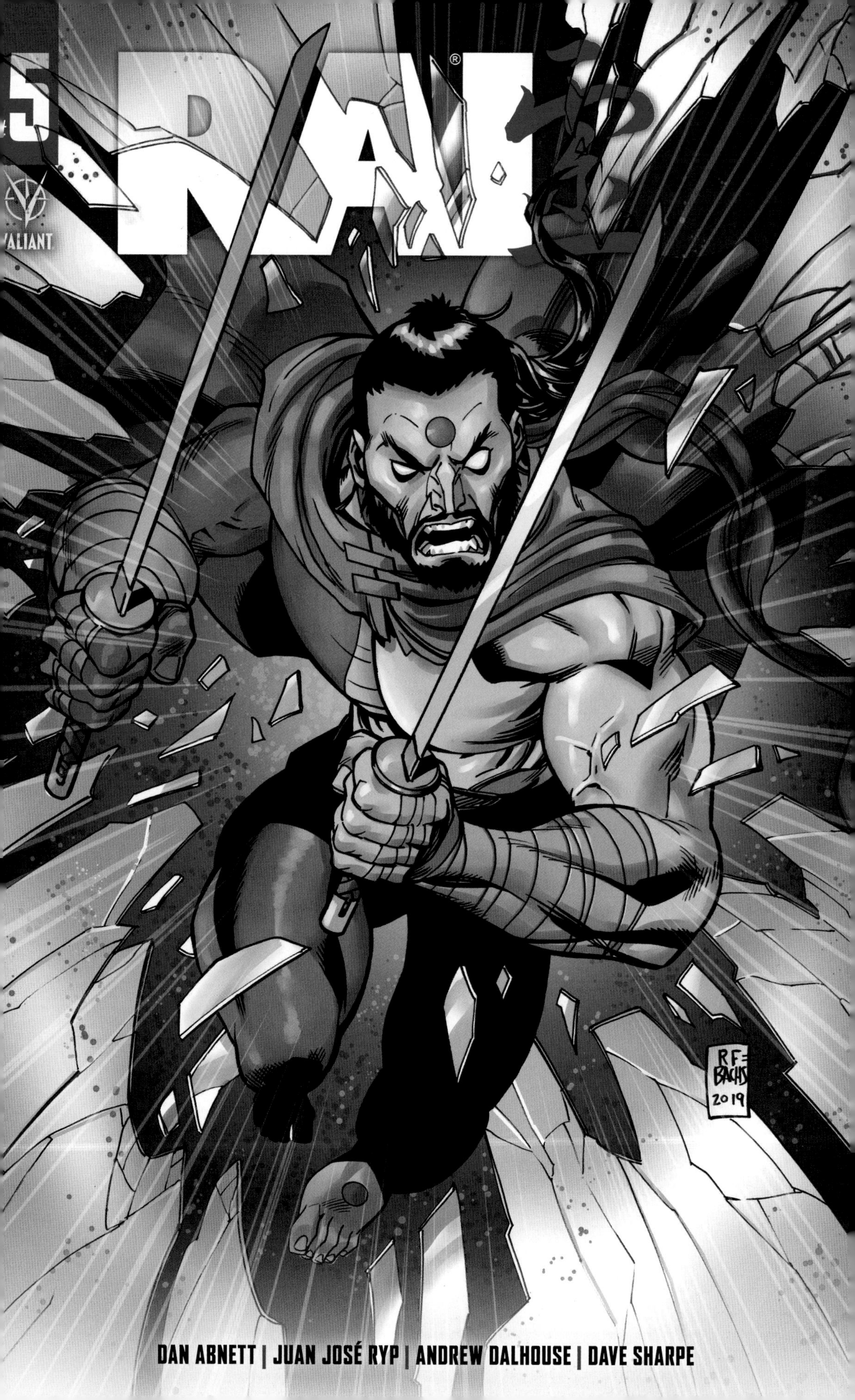
#5
RAI®
VALIANT
RF BACHS 2019
DAN ABNETT | JUAN JOSÉ RYP | ANDREW DALHOUSE | DAVE SHARPE

RAI #5

WRITER: DAN ABNETT
ARTIST: JUAN JOSÉ RYP
COLORIST: ANDREW DALHOUSE
LETTERER: DAVE SHARPE
COVER ARTIST: RAMÓN F. BACHS
ASSOCIATE EDITOR: DAVID MENCHEL
EDITOR: LYSA HAWKINS

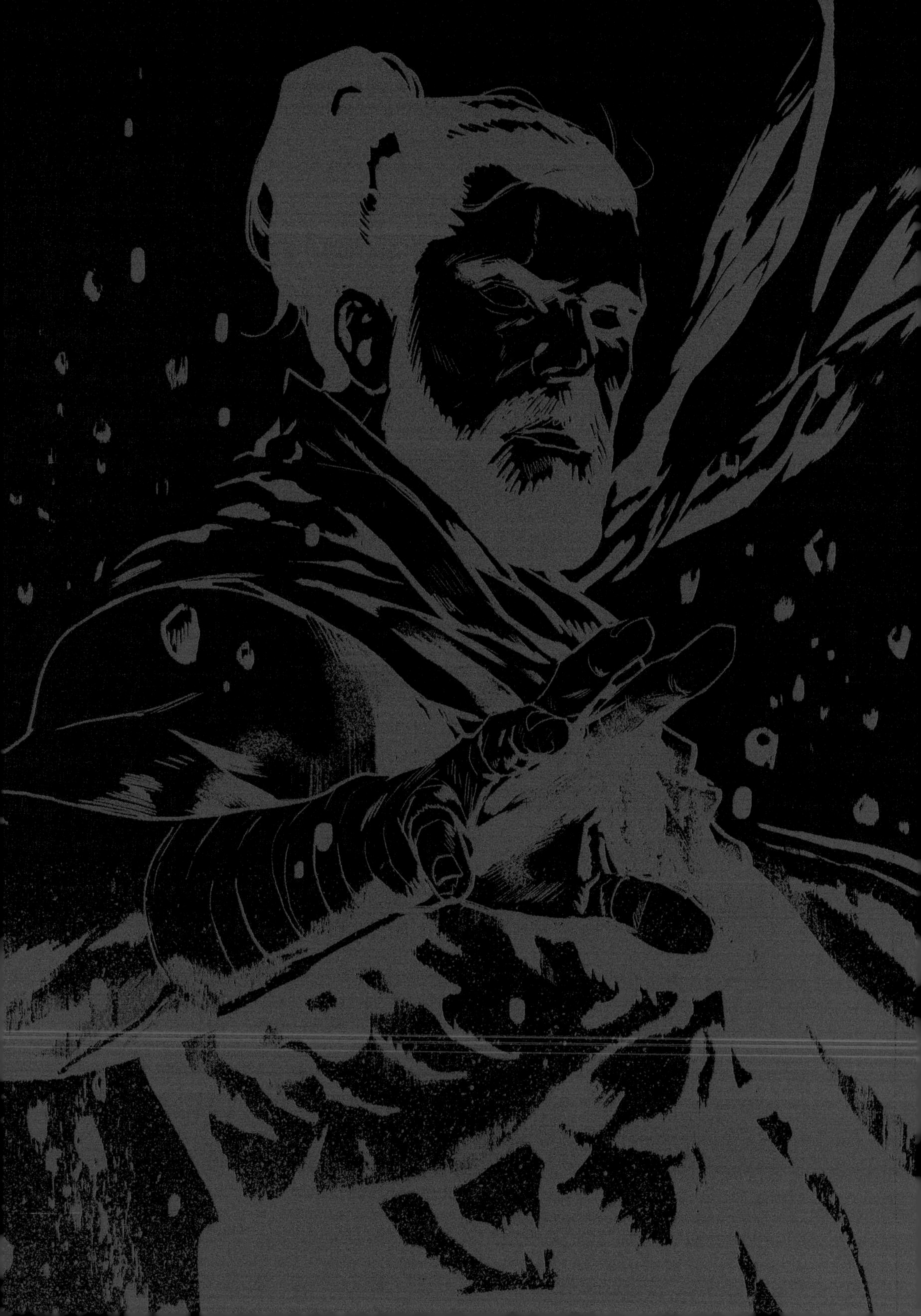

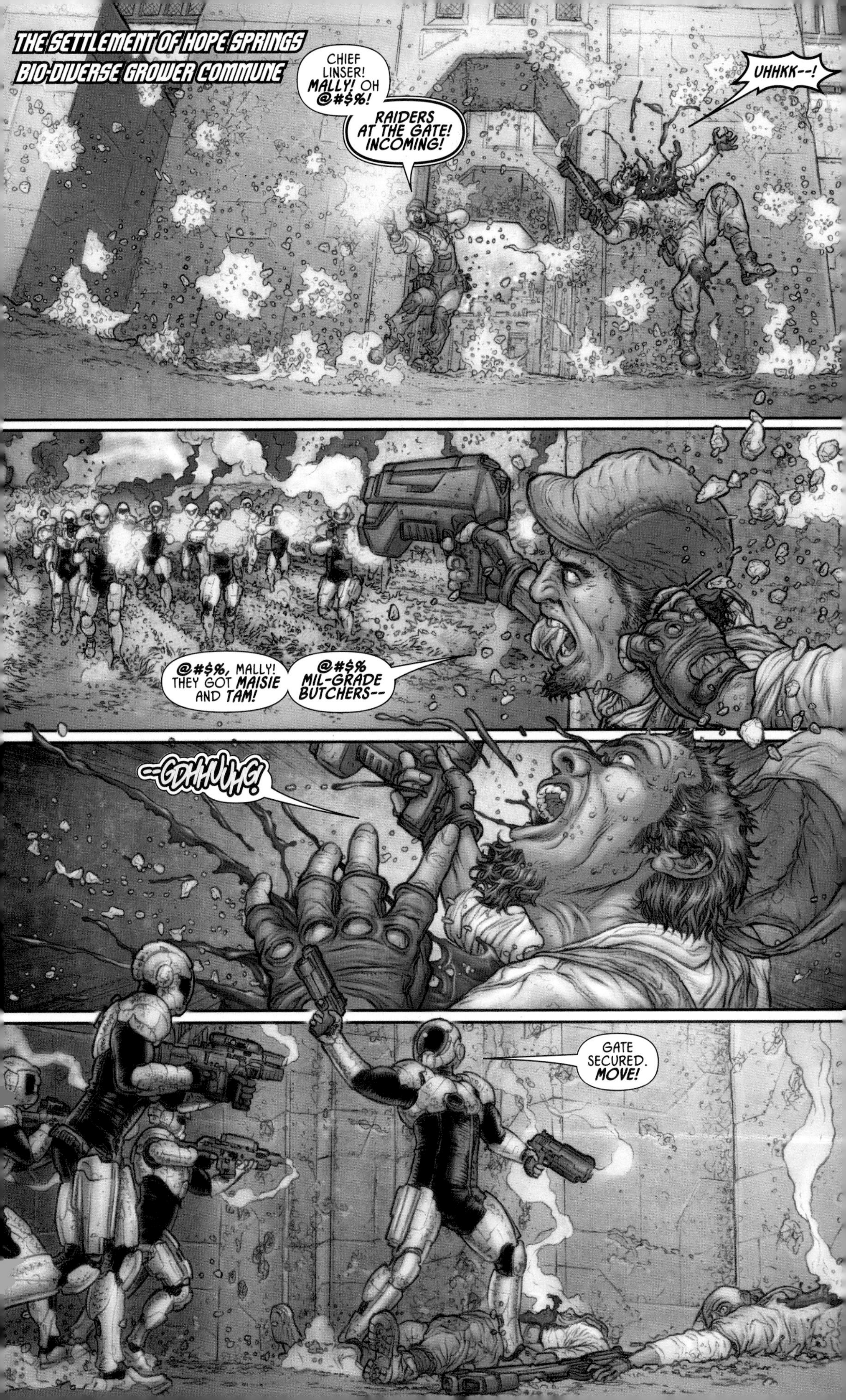
THE SETTLEMENT OF HOPE SPRINGS
BIO-DIVERSE GROWER COMMUNE
CHIEF LINSER! MALLY! OH @#$%!
RAIDERS AT THE GATE! INCOMING!
UHHKK--!
@#$%, MALLY! THEY GOT MAISIE AND TAM!
@#$% MIL-GRADE BUTCHERS--
--GDHHUUHG!
GATE SECURED. MOVE!

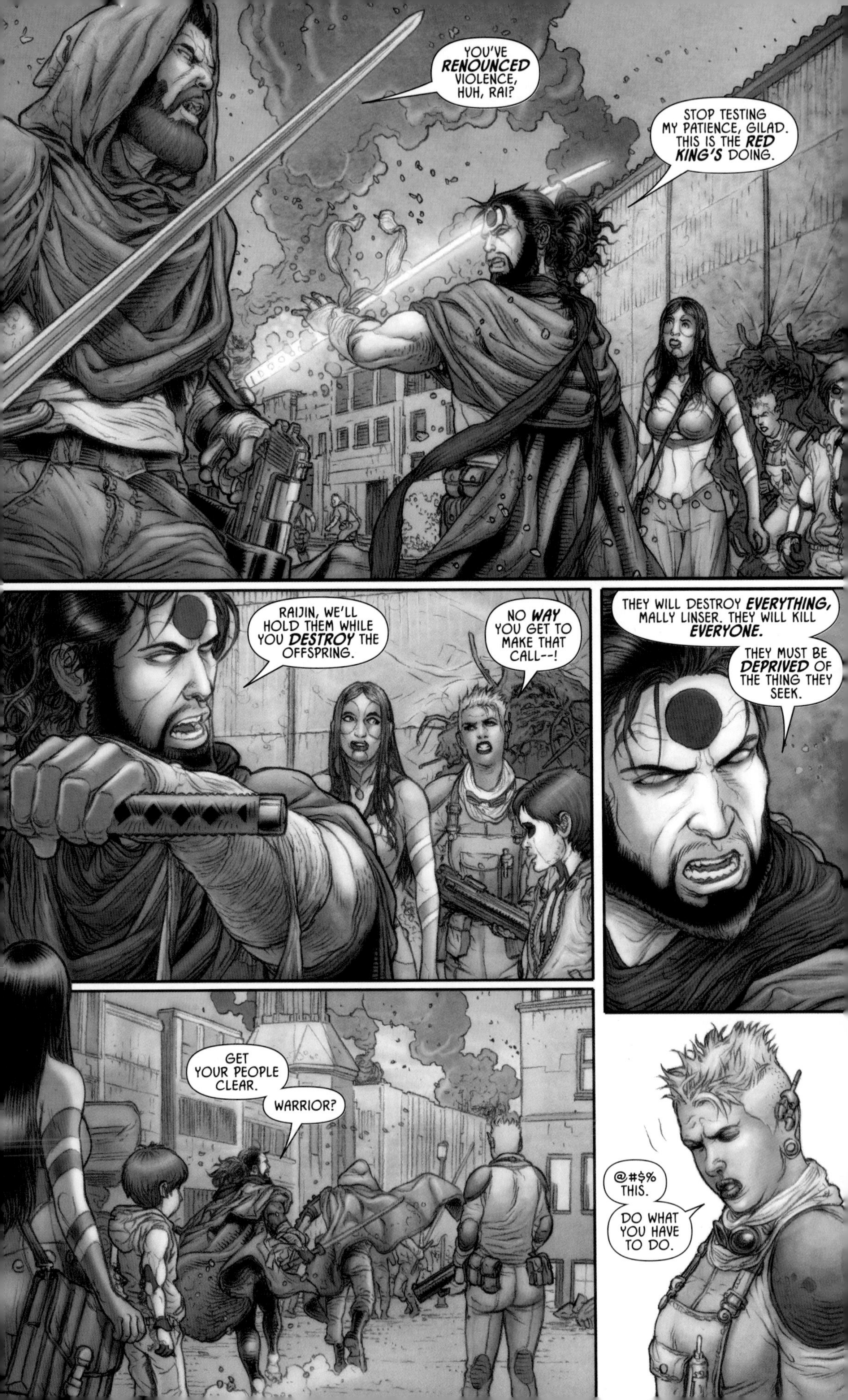

YOU'VE RENOUNCED VIOLENCE, HUH, RAI?
STOP TESTING MY PATIENCE, GILAD. THIS IS THE RED KING'S DOING.
RAIJIN, WE'LL HOLD THEM WHILE YOU DESTROY THE OFFSPRING.
NO WAY YOU GET TO MAKE THAT CALL--!
THEY WILL DESTROY EVERYTHING, MALLY LINSER. THEY WILL KILL EVERYONE.
THEY MUST BE DEPRIVED OF THE THING THEY SEEK.
GET YOUR PEOPLE CLEAR.
WARRIOR?
@#$% THIS.
DO WHAT YOU HAVE TO DO.

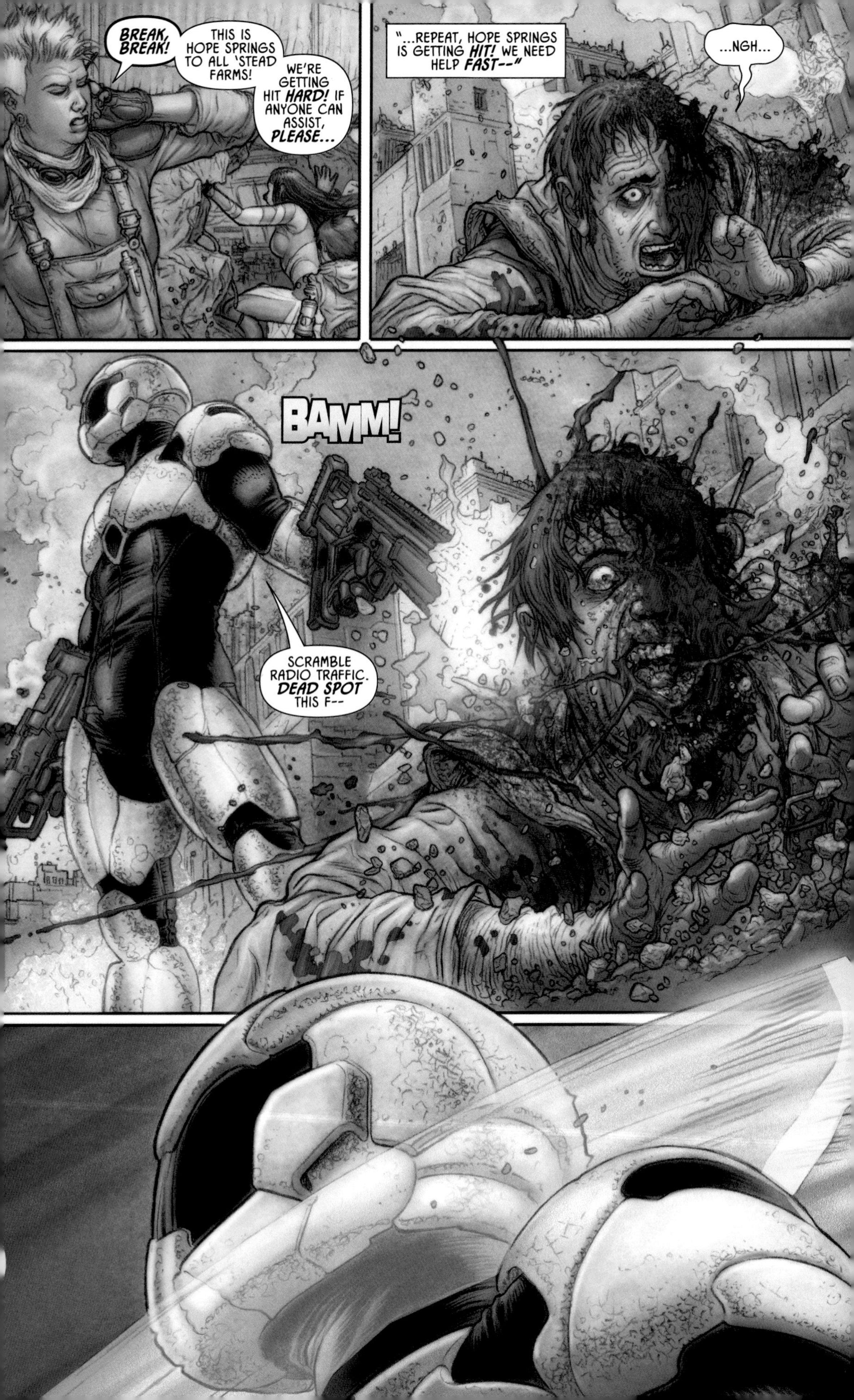
BREAK, BREAK!
THIS IS HOPE SPRINGS TO ALL 'STEAD FARMS!
WE'RE GETTING HIT HARD! IF ANYONE CAN ASSIST, PLEASE...
"...REPEAT, HOPE SPRINGS IS GETTING HIT! WE NEED HELP FAST--"
...NGH...
BAMM!
SCRAMBLE RADIO TRAFFIC. DEAD SPOT THIS F--

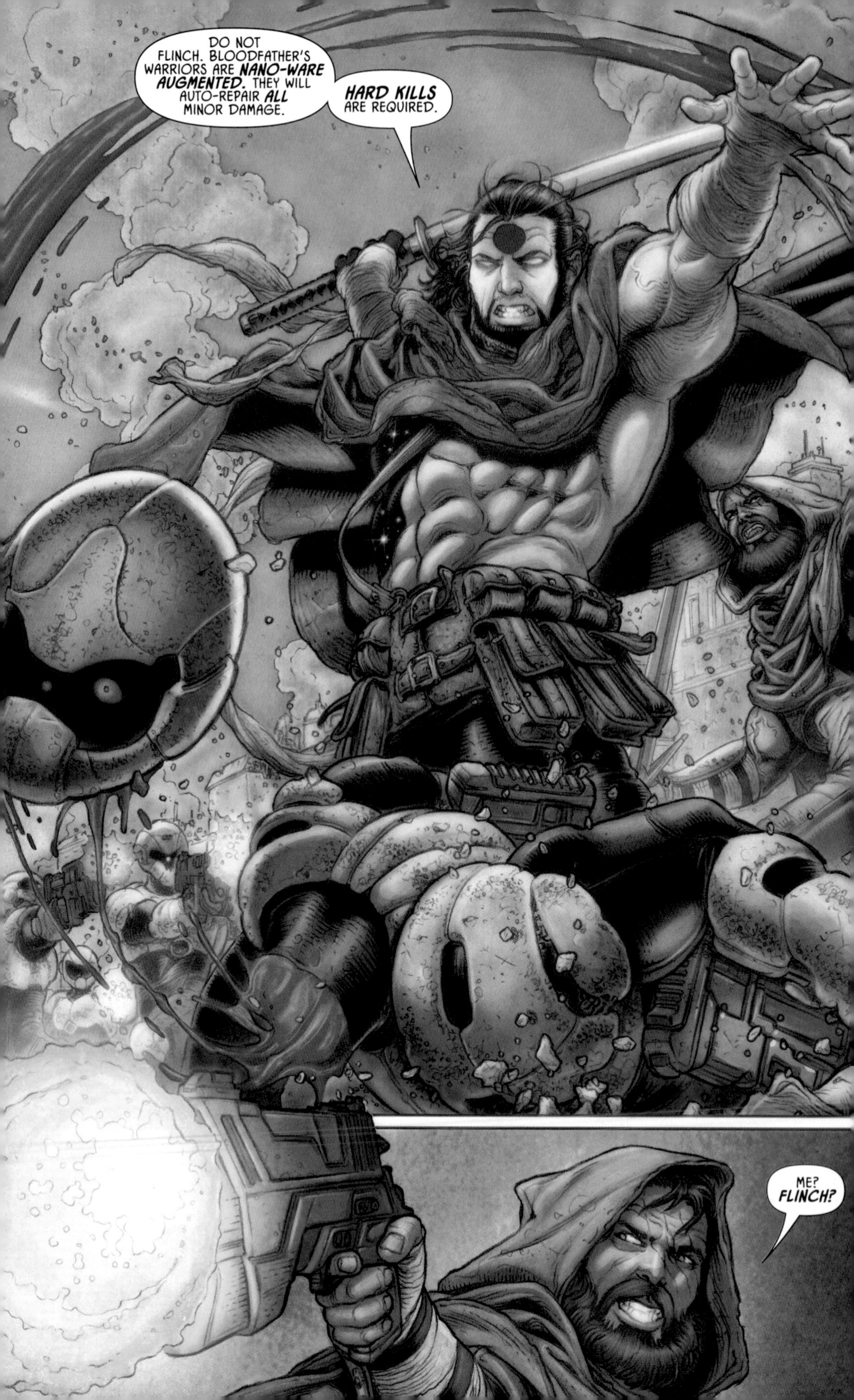
DO NOT FLINCH. BLOODFATHER'S WARRIORS ARE NANO-WARE AUGMENTED. THEY WILL AUTO-REPAIR ALL MINOR DAMAGE.
HARD KILLS ARE REQUIRED.
ME? FLINCH?

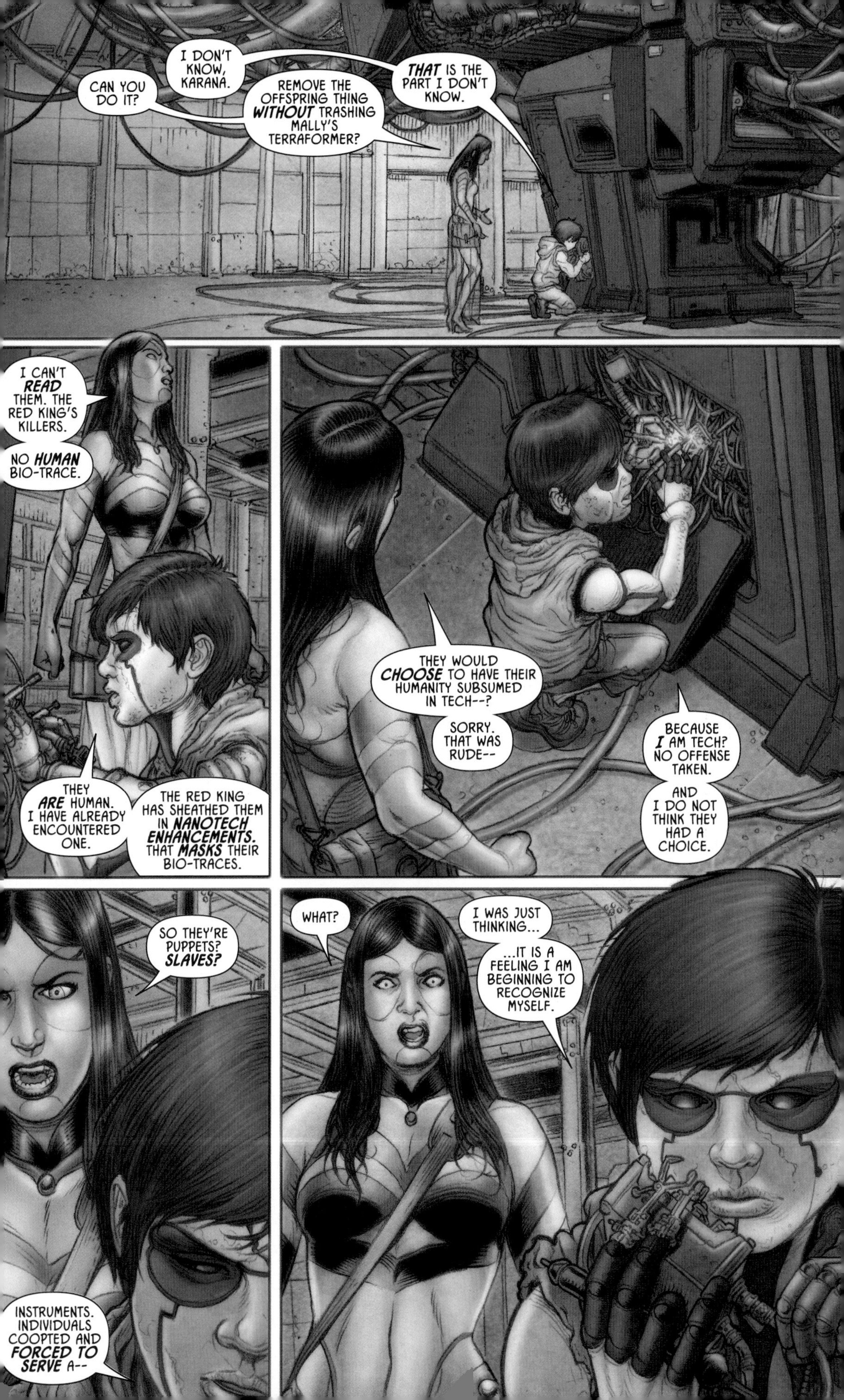
CAN YOU DO IT?
I DON'T KNOW, KARANA.
REMOVE THE OFFSPRING THING WITHOUT TRASHING MALLY'S TERRAFORMER?
THAT IS THE PART I DON'T KNOW.
I CAN'T READ THEM. THE RED KING'S KILLERS.
NO HUMAN BIO-TRACE.
THEY ARE HUMAN. I HAVE ALREADY ENCOUNTERED ONE.
THE RED KING HAS SHEATHED THEM IN NANOTECH ENHANCEMENTS. THAT MASKS THEIR BIO-TRACES.
THEY WOULD CHOOSE TO HAVE THEIR HUMANITY SUBSUMED IN TECH--?
SORRY. THAT WAS RUDE--
BECAUSE I AM TECH? NO OFFENSE TAKEN.
AND I DO NOT THINK THEY HAD A CHOICE.
SO THEY'RE PUPPETS? SLAVES?
INSTRUMENTS. INDIVIDUALS COOPTED AND FORCED TO SERVE A--
WHAT?
I WAS JUST THINKING...
...IT IS A FEELING I AM BEGINNING TO RECOGNIZE MYSELF.

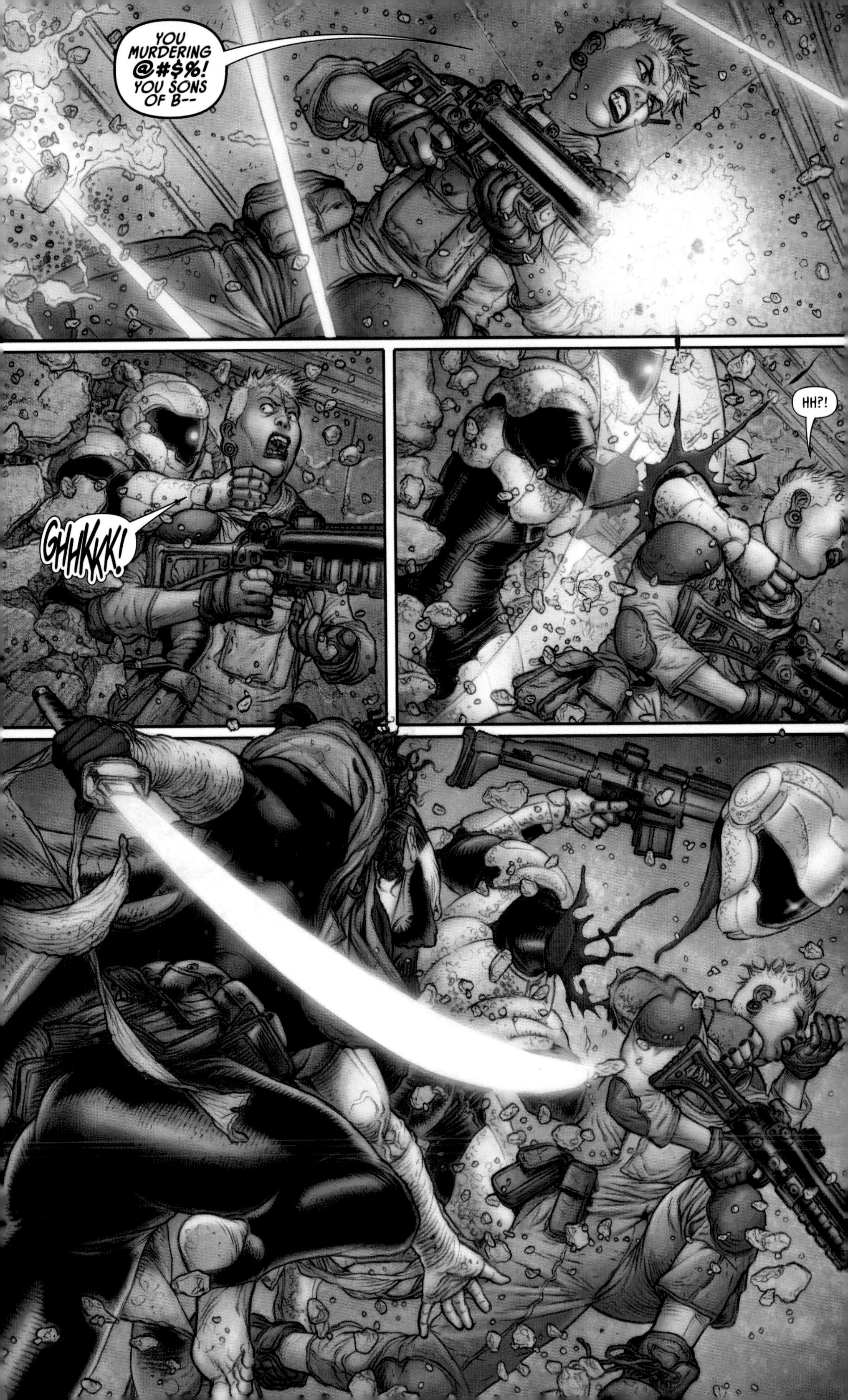
YOU MURDERING @#$%! YOU SONS OF B--
GHHKKK!
HH?!

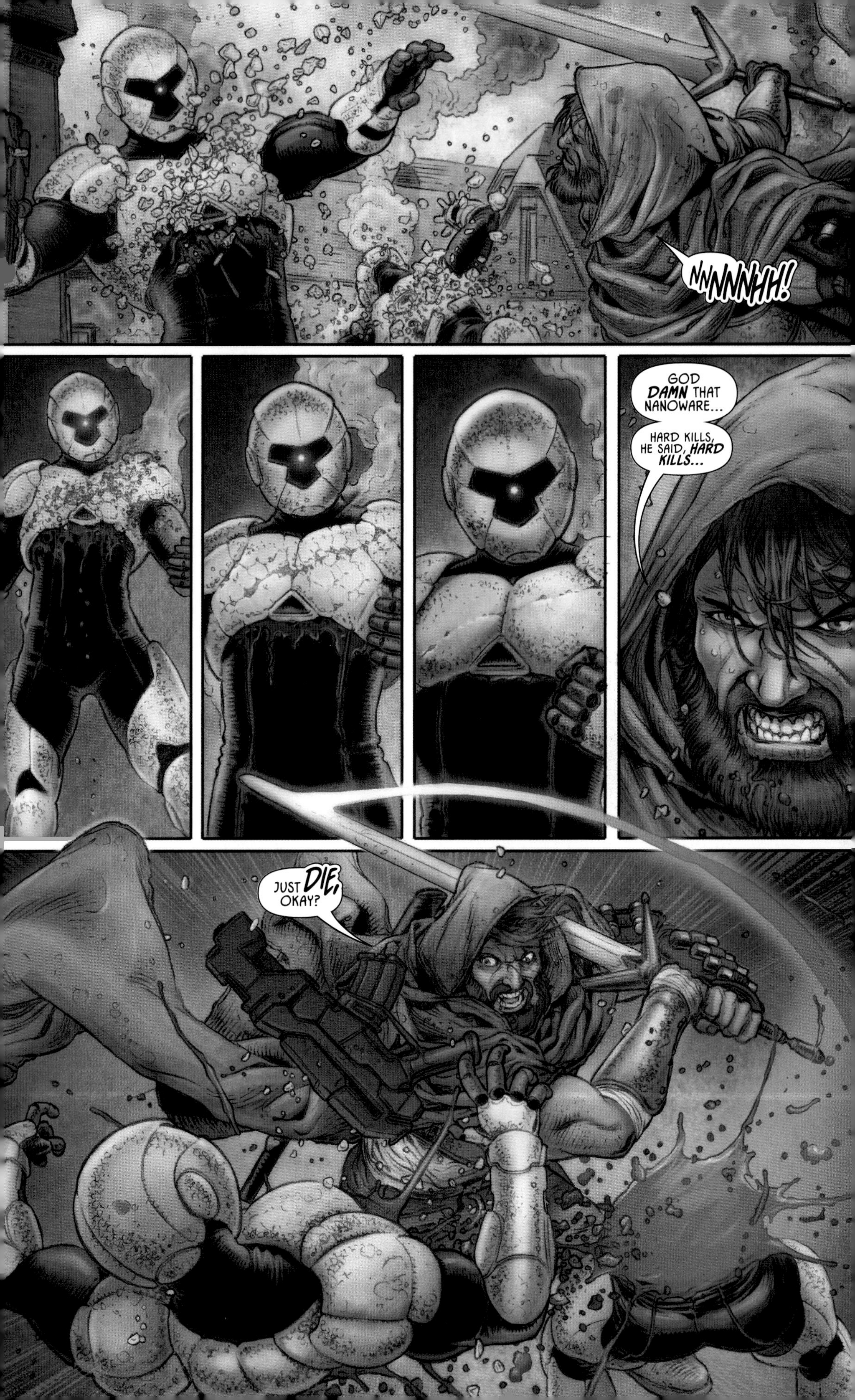
NNNNNHH!
GOD DAMN THAT NANOWARE...
HARD KILLS, HE SAID, HARD KILLS...
JUST DIE, OKAY?

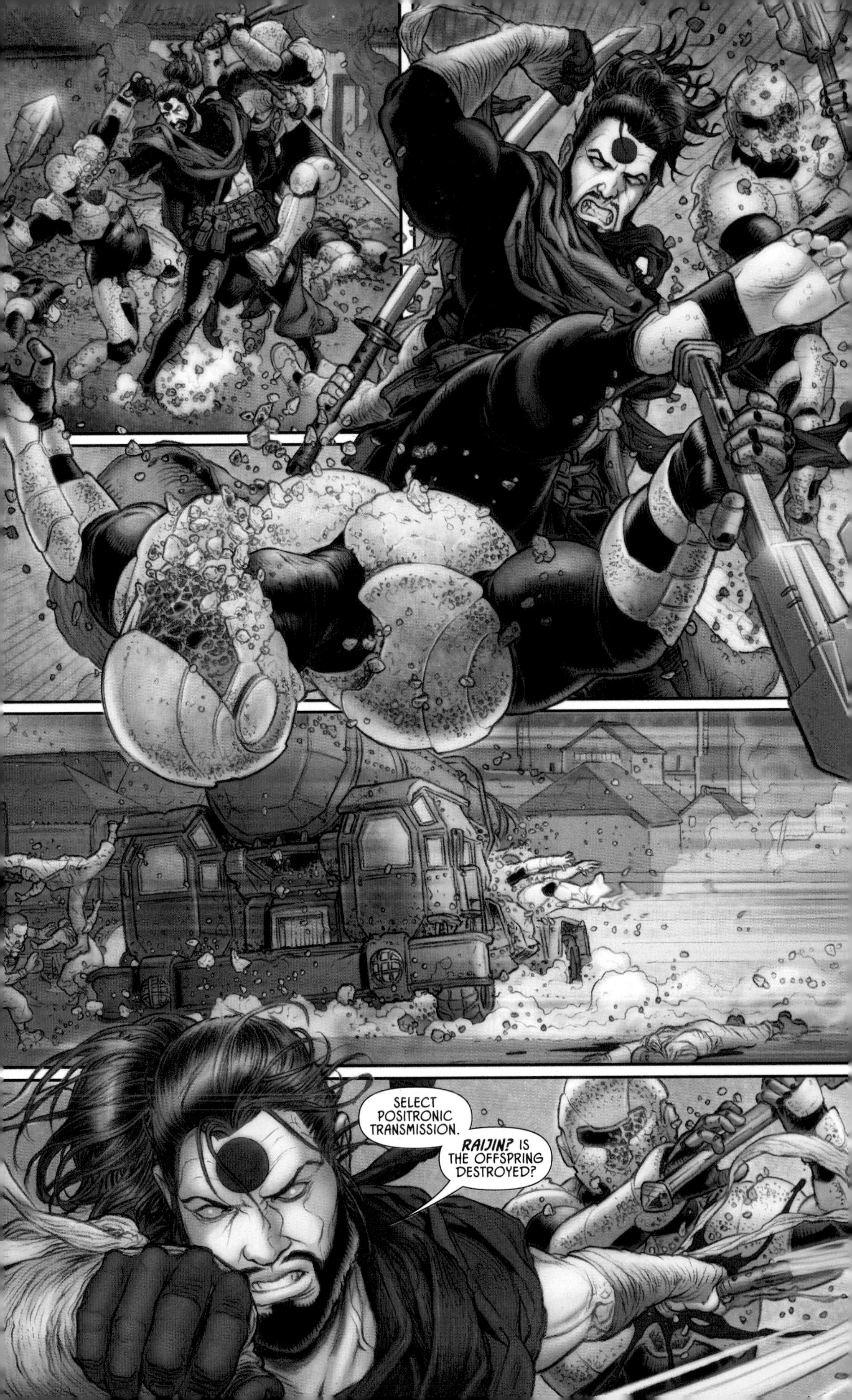
SELECT POSITRONIC TRANSMISSION.
RAIJIN? IS THE OFFSPRING DESTROYED?

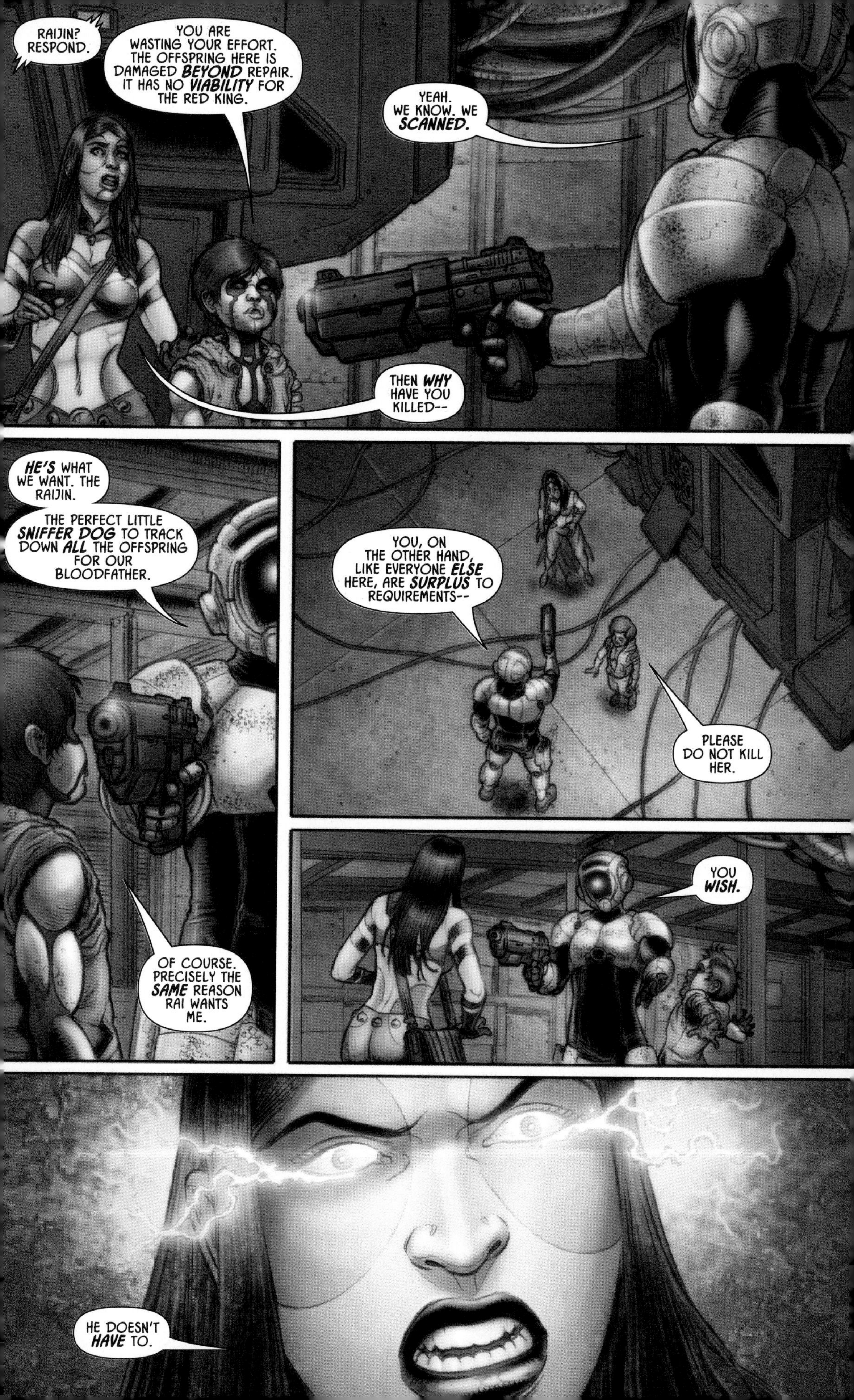
RAIJIN? RESPOND.
YOU ARE WASTING YOUR EFFORT. THE OFFSPRING HERE IS DAMAGED BEYOND REPAIR. IT HAS NO VIABILITY FOR THE RED KING.
YEAH. WE KNOW. WE SCANNED.
THEN WHY HAVE YOU KILLED--
HE'S WHAT WE WANT. THE RAIJIN.
THE PERFECT LITTLE SNIFFER DOG TO TRACK DOWN ALL THE OFFSPRING FOR OUR BLOODFATHER.
OF COURSE. PRECISELY THE SAME REASON RAI WANTS ME.
YOU, ON THE OTHER HAND, LIKE EVERYONE ELSE HERE, ARE SURPLUS TO REQUIREMENTS--
PLEASE DO NOT KILL HER.
YOU WISH.
HE DOESN'T HAVE TO.

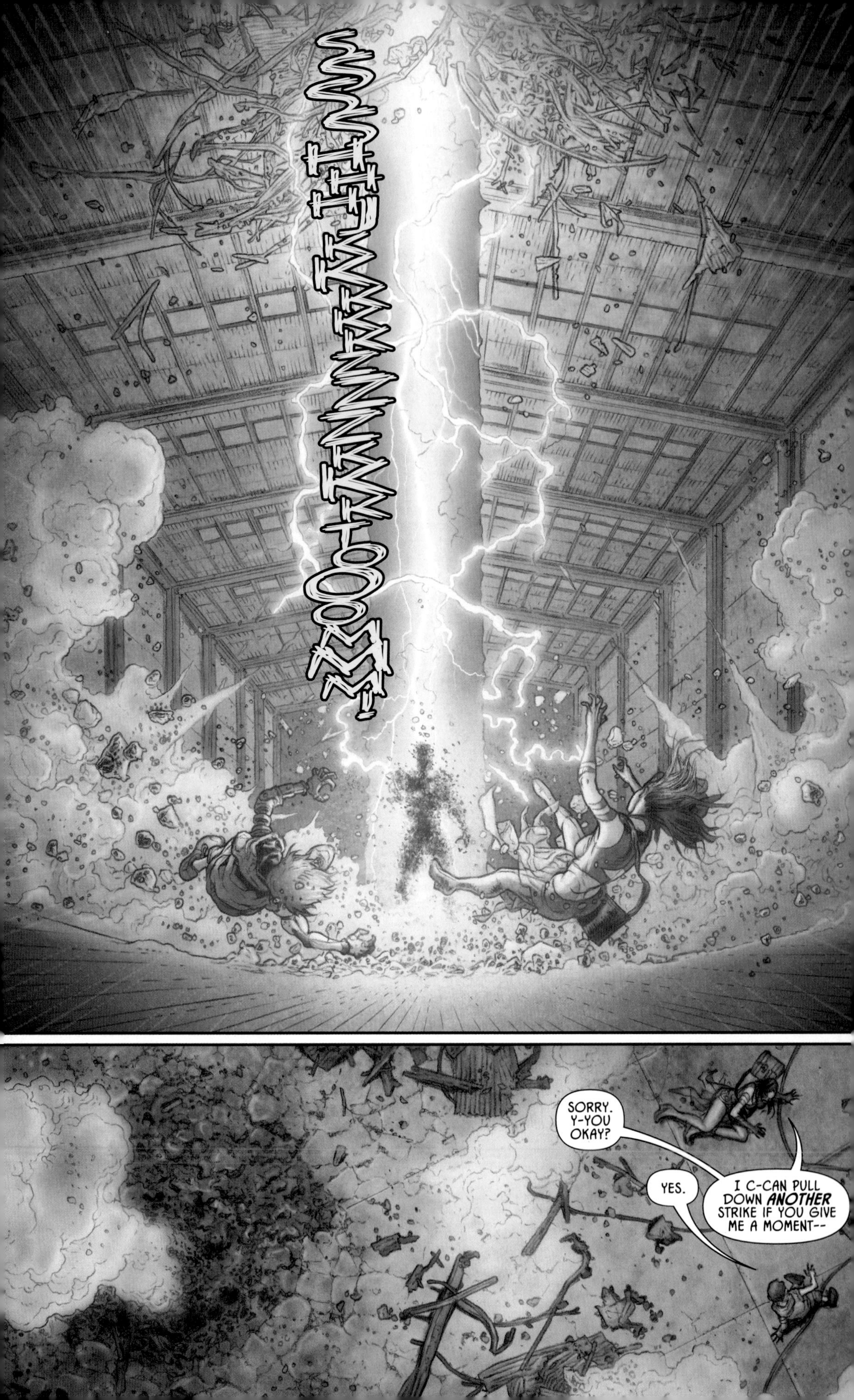
SORRY. Y-YOU OKAY?
YES.
I C-CAN PULL DOWN **ANOTHER** STRIKE IF YOU GIVE ME A MOMENT--

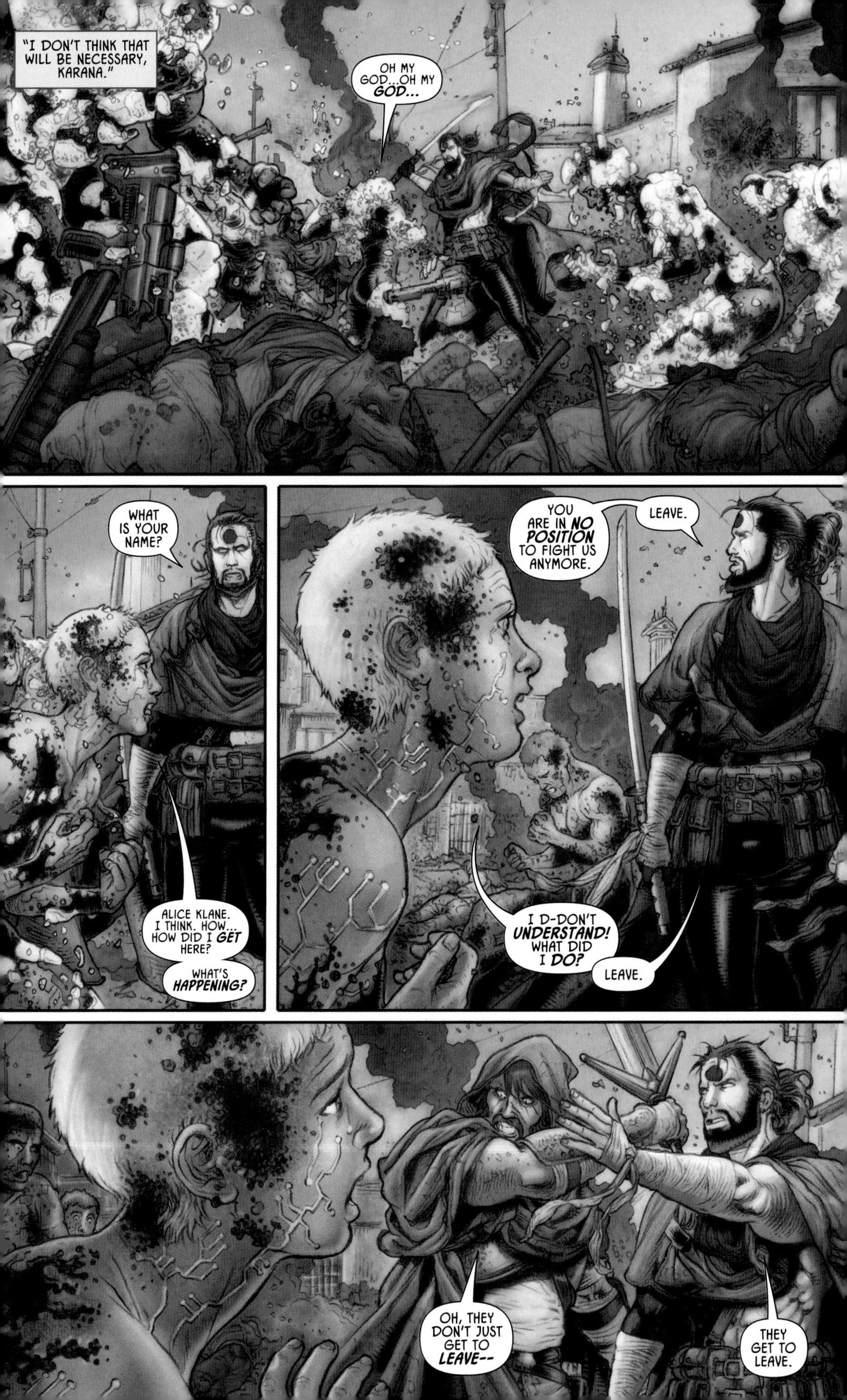
"I DON'T THINK THAT WILL BE NECESSARY, KARANA."
OH MY GOD...OH MY GOD...
WHAT IS YOUR NAME?
ALICE KLANE. I THINK. HOW... HOW DID I GET HERE?
WHAT'S HAPPENING?
YOU ARE IN NO POSITION TO FIGHT US ANYMORE.
LEAVE.
I D-DON'T UNDERSTAND! WHAT DID I DO?
LEAVE.
OH, THEY DON'T JUST GET TO LEAVE--
THEY GET TO LEAVE.

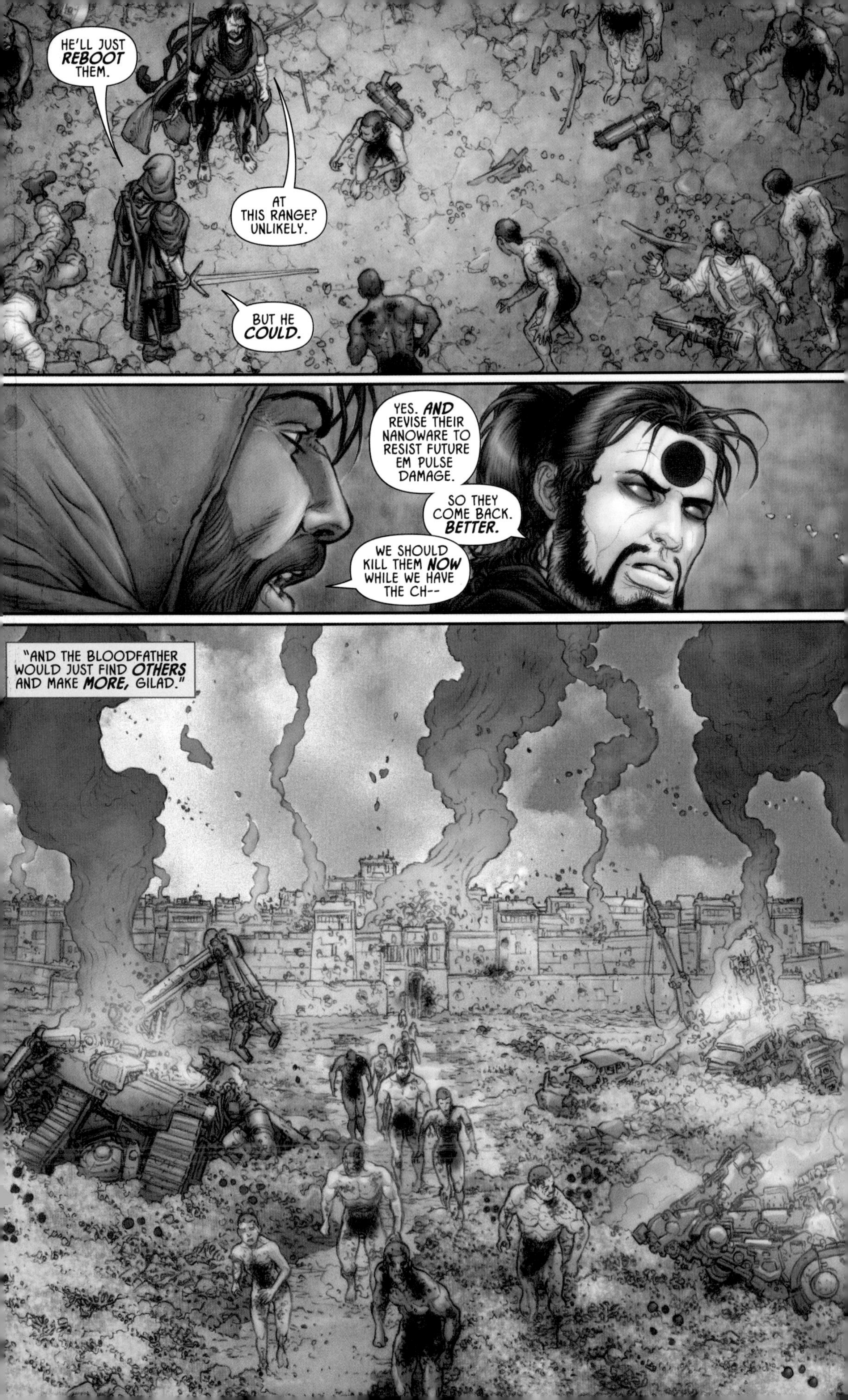
HE'LL JUST REBOOT THEM.
AT THIS RANGE? UNLIKELY.
BUT HE COULD.
YES. AND REVISE THEIR NANOWARE TO RESIST FUTURE EM PULSE DAMAGE.
SO THEY COME BACK. BETTER.
WE SHOULD KILL THEM NOW WHILE WE HAVE THE CH--
"AND THE BLOODFATHER WOULD JUST FIND OTHERS AND MAKE MORE, GILAD."

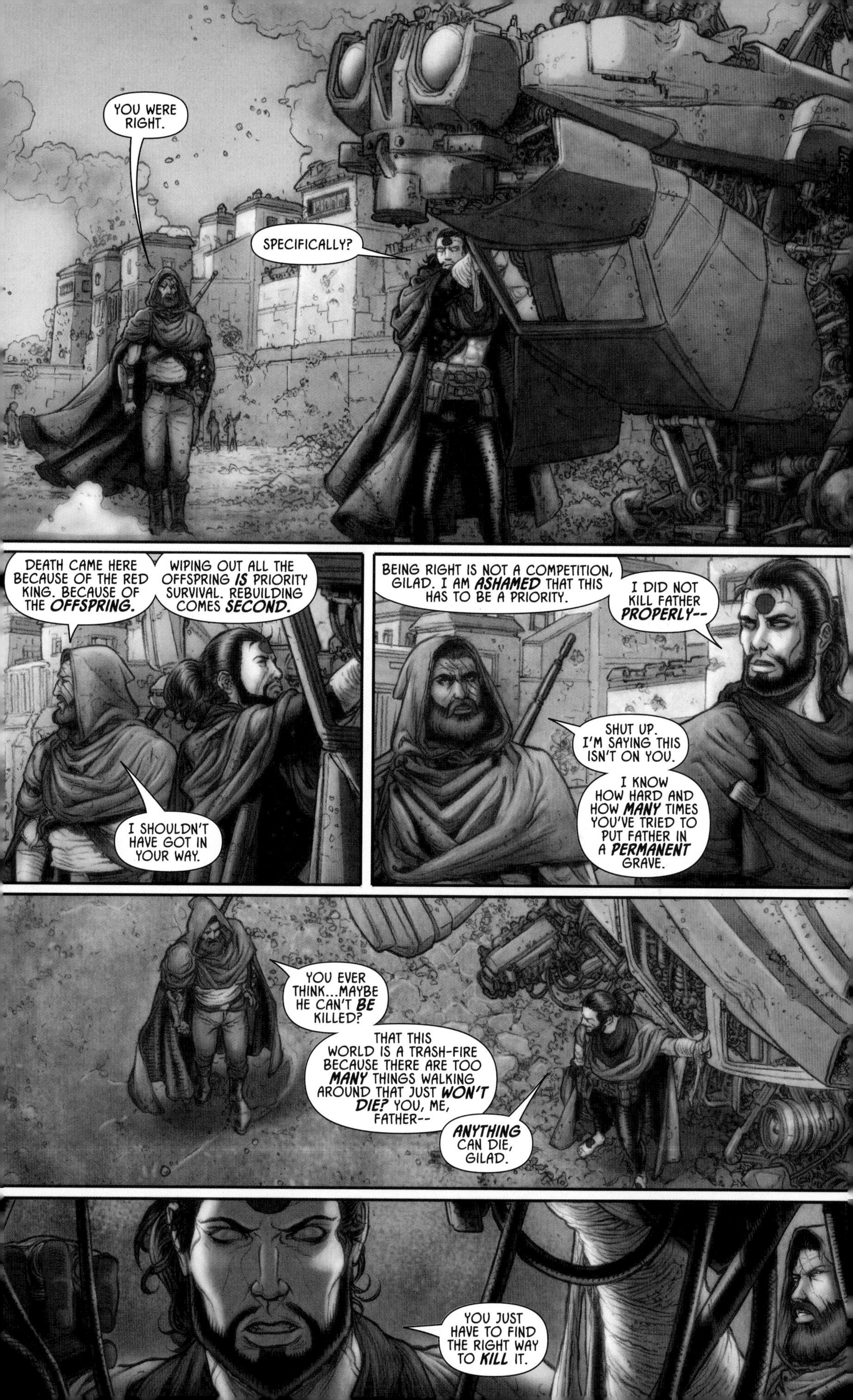
YOU WERE RIGHT.
SPECIFICALLY?
DEATH CAME HERE BECAUSE OF THE RED KING. BECAUSE OF THE OFFSPRING.
WIPING OUT ALL THE OFFSPRING IS PRIORITY SURVIVAL. REBUILDING COMES SECOND.
I SHOULDN'T HAVE GOT IN YOUR WAY.
BEING RIGHT IS NOT A COMPETITION, GILAD. I AM ASHAMED THAT THIS HAS TO BE A PRIORITY.
I DID NOT KILL FATHER PROPERLY--
SHUT UP. I'M SAYING THIS ISN'T ON YOU.
I KNOW HOW HARD AND HOW MANY TIMES YOU'VE TRIED TO PUT FATHER IN A PERMANENT GRAVE.
YOU EVER THINK...MAYBE HE CAN'T BE KILLED?
THAT THIS WORLD IS A TRASH-FIRE BECAUSE THERE ARE TOO MANY THINGS WALKING AROUND THAT JUST WON'T DIE? YOU, ME, FATHER--
ANYTHING CAN DIE, GILAD.
YOU JUST HAVE TO FIND THE RIGHT WAY TO KILL IT.

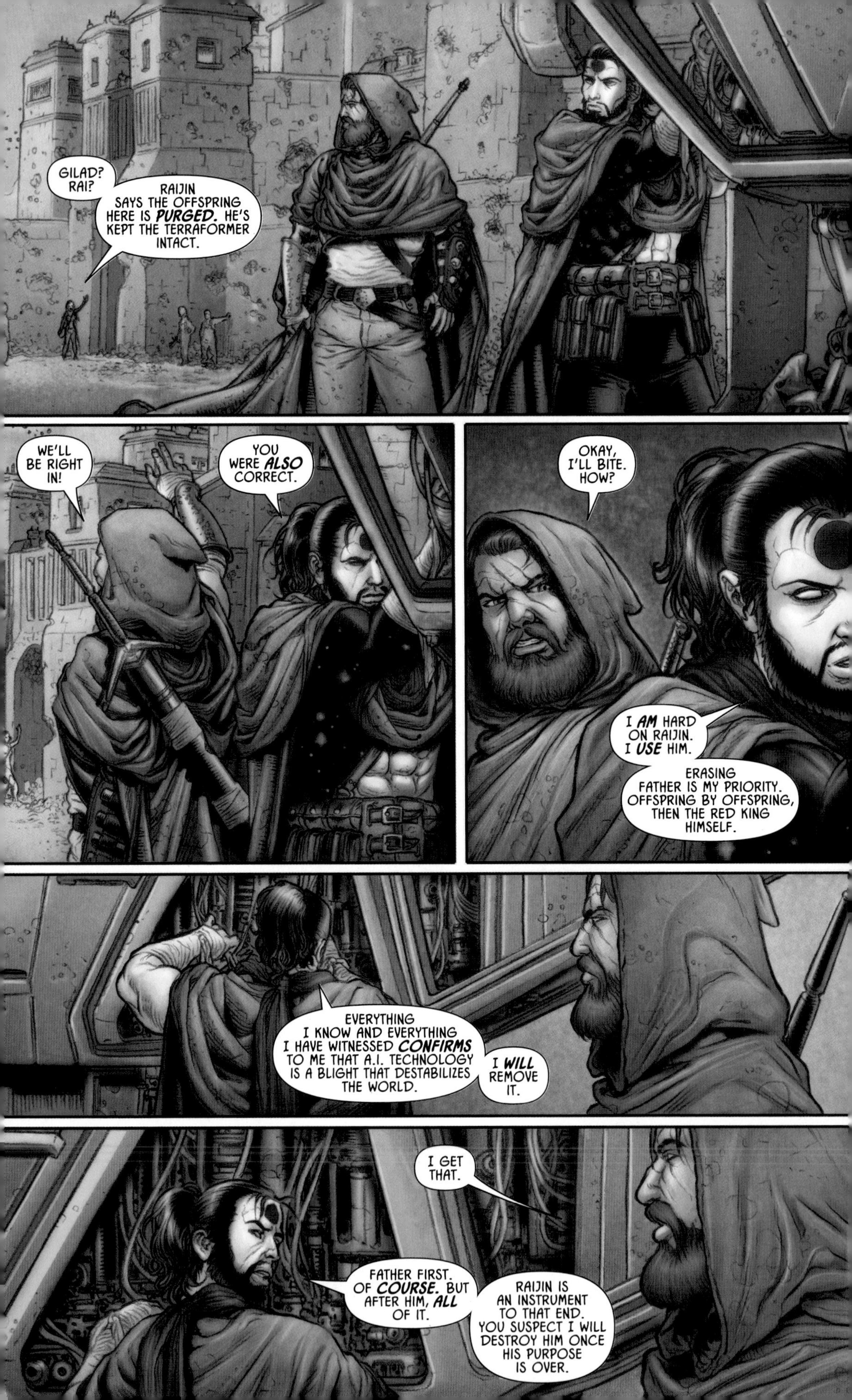

GILAD? RAI?
RAIJIN SAYS THE OFFSPRING HERE IS **PURGED.** HE'S KEPT THE TERRAFORMER INTACT.
WE'LL BE RIGHT IN!
YOU WERE **ALSO** CORRECT.
OKAY, I'LL BITE. HOW?
I **AM** HARD ON RAIJIN. I **USE** HIM.
ERASING FATHER IS MY PRIORITY. OFFSPRING BY OFFSPRING, THEN THE RED KING HIMSELF.
EVERYTHING I KNOW AND EVERYTHING I HAVE WITNESSED **CONFIRMS** TO ME THAT A.I. TECHNOLOGY IS A BLIGHT THAT DESTABILIZES THE WORLD.
I **WILL** REMOVE IT.
I GET THAT.
FATHER FIRST. OF **COURSE.** BUT AFTER HIM, **ALL** OF IT.
RAIJIN IS AN INSTRUMENT TO THAT END. YOU SUSPECT I WILL DESTROY HIM ONCE HIS PURPOSE IS OVER.

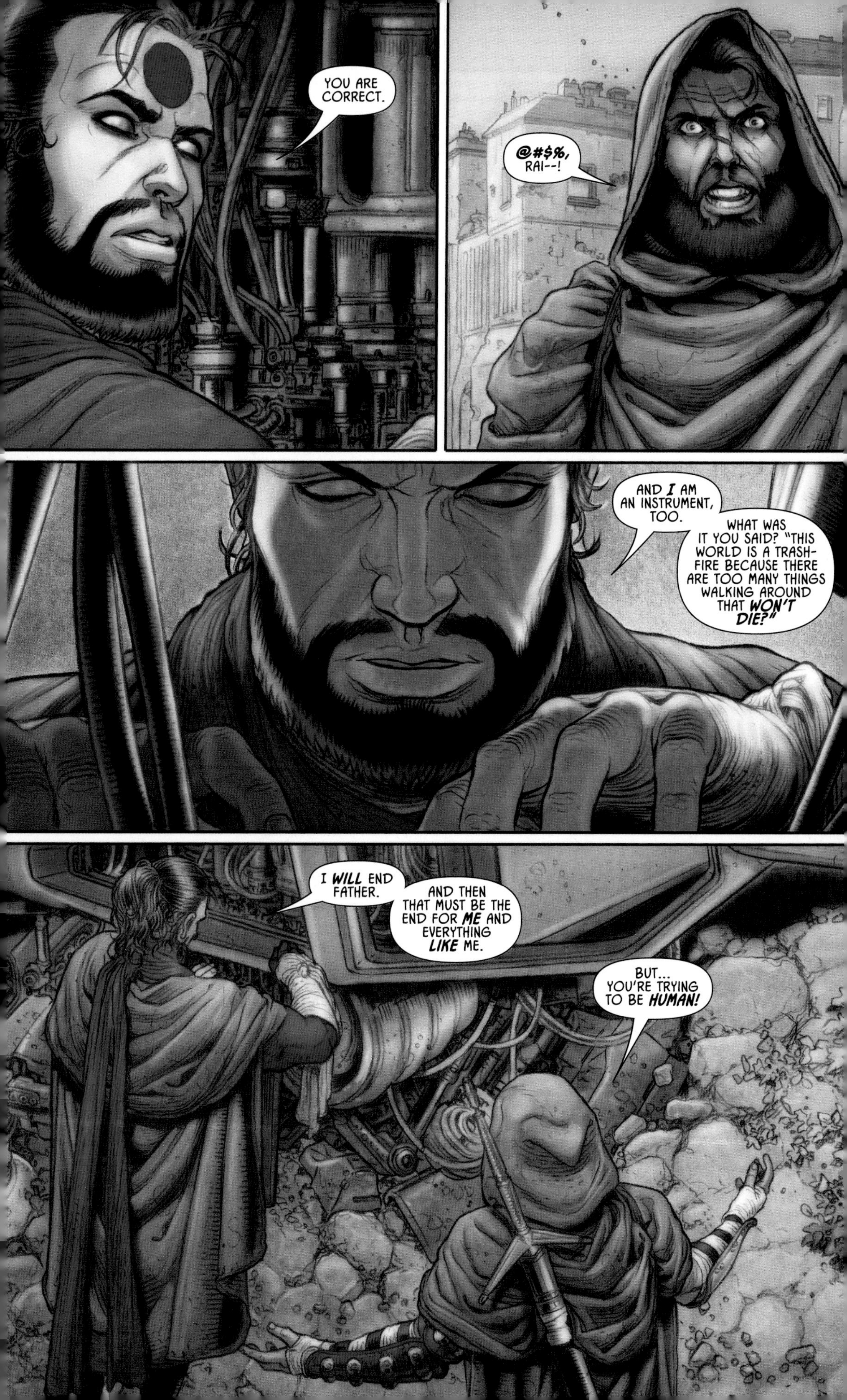
YOU ARE CORRECT.
@#$%, RAI--!
AND I AM AN INSTRUMENT, TOO.
WHAT WAS IT YOU SAID? "THIS WORLD IS A TRASH-FIRE BECAUSE THERE ARE TOO MANY THINGS WALKING AROUND THAT WON'T DIE?"
I WILL END FATHER.
AND THEN THAT MUST BE THE END FOR ME AND EVERYTHING LIKE ME.
BUT... YOU'RE TRYING TO BE HUMAN!

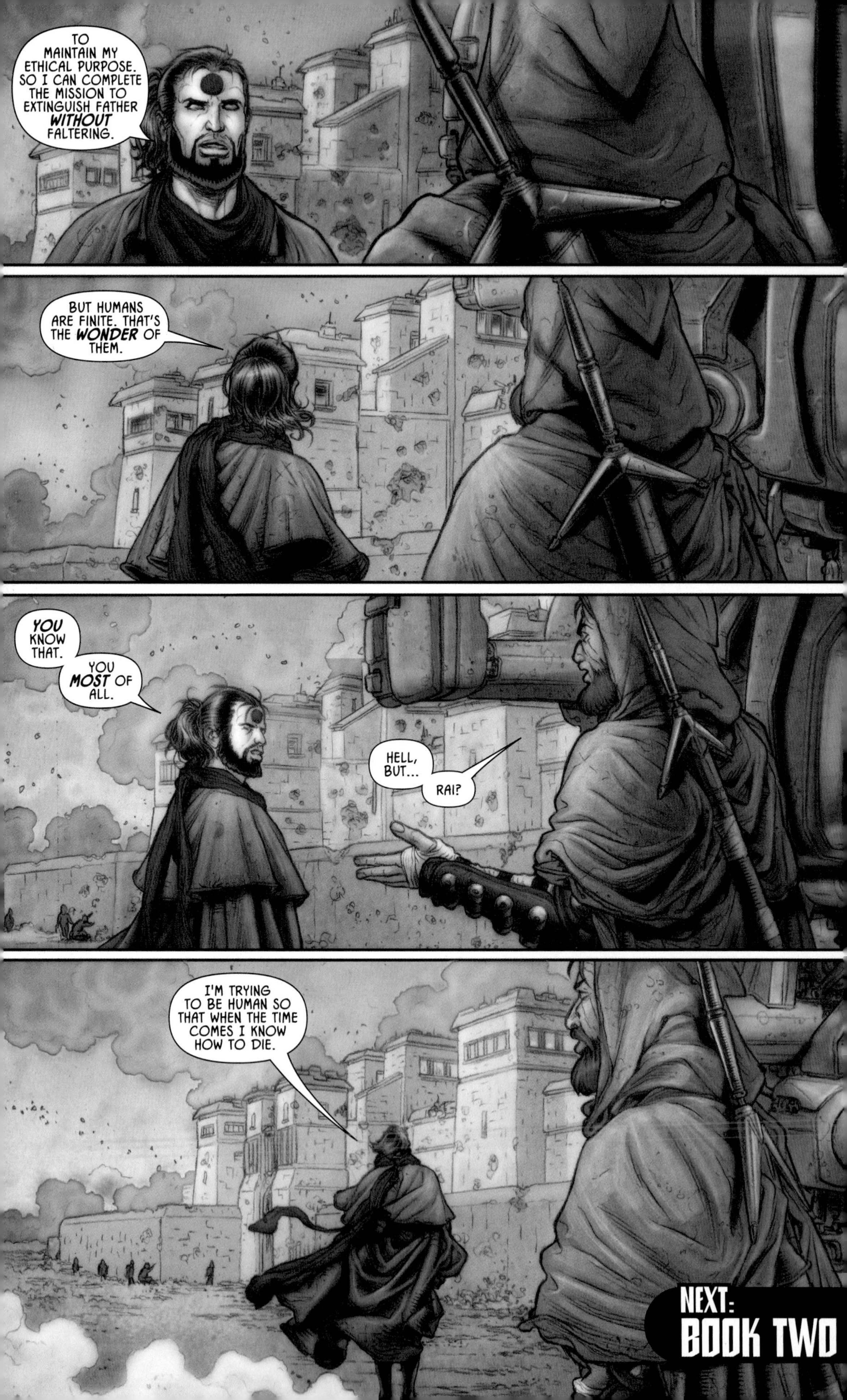
TO MAINTAIN MY ETHICAL PURPOSE. SO I CAN COMPLETE THE MISSION TO EXTINGUISH FATHER WITHOUT FALTERING.
BUT HUMANS ARE FINITE. THAT'S THE WONDER OF THEM.
YOU KNOW THAT.
YOU MOST OF ALL.
HELL, BUT...
RAI?
I'M TRYING TO BE HUMAN SO THAT WHEN THE TIME COMES I KNOW HOW TO DIE.
NEXT: BOOK TWO

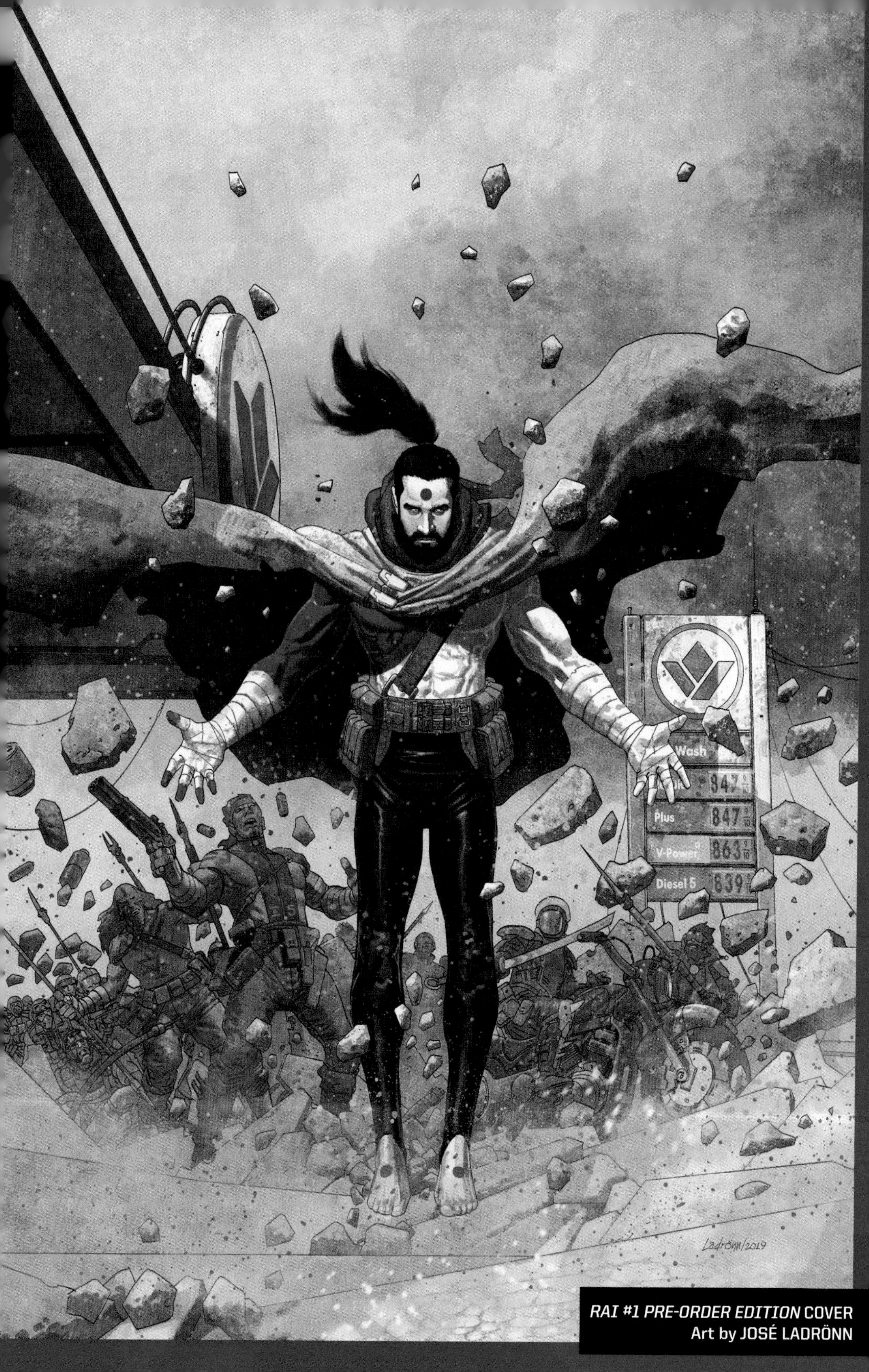
Wash
847
Plus 847
V-Power 863
Diesel 5 839
Ladrönn/2019

RAI #1 PRE-ORDER EDITION COVER
Art by JOSÉ LADRÖNN

RAI #2 COVER B
Art by DAVE JOHNSON

RAI #3 COVER B
Art by MICHAEL WALSH

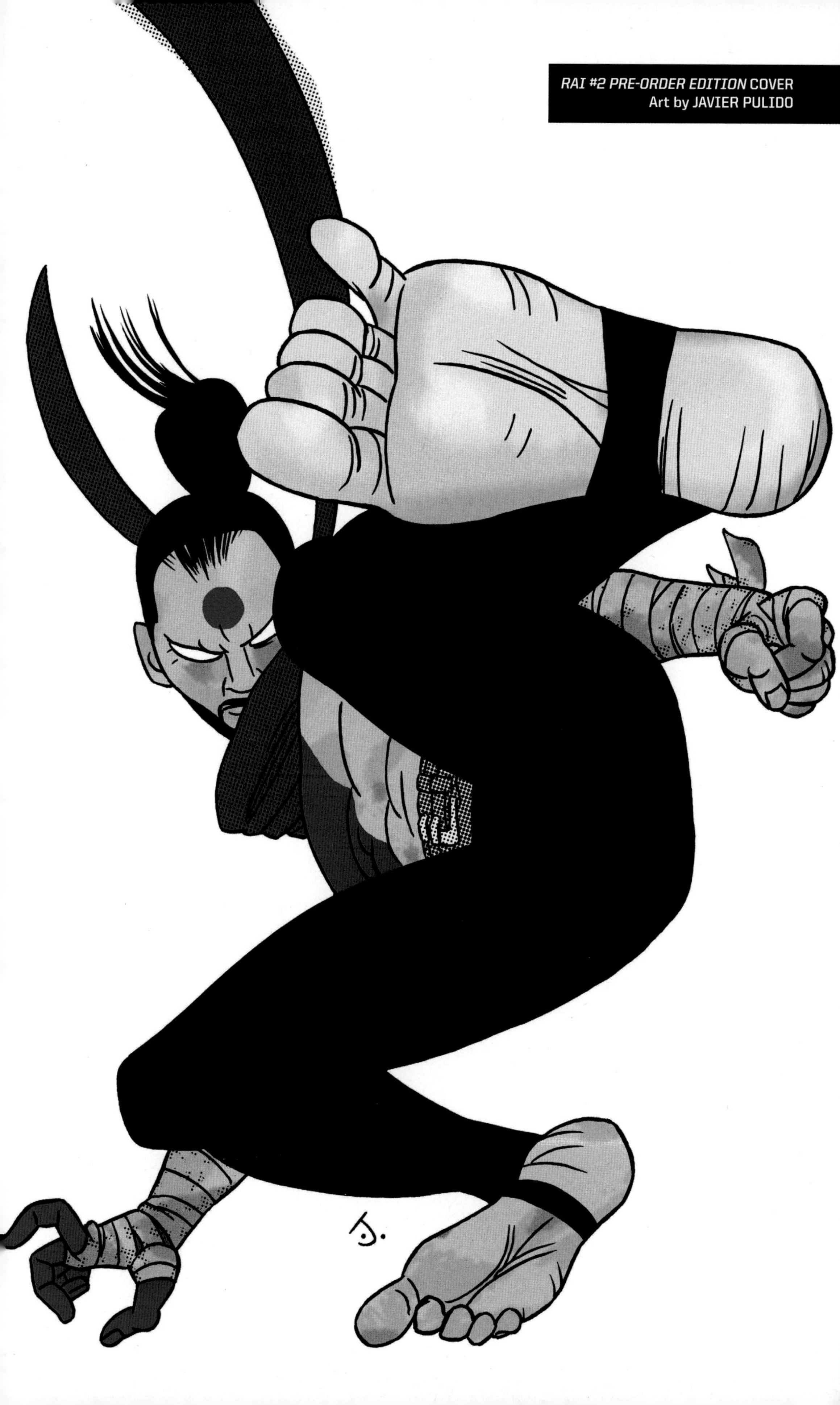

RAI #2 PRE-ORDER EDITION COVER
Art by JAVIER PULIDO

RAI #4 COVER B
Art by SIMON BISLEY

RAI #4 PRE-ORDER EDITION COVER
Art by ADAM GORHAM with MICHAEL GARLAND

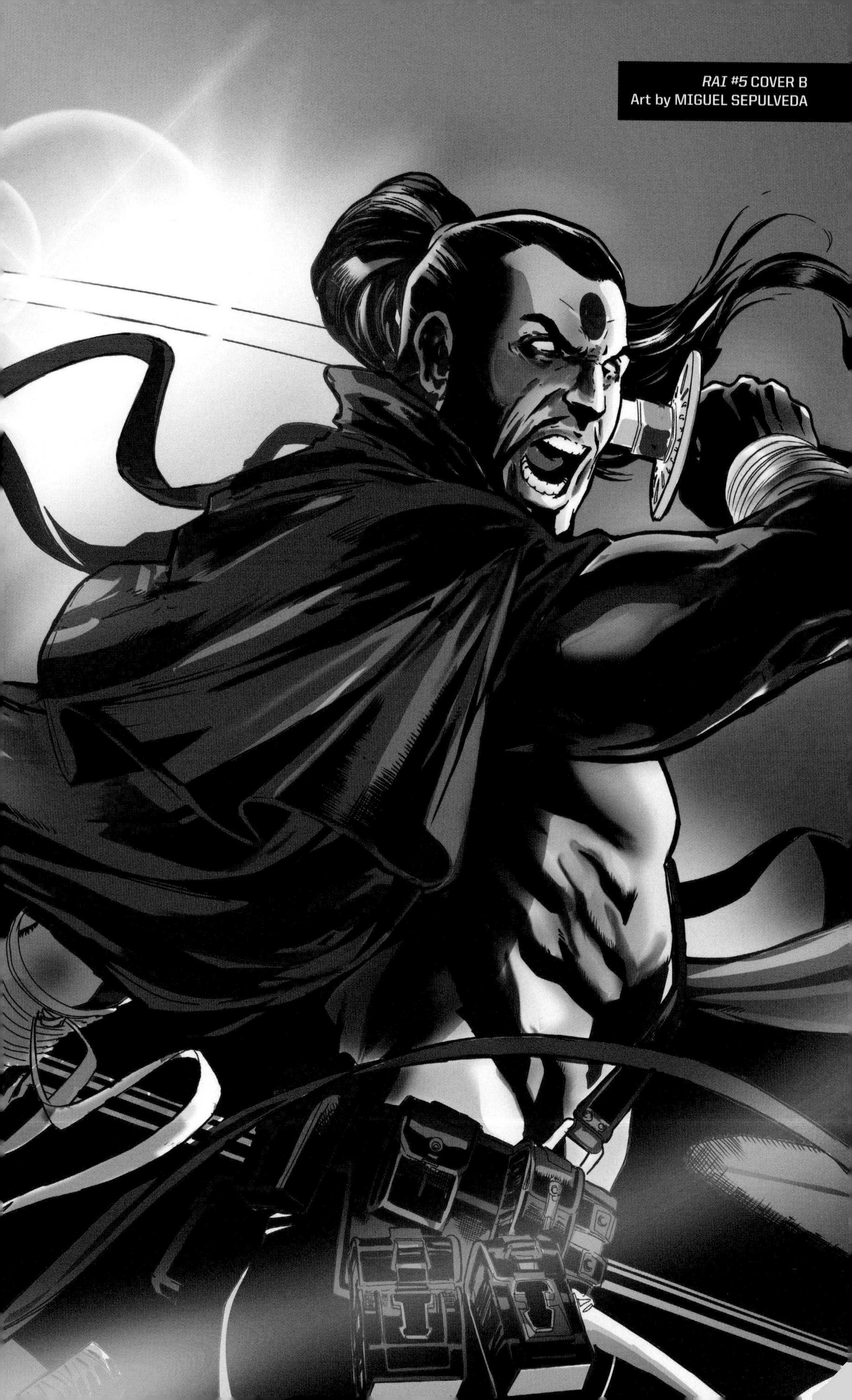

RAI #5 COVER B
Art by MIGUEL SEPULVEDA

RAI #1, pages 10, 11, and (facing) 12
Art by JUAN JOSÉ RYP

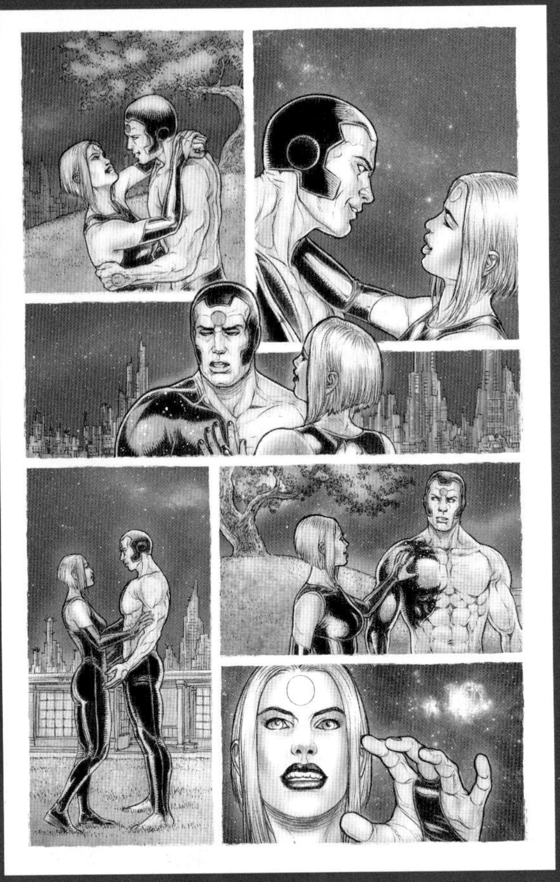

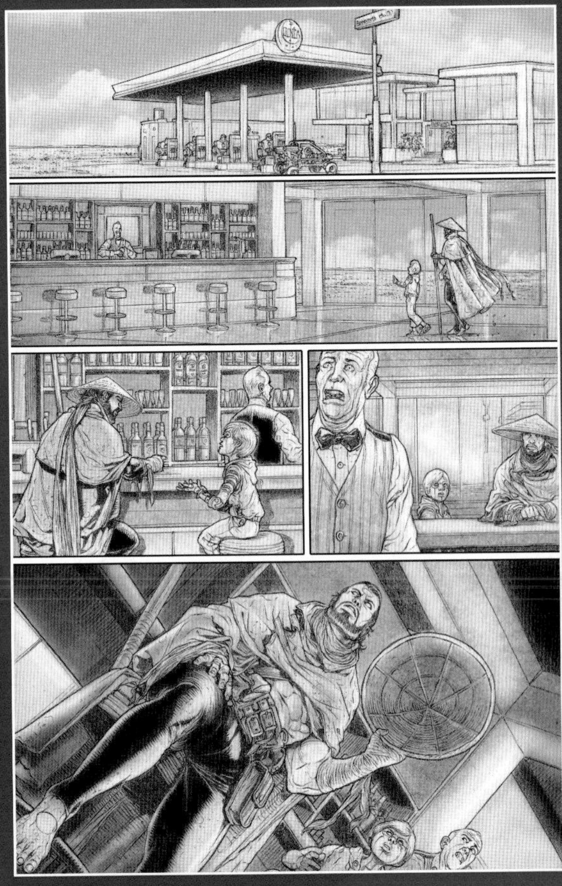

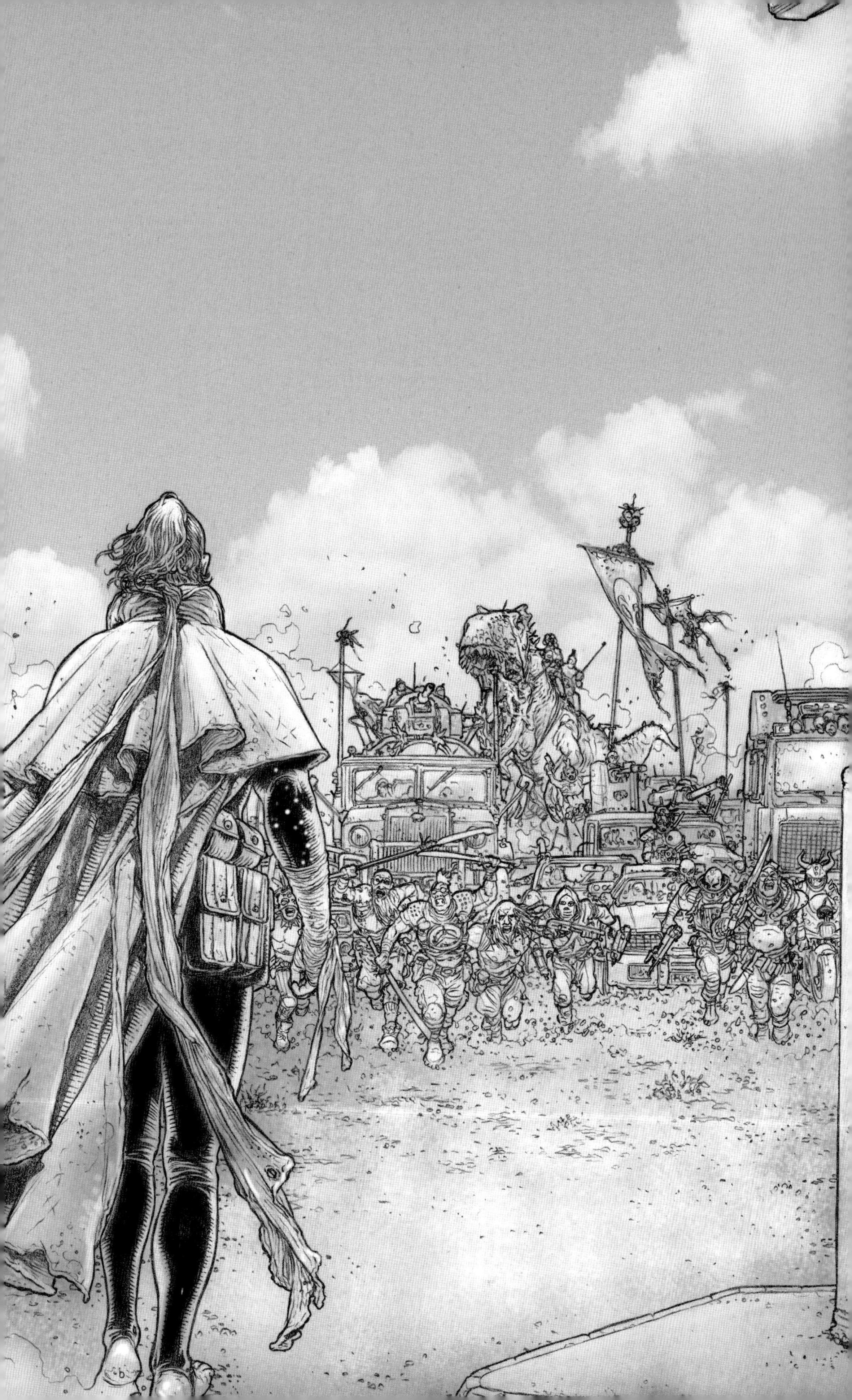

RAI #3, pages 17, 18, and (facing) 19
Art by JUAN JOSÉ RYP

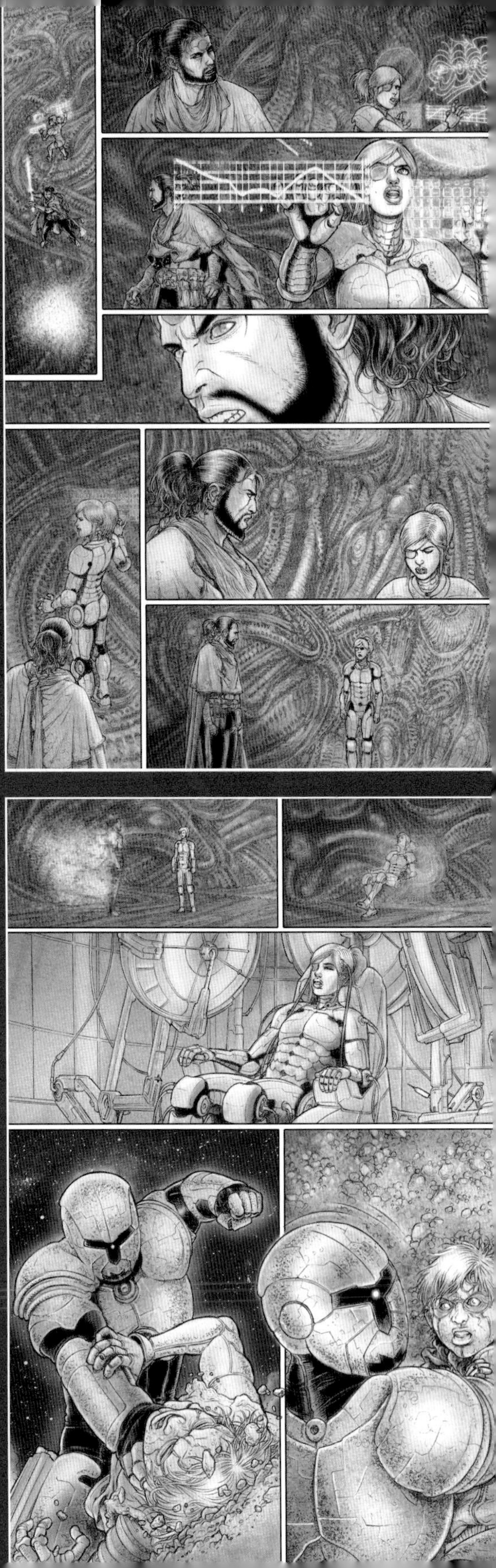

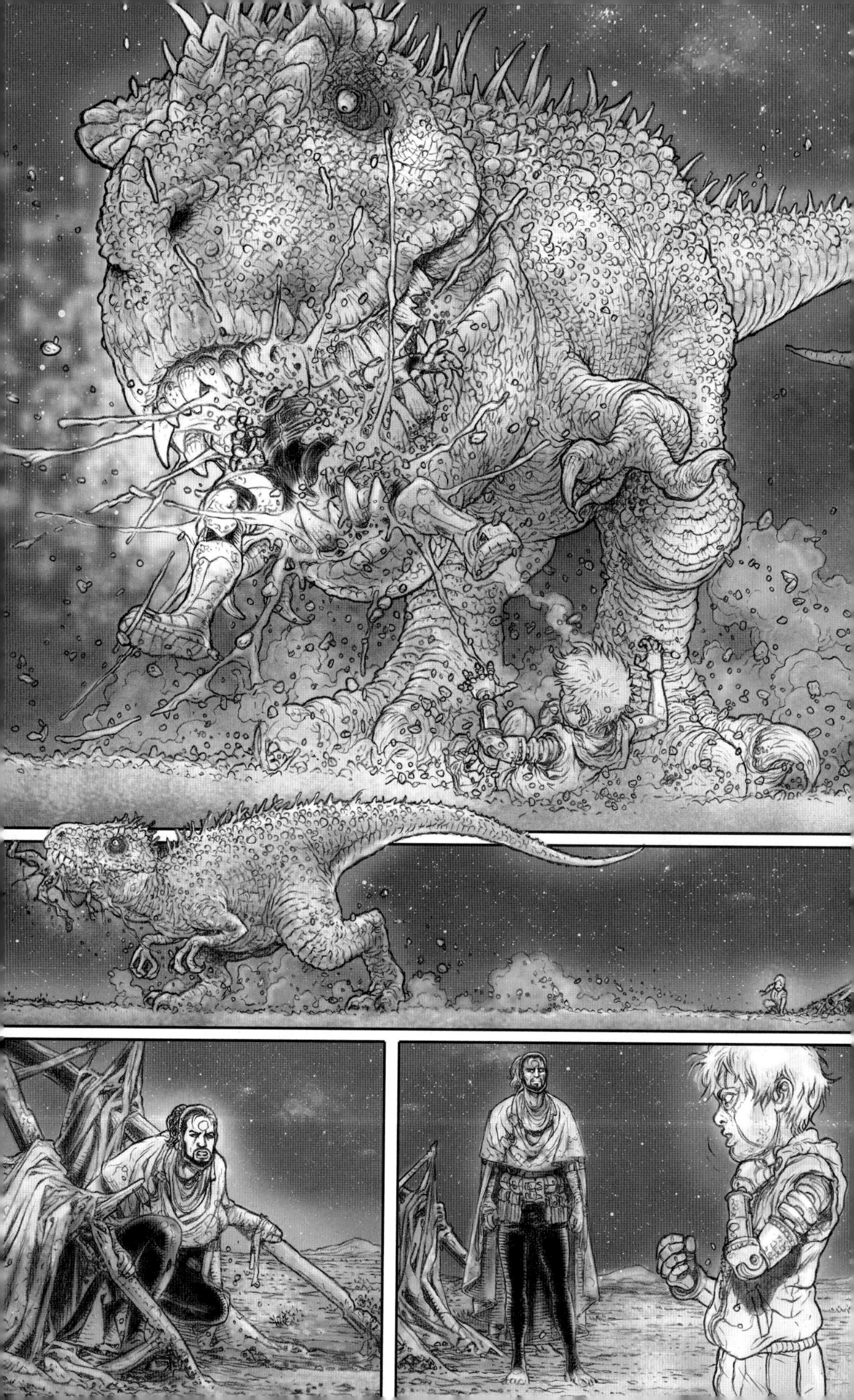

RAI #4, pages 3, 4, and (facing) 5
Art by JUAN JOSÉ RYP

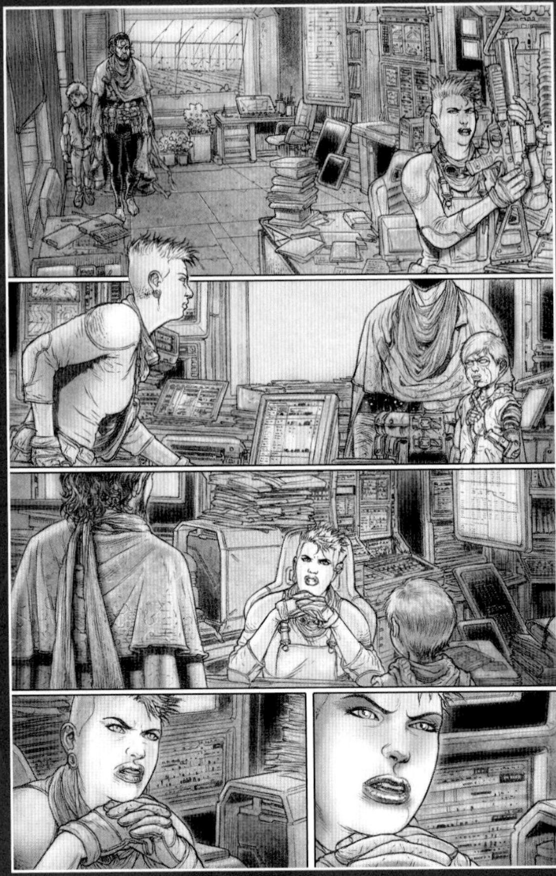

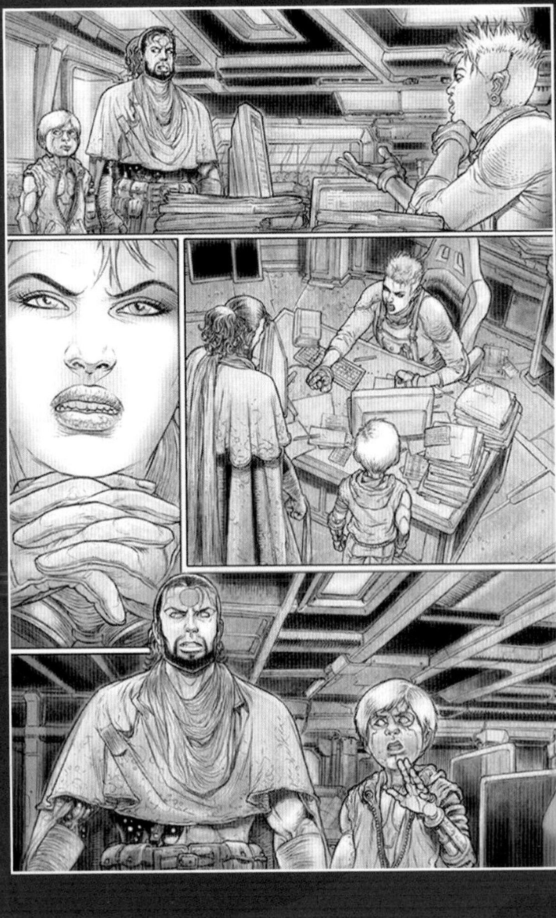

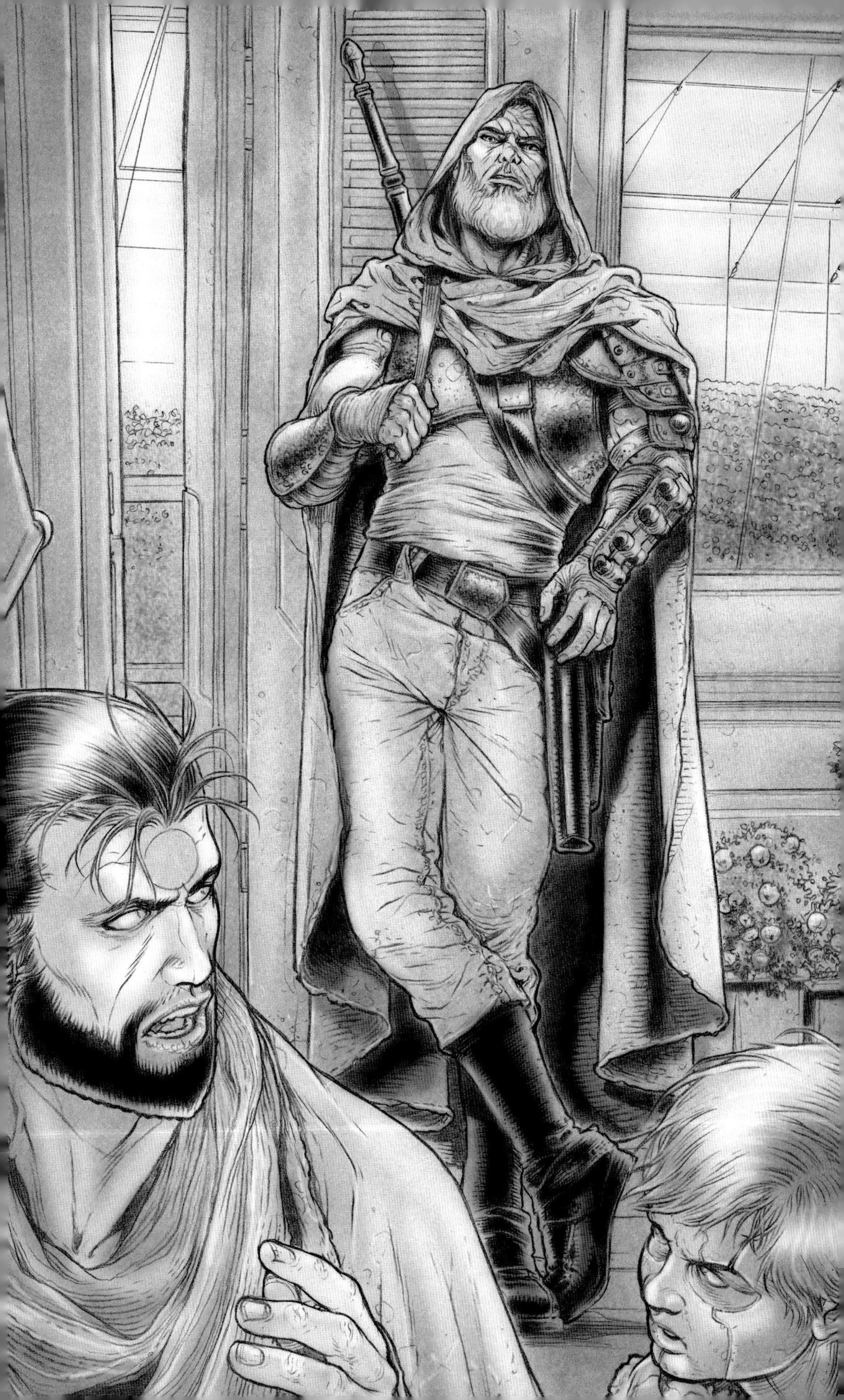

EXPLORE THE VALIANT U|

ACTION & ADVENTURE

BLOCKBUSTER ADVENTURE

COMEDY

BLOODSHOT BOOK ONE
ISBN: 978-1-68215-255-3
NINJA-K VOL. 1: THE NINJA FILES
ISBN: 978-1-68215-259-1
SAVAGE
ISBN: 978-1-68215-189-1
WRATH OF THE ETERNAL WARRIOR VOL. 1: RISEN
ISBN: 978-1-68215-123-5
X-O MANOWAR (2017) VOL. 1: SOLDIER
ISBN: 978-1-68215-205-8

4001 A.D.
ISBN: 978-1-68215-143-3
ARMOR HUNTERS
ISBN: 978-1-939346-45-2
BOOK OF DEATH
ISBN: 978-1-939346-97-1
FALLEN WORLD
ISBN: 978-1-68215-331-4
HARBINGER WARS
ISBN: 978-1-939346-09-4
HARBINGER WARS 2
ISBN: 978-1-68215-289-8
INCURSION
ISBN: 978-1-68215-303-1
THE VALIANT
ISBN: 978-1-939346-60-5

A&A: THE ADVENTURES OF ARCHER & ARMSTRONG VOL. 1: IN THE BAG
ISBN: 978-1-68215-149-5
THE DELINQUENTS
ISBN: 978-1-939346-51-3
QUANTUM AND WOODY! (2017) VOL. 1: KISS KISS, KLANG KLANG
ISBN: 978-1-68215-269-0

IVERSE STARTING AT  $9.99

HORROR & MYSTERY

SCIENCE FICTION & FANTASY

TEEN ADVENTURE

BRITANNIA
ISBN: 978-1-68215-185-3
DOCTOR MIRAGE
ISBN: 978-1-68215-346-8
PUNK MAMBO
ISBN: 978-1-68215-330-7
RAPTURE
ISBN: 978-1-68215-225-6
SHADOWMAN (2018) VOL. 1:
FEAR OF THE DARK
ISBN: 978-1-68215-239-3

DIVINITY
ISBN: 978-1-939346-76-6
THE FORGOTTEN QUEEN
ISBN: 978-1-68215-324-6
IMPERIUM VOL. 1: COLLECTING MONSTERS
ISBN: 978-1-939346-75-9
IVAR, TIMEWALKER VOL. 1: MAKING HISTORY
ISBN: 978-1-939346-63-6
RAI BOOK ONE
ISBN: 978-1-682153-60-4
WAR MOTHER
ISBN: 978-1-68215-237-9

FAITH VOL. 1: HOLLYWOOD AND VINE
ISBN: 978-1-68215-121-1
GENERATION ZERO VOL. 1:
WE ARE THE FUTURE
ISBN: 978-1-68215-175-4
HARBINGER RENEGADE VOL. 1:
THE JUDGMENT OF SOLOMON
ISBN: 978-1-68215-169-3
LIVEWIRE VOL. 1: FUGITIVE
ISBN: 978-1-68215-301-7
SECRET WEAPONS
ISBN: 978-1-68215-229-4

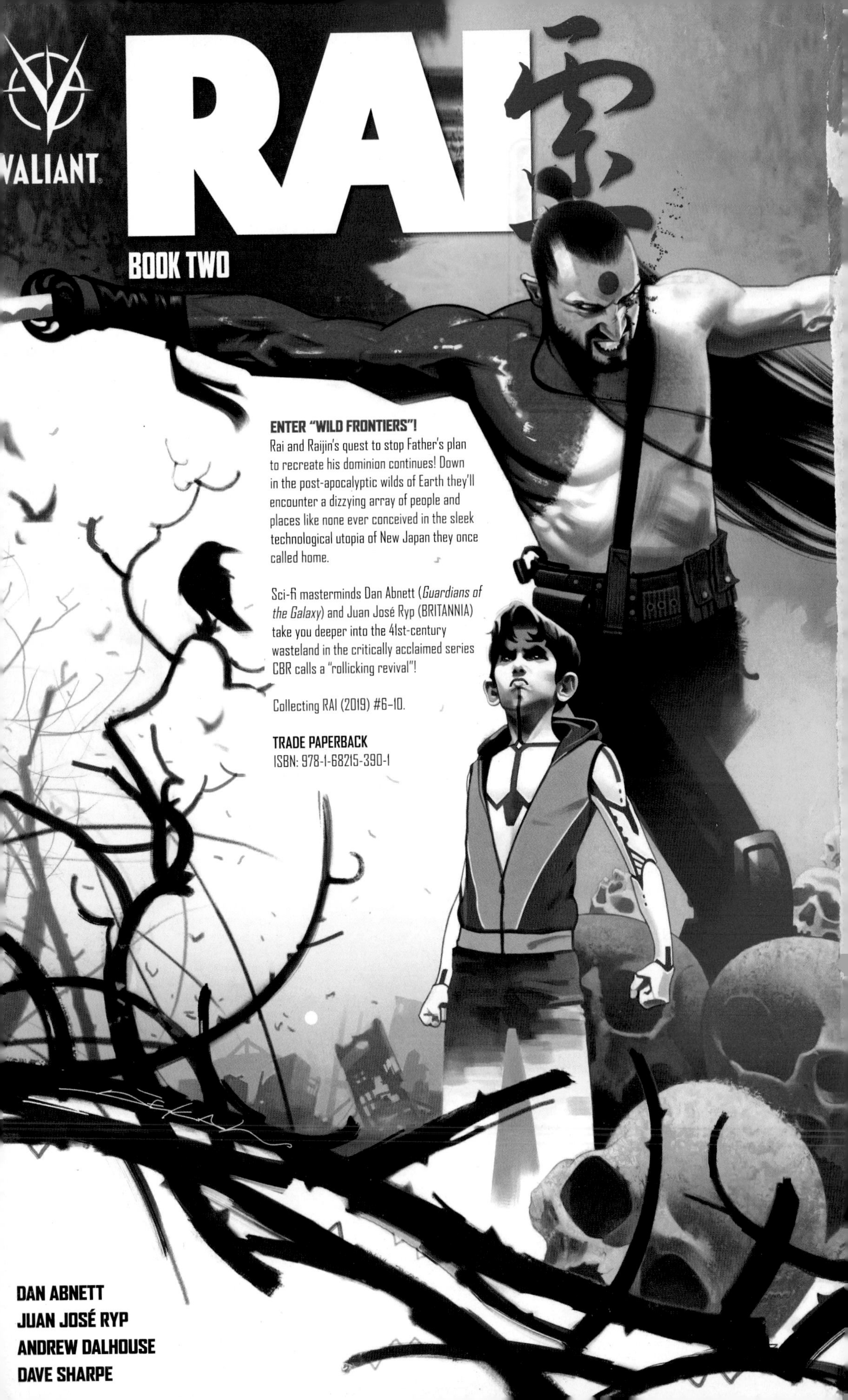

VALIANT

RAI

BOOK TWO

ENTER "WILD FRONTIERS"!

Rai and Raijin's quest to stop Father's plan to recreate his dominion continues! Down in the post-apocalyptic wilds of Earth they'll encounter a dizzying array of people and places like none ever conceived in the sleek technological utopia of New Japan they once called home.

Sci-fi masterminds Dan Abnett (*Guardians of the Galaxy*) and Juan José Ryp (BRITANNIA) take you deeper into the 41st-century wasteland in the critically acclaimed series CBR calls a "rollicking revival"!

Collecting RAI (2019) #6–10.

TRADE PAPERBACK
ISBN: 978-1-68215-390-1

DAN ABNETT
JUAN JOSÉ RYP
ANDREW DALHOUSE
DAVE SHARPE